Praise for Jason Hribal's *Fear of the Animal Planet*

"Animal fables, jungle books, Aesopian tales were the discursive evidence of cross-species interaction that survived into modernity as children's literature. When the carceral replaced the domestic system, as the zoos, circuses, and laboratories became the primary site of interaction replacing the barnyard and the wild wood, the animals began to resist. Here are their hidden stories. Jason Hribal takes us behind the zoo scenes, the phoney exhibits, and cute displays to reveal an ugly economy of exploitation, international trafficking in exotic animals, over-work, cruelty in training, incessant and insolent teasing from the public. He chronicles the escapes, the assaults, the demand of food, and the refusals to reproduce that resulted. Here is animal resistance neither 'wild' nor 'instinctual' but responses to specific injustices. Single-minded, eccentric, and delightfully cranky, Hribal is the annalist non pareil of animal escape. With light but unforgiving misanthropy he carefully names the animals (the pachyderms – Jumbo and Tinkerbelle, the primates – Moe, Kumang, Little Joe, the sea lions, dolphins, and Orcas (Corky, Kasatka) while leaving the keepers, trainers, and showmen in shameful anonymity. From the escape of Tatiana, the Siberian tiger from the San Francisco zoo, to the latest orca killing Hribal relentlessly gathers the evidence to witness these risings of the creatures."

— Peter Linebaugh, author of *The Magna Carta Manifesto* and *The London Hanged*

"'Vengeance is mine,'" sayeth the captive beast. Prepare to have your illusions of security shattered as Jason Hribal shows us that a revolution is brewing among those frustrated leaping orcas, elephants in head-dresses, and tigers kept behind bars. Animal spectacles, shows, and exhibits, it turns out, pose a deep, dark threat not only to nature herself but also to those who impose their will on wild spirits and those who pop in for a few hours to watch. A riveting, eye-opening book."

— Ingrid Newkirk, president and co-founder of PETA

"Jason Hribal stacks up the evidence, and the conclusions are inescapable. Zoos, circuses and theme parks are the strategic hamlets of Americans' long war against nature itself."

— Susan Davis, author *Spectacular Nature: Corporate Culture and the Sea World Experience*

"Zoos, Circuses and Guantanamo Bay...Beatened, whiped and shot! *Oh why?!* Jason Hribal exposes the perverted species *we* really are. Life, liberty and the pursuit of happiness is but a dream. Especially for our fellow beings."

— Allison Lance, founder of Galapagos Preservation Society

"Jason Hribal's *Fear of the Animal Planet* does a great service in chronicling the resistance of nonhuman animals against the multiplicity of human institutions of exploitation and oppression. It is a timely and vitally important book that promises to dramatically reshape debates in science, law, philosophy, and the burgeoning — but largely sterile — field of animal studies. One radical upshot of the book is to extend the notion of agency to nonhuman animals and to show many of them — such as elephants, tigers, and orcas — to be political in their revolt against human oppression. Moreover, humanists and leftists of all stripes, cannot, without embarrassment, persist in reducing nonhuman animals to the status of objects while restricting the discourse of intentionality, rebellion, autonomy, and liberation to human actors only. In addition, "animal advocates" will have to check their own historical biases and speciesist distortions upon learning that moral progress and the animal ethics paradigm shift was not brought about solely through their own campaigns. Progressive change is also driven by nonhuman animals themselves in their revolt against their captors and in the evolving awareness in human society their resistance precipitates. Unfortunately, as fascinating and chronic as their self-liberation struggles have been throughout the world — in zoos, circuses, and other exploitative institutions — their defiance to human supremacism cannot amount to a revolution without the organized radical politics of enlightened and militant sectors of humanity. The fate of nonhuman animal species continues to hang on whether or not humans can over-come the violent proclivities of their own animality and dismantle the omnicidal machines of global capitalism. This book, however, takes us far in the right direction toward grasping the complexity of nonhuman animals' emotions, minds, and social life such that we can recognize them as *political agents* and shapers of history in their own right."

— Dr. Steven Best, Associate Professor of Philosophy, University of Texas, El Paso, co-editor of *Terrorists or Freedom Fighters: Reflections on the Liberation of Animals*

"Hribal skillfully excavates the hidden history of captive animals as active agents in their own liberation. His book is a harrowing, and curiously uplifting, chronicle of resistance against some of the cruelest forms of torture and oppression this side of Abu Ghraib prison."

— Jeffrey St. Clair, from "Let Us Now Praise Infamous Animals," author of *Born Under a Bad Sky*

FEAR OF THE
ANIMAL PLANET
THE HIDDEN HISTORY OF
ANIMAL RESISTANCE

First published by
CounterPunch and AK Press 2010

CounterPunch
PO Box 228, Petrolia, California 95558

AK Press
674-A 23rd St, Oakland, California 94612-1163

ISBN 978-1-84935-026-6

A catalog record for this book is available from the Library of Congress.
Library of Congress Control Number: 2010925758

Design and typography by Tiffany Wardle de Sousa.

Typeset in Minion Pro, designed by Robert Slimbach for Adobe Systems Inc.;
Futura, originally designed by Paul Renner; and Compacta, designed by Fred Lambert.
Cover and title pages use Tungsten, designed by Hoefler & Frere-Jones.

Printed and bound in Canada.

FEAR OF THE ANIMAL PLANET

THE HIDDEN HISTORY OF ANIMAL RESISTANCE

JASON HRIBAL

Introduction by Jeffrey St. Clair

CounterPunch
PETROLIA

For William Maugham, who encouraged me to read.

TABLE OF CONTENTS

LET US NOW PRAISE INFAMOUS ANIMALS

BY JEFFREY ST. CLAIR

In the spring of 1457, a gruesome murder took place in the French village of Savigny-sur-Etang. A five-year-old boy had been killed and his body partially consumed. A local family was accused of this frightful crime by local residents who claimed to have witnessed the murder. The seven suspects, a mother and her six children, were soon tracked down by local authorities, who discovered them still stained by the boy's blood. They were arrested, indicted on charges of infanticide and held in the local jail for trial.

The defendants were indigent and the court appointed a lawyer to represent them. A few weeks later a trial was convened in Savigny's seigneurial court. Before a crowded room, witnesses were called. Evidence was presented and legal arguments hotly debated. The justices considered the facts and the law and rendered a verdict and a sentence. The mother was pronounced guilty and ordered to be hanged to death by her legs from the limb of the gallows tree. Her six children, however, received a judicial pardon. The court accepted the defense lawyer's argument that the youngsters lacked the mental competence to have committed a crime in the eyes of the law. The orphaned children were sent into custodial care at the expense of the state.

This is an interesting case to be sure, featuring important lessons about the legal rights of the poor and the historic roots of juvenile justice in western jurisprudence, lessons that seem entirely lost on our current "tradition-obsessed" Supreme Court. But here's the kicker: the defendants in these proceedings were not members of our species. They were, it must be said, a family of pigs.

The Savigny murder case, even in its ghastly particulars, was unexceptional. In medieval Europe (and even colonial America) thousands of animals were summoned to court and put on trial for a variety of offenses, ranging from trespassing, thievery and vandalism to rape, assault and murder. The defendants included cats, dogs, cows, sheep, goats, slugs, swallows, oxen, horses, mules, donkeys, pigs, wolves, bears, bees, weevils, and termites. These tribunals were not show trials or strange festivals like Fools Day. The tribunals were taken seriously by both the courts and the community.

Though now largely lost to history, these trials followed the same convoluted rules of legal procedure used in cases involving humans. Indeed, as detailed in E. P. Evans's remarkable book, *The Criminal Prosecution and Capital Punishment of Animals* (1906), humans and animals were frequently tried together in the same courtroom as co-conspirators, especially in cases of bestiality. The animal defendants were appointed their own lawyers at public expense. Animals enjoyed appeal rights and there are several instances when convictions were overturned and sentences reduced or commuted entirely. Sometimes, particularly in cases involving pigs, the animal defendants were dressed in human clothes during court proceedings and at executions.

Animal trials were held in two distinct settings: ecclesiastical courts and secular courts. Ecclesiastical courts were the venue of choice for cases involving the destruction of public resources, such as crops, or in crimes involving the corruption of public morals, such as witchcraft or sexual congress between humans and beasts. The secular and royal courts claimed jurisdiction over cases where animals were accused of causing bodily harm or death to humans or, in some instances, other animals.

When guilty verdicts were issued and a death sentence imposed, a professional executioner was commissioned for the lethal task. Animals were subjected to the same ghastly forms of torture and execution as were condemned humans. Convicted animals were lashed, put to the rack, hanged, beheaded, burned at the stake, buried alive, stoned to death and drawn-and-quartered. In 14th century Sardinia, trespassing livestock had an ear cut-off for each offense. In an early application of the three-strikes-and-you're-out rule, the third conviction resulted in immediate execution.

The flesh of executed animals was never eaten. Instead, the corpses of the condemned were either burned, dumped in rivers or buried next to human convicts in graveyards set aside for criminals and heretics. The heads of the condemned, especially in cases of bestiality, were often displayed on pikes in the town square adjacent to the heads of their human co-conspirators.

The first recorded murder trial involving an animal took place in 1266 at Fontenay-aux-Roses (birthplace of the painter Pierre Bonnard) on the outskirts of Paris. The case involved a murder of an infant girl. The defendant was a pig. Though the records have been lost, similar trials almost certainly date back to classical Greece, where, according to Aristotle, secular trials of animals were regularly held in the great Prytaneum of Athens.

Interestingly, Thomas Aquinas's *Summa Theologiae,* written in 1269, is in part an attack on Aristotle's ideas and his "radical acolytes" who had infiltrated the universities of thirteenth century Europe. In the *Summa,* Aquinas laboriously tried to explain the theological basis for the trials of animals.

While most of the animal trials, according the records unearthed by Evans, appear to have taken place in France, Germany and Italy, nearly every country in Europe seems to have put beasts on trial, including Russia, Poland, Romania, Spain, Scotland and Ireland. Anglophiles have long claimed that England alone resisted the idea of hauling cows, dogs and pigs before the royal courts. But Shakespeare suggests otherwise. In "The Merchant of Venice," Portia's friend, the young and impetuous Gratiano, abuses Shylock, comparing him to a wolf that had been tried and hanged for murder:

> "Thy currish spirit
> Govern'd a wolf, who, hang'd for human slaughter,
> Even from the gallows did his fell soul fleet,
> And, whilst thou lay'st in thy unhallow'd dam,
> Infus'd itself in thee.."

Even colonial Brazil got in on the act. In 1713 a rectory at the Franciscan monastery in Piedade no Maranhão collapsed, its foundation ravaged by termites. The friars lodged charges against the termites and an ecclesiastical inquest soon issued a summons demanding that the ravenous insects appear before the court to confront the allegations against their conduct. Often in such cases, the animals who failed to heed the warrant were summarily convicted in default judgments. But these termites had a crafty lawyer. He argued that the termites were industrious creatures, worked hard and enjoyed a God-given right to feed themselves. Moreover, the lawyer declared, the slothful habits of the friars had likely contributed to the disrepair of the monastery. The monks, the defense lawyer argued, were merely using the local termite community as an excuse for their own negligence. The judge returned to his chambers, contemplated the facts presented him and returned with a Solomonic ruling. The friars were compelled to provide a woodpile for the termites to dine at and the insects were commanded to leave the monastery and confine their eating to their new feedlot.

A similar case unfolded in the province of Savoy, France in 1575. The weevils of Saint Julien, a tiny hamlet in the Rhone Alps, were indicted for the crime of destroying the famous vineyards on the flanks of Mount Cenis. A lawyer, Pierre Rembaud, was appointed as defense counsel for the accused. Rembaud wasted no time in filing a motion for summary judgment, arguing that the weevils had every right to consume the grape leaves. Indeed, Rembaud asserted, the weevils enjoyed a prior claim to the vegetation on Mount Cenis, since, as detailed in the Book of Genesis, the Supreme Deity had created animals before he fashioned humans and God had promised animals all of the grasses, leaves and green herbs for their sustenance. Rembaud's argument stumped the court. As the judges deliberated, the villagers of Saint Julien seemed swayed by the lawyer's legal reasoning. Perhaps the bugs had legitimate grievances. The towns-folk scrambled to set aside a patch of open land away from the vineyards as a foraging ground for the weevils. The land was surveyed. Deeds were drawn up and the property was shown to counselor Rembaud for his inspection and approval. They called the weevil reserve La Grand Feisse. Rembaud walked the site, investigating the plant communities with the eyes of a seasoned botanist. Finally, he shook his head. No deal. The land was rocky and had obviously been overgrazed for decades. La Grand Feisse was wholly unsuitable for the discriminating palates of his clients. If only John Walker Lindh had been appointed so resolute an advocate!

The Perry Mason of animal defense lawyers was an acclaimed French jurist named Bartholomew Chassenée, who later became a chief justice in the French provincial courts and a preeminent legal theorist. One of Chassenée's most intriguing essays, the sixteenth-century equivalent of a law review article, was titled *De Excommunicatore Animalium Insectorium.* In another legal mongraph, Chassenée argued with persuasive force that local animals, both wild and domesticated, should be considered lay members of the parish community. In other words, the rights of animals were similar in kind to the rights of the people at large.

In the summer of 1522, Chassenée was called to the ancient village of Autun in Burgundy. The old town, founded during the reign of Augustus, had been recently overrun by rats. French maidens had been frightened, the barley crop destroyed, the vineyards placed in peril. The town crier issued a summons for the rats to appear before the court. None showed. The judge asked Chassenée why he should not find his clients guilty *in absentia.* The lawyer argued that the rat population was dispersed through the countryside and that his clients were almost certainly unaware of the charges pending against them. The judge agreed. The town crier was dispatched into the fields to repeat his urgent notice. Yet still the rats failed to appear at trial. Once again Chassenée jumped into action. Showing tactical skills that should impress Gerry Spence, Chassenée shifted his strategy. Now he passionately explained to the court that the rats remained hidden in their rural nests, paralyzed by the prospect of making a journey past the cats of Autun, who were well-known for their ferocious animosity toward rodents.

In the end, the rats were spared execution. The judge sternly ordered them to vacate the fields of Autun within six days. If the rats failed to heed this injunction, the animals would be duly anathematized, condemned to eternal torment. This sentence of damnation would be imposed, the court warned, regardless of any rodent infirmities or pregnancies.

Few animal trials were prosecuted as vigorously as those involving allegations of bestiality. In 1565, a man was indicted for engaging in sexual relations with a mule in the French city of Montpelier. The mule was also charged. Both stood trial together. They were duly convicted and sentenced to death at the stake. Because of the mule's angry disposition, the animal was subjected to additional torments. His feet were chopped off before the poor beast was pitched into the fire.

In 1598, the suspected sorceress Françoise Secretain was brought before the inquisitional court at St. Claude in the Jura Mountains of Burgundy to face charges of witchcraft and bestiality. Secretain was accused of communing with the devil and having sex with a dog, a cat and a rooster. The blood-curdling case is described in detail by her prosecutor, the Grand Justice Henri Boguet, in his strange memoir *Discours des Sorciers*. Secretain was stripped naked in her cell, as the fanatical Boguet inspected her for the mark of Satan. The animals were shaved and plucked for similar examinations. Secretain and her pets were put to various tortures, including having a hot poker plunged down their throats to see if they shed tears, for, as Boguet noted in his memoir:

> All the sorcerers whom I have examined in quality of Judge have never shed tears in my presence: or, indeed, if they have shed them it has been so parsimoniously that no notice was taken of them. I say this with regard to those who seemed to weep, but I doubt if their tears were not feigned. I am at least well assured that those tears were wrung from them with the greatest efforts. This was shown by the efforts which the accused made to weep, and by the small number of tears which they shed.

Alas, the poor woman and her animals did not weep. They perished together in flames at the stake.

In 1642 a teenage boy named Thomas Graunger stood accused of committing, in the unforgettable phrase of Cotton Mather, "infandous Buggeries" with farm animals in Plymouth, Massachusetts. Young master Graunger was hauled before an austere tribunal of Puritans headed by Gov. William Bradford. There he stood trial beside his co-defendants, a mare, a cow, two goats, four sheep, two calves and a turkey. All were found guilty. They were publicly tortured and executed. Their bodies were burned on a pyre, their ashes buried in a mass grave. Graunger was the first juvenile to be executed in colonial America.

In 1750, a French farmer named Jacques Ferron was espied sodomizing a female donkey in a field. Man and beast were arrested and hauled before a tribunal in the commune of Vanves near Paris. After a day-long trial, Ferron was convicted and sentenced to be burned at the stake. But the donkey's lawyers argued that their client was innocent. The defense maintained that the illicit acts were not consensual. The donkey, the defense pleaded, was a victim of rape and not a willing participant in carnal congress with Ferron. Character witnesses were called to testify on the donkey's behalf. Affidavits calling for mercy were filed with the court by several leading citizens of the town, including the head abbot at the local priory, attesting to the benign nature and good moral character of the animal. The abbot wrote that the four-year-old donkey was "in word and deed and in all her habits of life a most honorable creature." Here the court was compelled to evaluate matters of volition, free will and resistance. In short, did the donkey say no? After an intense deliberation, the court announced its verdict. The donkey was acquitted and duly released back to its pasture.

What are we to make of all this? Why did both the secular and religious courts of Europe devote so much time and money to these elaborate trials of troublesome animals? Some scholars, such as James Frazer, argue that the trials performed the function of the ancient rituals of sacrifice and atonement. Others, such as the legal theorist Hans Kelsen, view the cases as the last gasp of the animistic religions. Some have offered an economic explanation suggesting that animals were tried and executed during times of glut or seized in times of economic plight as property by the Church or Crown through the rule of deodand or "giving unto God." Still others have suggested that the trials and executions served a public health function, culling populations of farm animals and rodents that might contribute to the spread of infectious diseases.

Our interest here, however, is not with the social purpose of the trials, but in the qualities and rights the so-called medieval mind ascribed to the defendants: rationality, premeditation, free will, moral agency, calculation and motivation. In other words, it was presumed that animals acted with intention, that they could be driven by greed, jealousy and revenge. Thus the people of the Middle Ages, dismissed as primitives in many modernist quarters, were actually open to a truly radical idea: animal consciousness. As demonstrated in these trials, animals could be found to have *mens rea,* a guilty mind. But the courts also seriously considered exculpatory evidence aimed at proving that the actions of the accused, including murder, were justifiable owing to a long train of abuses. In other words, if animals could commit crimes, then crimes could also be committed against them.

The animal trials peaked in the late-sixteenth and early-seventeenth centuries, then faded away. They came to be viewed through the lens of modern historians as comical curiosities, grotesquely odd relics of the Dark Ages. The legal scholar W. W. Hyde succinctly summed up the smug, self-aggrandizing view of the legal scholars of the 20th century: "the savage in his rage at an animal's misdeeds obliterates all distinctions between man and beast, and treats the latter in all respects as the former."

Of course, the phasing out of animal trials didn't mean that the cruel treatment of domesticated animals improved or that problematic beasts stopped being put to death in public extravaganzas. While the trials ceased, the executions increased.

Recall the death warrant issued in 1903 against Topsy the Elephant, star of the Forepaugh Circus at Coney Island's Luna Park. Topsy had killed three handlers in a three-year period. One of her trainers was a sadist, who tortured the elephant by beating her with clubs, stabbing her with pikes and feeding her lit cigarettes.

Tospy was ordered to be hanged, but then Thomas Edison showed up and offered to electrocute Topsy. She was shackled, fed carrots laced with potassium cyanide and jolted with 6,600 volts of alternating current. Before a crowd of 1,500 onlookers, Topsy shivered, toppled and died in a cloud of dust. Edison filmed the entire event. He titled his documentary short, "Electrocuting the Elephant."

Topsy received no trial. It was not even imagined that she had grievances, a justification for her violent actions. Topsy was killed because she'd become a liability. Her death was a business decision, pure and simple.

So what happened? How did animals come to be viewed as mindless commodities? One explanation is that modernity rudely intruded in the rather frail form of René Descartes. The great Cartesian disconnect not only cleaved mind from body, but also severed humans from the natural world. Descartes postulated that animals were mere physical automatons. They were biological machines whose actions were driven solely by bio-physical instincts. Animals lacked the power of cognition, the ability to think and reason. They had a brain but no mind. At Port-Royal the Cartesians cut up living creatures with fervor, and in the words of one of Descartes's biographers, "kicked about their dogs and dissected their cats without mercy, laughing at any compassion for them and calling their screams the noise of breaking machinery." Across the Channel Francis Bacon declared in the *Novum Organum* that the proper aim of science was to restore the divinely ordained dominance of man over nature, "to extend more widely the limits of the power and greatness of man and so to endow him with "infinite commodities." Bacon's doctor, William Harvey, was a diligent vivisector of living animals.

Thus did the great sages of the Enlightenment assert humanity's ruthless primacy over the Animal Kingdom. The materialistic view of history, and the fearsome economic and technological pistons driving it, left no room for either the souls or consciousness of animals. They were no longer our fellow beings. They had been rendered philosophically and literally in resources for guiltless exploitation, turned into objects of commerce, labor, entertainment and food.

Conveniently for humans, the philosophers of the Industrial Age declared that animal had no sense of their miserable condition. They could not understand abuse, they had no conception of suffering, they could not feel pain. When captive animals bit, trampled or killed their human captors, it wasn't an act of rebellion against abusive treatment but merely a reflex. There was no need, therefore, to investigate the motivations behind these violent encounters because there could be no pre-meditation at all on the animal's part. The confrontations could not be crimes. They were mere accidents, nothing more.

One wonders what Descartes would have made of the group of orangutans, who stole crowbars and screwdrivers from zookeepers in

San Diego to repeatedly break out of their enclosures? How's that for cognition, cooperation and tool use, Monsieur Descartes?

In 1668, Jean Racine, a playwright not known for his facility with farce, wrote a comedy satirizing the trials of animals. Written eighteen years after the death of Descartes, *Les Plaideurs* (The Litigants) tells the story of a senile old man obsessed with judging, who eventually places the family dog on trial for stealing a capon from the kitchen table. The mutt is convicted and sentenced to death. Then the condemned canine's lawyer makes a last minute plea for mercy and reveals a litter of puppies before the judge. The old man is moved and the harsh hand of justice is stayed.

Racine's comedy, loosely based on Aristophanes's *The Wasps,* bombed, playing only two nights before closing, perhaps because the public had not yet been convinced by the solons of Europe to fully renounce their kinship with natural creatures. Revealingly, the play was resurrected a century later by the Comedie-Française to packed houses. By then public attitudes toward animals had shifted decisively in favor of human exceptionalism. According some accounts, the play has now become the most frequently performed French comedy, having been presented in more than 1,400 different productions.

Contrast Descartes's sterile, homocentric view with that of a much greater intellect, Michel de Montaigne. Writing a mere fifty years before Descartes, Montaigne, the most gifted French prose stylist, declared: "We understand them no more than they us. By the same token they may as well esteem us beasts as we them." Famously, he wrote in the "Apology for Raymond Sebond", "When I play with my cat, who knows if I am not a pastime to her more than she is to me?" Montaigne was distressed by the barbarous treatment of animals: "If I see but a chicken's neck pulled off or a pig sticked, I cannot choose but grieve; and I cannot well endure a silly dew-bedabbled hare to groan when she is seized upon by the hounds."

But the materialists held sway. Descartes was backed up the grim John Calvin, who proclaimed that the natural world was a merely a material resource to be exploited for the benefit of humanity, "True it is that God hath given us the birds for our food," Calvin declared. "We know he hath made the whole world for us."

John Locke, the father of modern liberal thinking, described animals as "perfect machines" available for unregulated use by man. The animals could be sent to the slaughterhouse with no right of appeal. In Locke's coldly utilitarian view, cows, goats, chickens and sheep were simply meat on feet.

Thus was the Great Chain of Being ruthlessly transmuted into an iron chain with a manacle clasped round the legs and throats of animals, hauling them off to zoos, circuses, bull rings and abattoirs.

Karl Marx, that supreme materialist, ridiculed the Romantic poets for their "deification of Nature" and chastised Darwin for his "natural, zoological way of thinking." Unfortunately, Marx's great intellect was not empathetic enough to extend his concepts of division of labor, alienation and worker revolt to the animals harnessed into grim service by the lords of capital. By the 1930s, so Matt Cartmill writes in his excellent history of hunting, *A View to a Death in the Morning*, "some Marxist thinkers… urged that it was time to put an end to nature and that animals and plants that serve no human purpose ought to be exterminated."

Marx liked to disparage his enemies by calling them baboons. But what would Marx have made of the baboons of northern Africa, hunted down by animal traders, who slaughtered nursing mother baboons and stole their babies for American zoos and medical research labs. The baboon communities violently resisted this risible enterprise, chasing the captors through the wilderness all the way to the train station. Some of the baboons even followed the train for more than a hundred miles and at distant stations launched raids on the cars in an attempt to free the captives. How's that for fearless solidarity?

Fidel Castro, one of Marx's most ardent political practitioners, reinvented himself in his 80s as a kind of eco-guerilla, decrying the threat of global warming and advocating green revolutions. Yet Castro likes nothing more than to take visiting journalists to the Acuario Nacional de la Habana to watch captive dolphins perform tricks. The cetaceans are kept in wretched conditions, often trapped in waters so saturated with chlorine that it burns ulcers in the skin and peels the corneas off the eyeballs. Cuba captures and breeds dolphins for touring exhibitions and for sale to notoriously noxious aquatic parks throughout South America. The captive dolphins in Havana are trained by Celia Guevara, daughter of Che. There, as in other dolphin parks, food is used as a weapon in the pitiless reconditioning of the brainy sea mammals. Do the trick right or you don't get fed. Is it any wonder then that many captive dolphins have chosen to bite the hand that starves them?

In this respect, at least, Adam Smith comes out a little more humane than the Marxists. Although he viewed animals as property, Smith recoiled at the sight of the abattoir: "The trade of a butcher is a brutal and odious business."

Through the ages, it's been the poets who have largely held firm in their affinity with the natural world. Consider the *Metamorphoses* composed by the Roman poet and political dissident Ovid around the time of Christ's birth. In the final book of this epic, where humans are routinely transformed into animals, Ovid summons the spirit of Pythagoras. The great sage of Samos, whom Aristotle hailed as the father of philosophy, gives the most important speech in the poem. But the author of the famous Theorem forsakes the opportunity to proclaim that mathematics is the foundation of nature. Instead, Ovid's Pythagoras denounces the killing of animals for food and asserts the sanctity of all life forms.

> "What evil they contrive, how impiously they prepare to shed human blood itself, who rip at a calf's throat with the knife, and listen unmoved to its bleating, or can kill a kid goat to eat, that cries like a child, or feed on a bird, that they themselves have fed! How far does that fall short of actual murder? Where does the way lead on from there?"

Where indeed. To hell, perhaps? That's what John Milton thought. Milton's God advises Adam that animals have the power of cognition and indeed they "reason not contemptibly."

Crusty Robert Burns tells a frightened field mouse:

> I'm truly sorry Man's dominion
> Has broken Nature's social union,
> An' justifies that ill opinion,
> Which makes thee startle,

> At me, thy poor, earth-born companion,
> An' fellow-mortal!

Samuel Taylor Coleridge expressed similar fraternal sentiments to a donkey chained in a field:

> Poor Ass! thy master should have learnt to show Pity –
> best taught by fellowship of Woe!
> For much I fear me that *He* lives like thee,
> Half famished in a land of Luxury!
> How *askingly* its footsteps hither bend!
> It seems to say, "And have I then *one* friend?"
> Innocent foal! thou poor despised forlorn!
> I hail thee *Brother* — spite of the fool's scorn!
> And fain would take thee with me, in the Dell
> Of Peace and mild Equality to dwell …

Lord Byron objected to angling, saying it inflicted unnecessary pain on trout, and ridiculed Izaak Walton for debasing poetry in promotion of this "cruel" hobby. His Lordship would, no doubt, have been outraged by the inane past-time of "catch-and-release" fishing.

Byron's arch-nemesis William Wordsworth wrote a stunning poem titled "Hart-Leap Well," tracking the last moments in the life a mighty stag chased "for thirteen hours" to its death by a horse-riding knight and his hounds. The ballad closes with a stark denunciation of hunting for sport:

> "This Beast not unobserved by Nature fell;
> His death was mourned by sympathy divine.
>
> "The Being, that is in the clouds and air,
> That is in the green leaves among the groves,
> Maintains a deep and reverential care
> For the unoffending creatures whom he loves.
> …
> "One lesson, Shepherd, let us two divide,
> Taught both by what she [ie. Nature' shows, and what conceals;
> Never to blend our pleasure or our pride
> With sorrow of the meanest thing that feels."

The great, though mad, naturalist-poet John Clare openly worshipped "the religion of the fields," while William Blake, the poet of revolution, simply said:

> For every thing that lives is Holy,
> Life delights in life.

And, finally, there is the glorious precedent of Geoffrey Chaucer, who reveals himself to be an animal liberationist. In the "General Prologue" to *The Canterbury Tales*, Chaucer describes the Prioress as a woman who cannot abide the abuse of animals.

> But for to speken of hir conscience,
> She was so charitable and so pious
> She wolde wepe, if that she sawe a mous
> Caught in a trappe, if it were deed or bledde.
> Of smaule houndes hadde she that she fedde
> With rosted flessh, or milk and wastel-breed.
> But soore wepte she if oon of hem were deed,
> Or if men smoot it with a yerde smerte;
> And al was conscience and tender herte.

Later in the remarkable "Tale of the Manciple," Chaucer goes all the way, arguing forcefully against the caging of wild songbirds. The English language's first great poet concludes that no matter how well you treat the captives, the birds desire their freedom:

> "Taak any bryd, and put it in a cage,
> And do al thyn entente and thy corage
> To fostre it tendrely with mete and drynke,
> Of alle deyntees that thou kanst bithynke;
> And keepe it al so clenly as thou may,
> Although his cage of gold be nevere so gay,
> Yet hath this bryd, by twenty thousand foold,
> Levere in a forest that is rude and coold
> Goon ete wormes, and swich wrecchednesse;
> For evere this bryd wol doon his bisynesse
> To escape out of his cage, whan he may.
> His libertee this brid desireth ay."

It would take the philosophers nearly six hundred years to catch up with Chaucer's enlightened sentiments. In 1975, the Australian Peter

Singer published his revolutionary book *Animal Liberation.* Singer demolished the Cartesian model that treated animals as mere machines. Blending science and ethics, Singer asserted that most animals are sentient beings, capable of feeling pain. The infliction of pain was both unethical and immoral. He argued that the progressive credo of providing "the greatest good for the greatest number" should be extended to animals and that animals should be liberated from their servitude in scientific labs, factory farms, circuses and zoos.

A quarter century after the publication of *Animal Liberation,* Peter Singer revisited the great taboo of bestiality in an essay titled "Heavy Petting." Expressing sentiments that would have shocked Grand Inquisitor Boguet, Singer argued that sexual relations between humans and animals should not automatically be considered acts of abuse. According to Singer, it all comes down to the issue of harm. In some cases, Singer suggested, animals might actually feel excitement and pleasure in such inter-species couplings. Even for the most devoted animal rights advocates this might be taking E. O. Wilson's concept of biophilia a little too literally.

In *Fear of the Animal Planet,* historian Jason Hribal takes a radical, but logical, step beyond Singer. Hribal reverses the perspective and tells the story of liberation from the animals' points-of-view. This is history written from the end of the chain, from inside the cage, from the depths of the tank. Hribal's chilling investigation travels much further than Singer dared to go. For Hribal, the issue isn't merely harm and pain, but consent. The confined animals haven't given their permission to be held captive, forced to work, fondled or publicly displayed for profit.

Hribal skillfully excavates the hidden history of captive animals as active agents in their own liberation. His book is a harrowing, and curiously uplifting, chronicle of resistance against some of the cruelest forms of torture and oppression this side of Abu Ghraib prison.

Hribal takes us behind the scenes of the circus and the animal park, exposing methods of training involving sadistic forms of discipline and punishment, where elephants and chimps are routinely beaten and terrorized into submission.

We witness from the animals' perspective the tyrannical trainers, creepy dealers in exotic species, arrogant zookeepers and sinister
hunters, who slaughtered the parents of young elephants and apes in
front of their young before they captured them. We are taken inside the
cages, tents and tanks, where captive elephants, apes and sea mammals
are confined in wretched conditions with little medical care.

All of this is big business, naturally. Each performing dolphin can
generate more than a million dollars a year in revenue, while orcas can
produce twenty times that much.

This is a history of violent resistance to such abuses. Here are stories
of escapes, subterfuges, work stoppages, gorings, rampages, bitings, and,
yes, revenge killings. Each trampling of a brutal handler with a bull-hook,
each mauling of a taunting visitor, each drowning of a tormenting trainer
is a crack in the old order that treats animals as property, as engines of
profit, as mindless objects of exploitation and abuse. The animal rebels
are making their own history and Jason Hribal serves as their Michelet.

Hribal's heroic profiles in animal courage show how most of these
violent acts of resistance were motivated by their abusive treatment
and the miserable conditions of their confinement. These animals are
far from mindless. Their actions reveal memory not mere conditioning,
contemplation not instinct, and, most compellingly, discrimination not
blind rage. Again and again, the animals are shown to target only their
abusers, often taking pains to avoid trampling bystanders. Animals, in
other words, acting with a moral conscience.

So let us now praise infamous animals.

Consider the case of Jumbo the Elephant, the world's most famous
animal. Captured in eastern Africa in 1865, Jumbo would become the
star attraction of P.T. Barnums' Circus. Jumbo earned millions for his
owners, but he was treated abysmally for most of his brief life. The giant
pachyderm was confined to a small compartment with a concrete floor
that damaged his feet and caused his joints to become arthritic. He
was trained using unspeakably brutal methods, he was shackled in leg-
chains, jabbed with a lance, beaten with ax handles, drugged and fed
beer to the point of intoxication. He was endlessly shipped back-and-
forth across the country on the circus's train and made to perform two

shows a day, six days a week. At the age of 24 Jumbo was finally fed up. He could tolerate it no more. On a September night in Ontario, Jumbo and his sidekick, the small elephant called Tom Thumb, broke free from their handlers and wondered away from the tent and towards the train tracks. As P.T. Barnum later told the story, Jumbo pushed his pal Thom Thumb safely off the tracks and tried to ram an oncoming train. After Jumbo died an autopsy was performed. His stomach contents revealed numerous metallic objects that he had been fed over the years, including keys, screws, bolts, pennies and nickels—his reward for entertaining hundreds of thousands of people.

Tatiana the Tiger, confined for years in a small enclosure at the San Francisco Zoo, finally reached her limit after being tormented by three teenaged boys on Christmas day 2006. She leapt the twelve-foot high wall, snatched one of the lads in her paws and eviscerated him. She stalked the zoo grounds for the next half-hour, by-passing many other visitors, until she tracked down the two other culprits and mauled them both before being gunned down by police.

There is Ken the Orangutan who pelted an intrusive TV news crew with his own shit from his enclosure at the San Diego Zoo.

Moe the Chimpanzee, an unpaid Hollywood actor who, when he wasn't working, was locked in a tiny cage in West Covina. Moe made multiple escapes and fiercely resisted his recapture. He bit four people and punched at least one police officer. After his escape, he was sent off to a miserable confinement at a dreary place called Jungle Exotics. Moe escaped again, this time into the San Bernadino Mountains, where he's never been heard from since.

Speaking of Hollywood, let's toast the memory of Buddha the Orangutan (aka Clyde), who co-starred with Clint Eastwood in the movie *Every Which Way But Loose*. On the set, Buddha simply stopped working one day. He refused to perform his silly routines any more and his trainer repeatedly clubbed him in the head with a hard cane in front of the crew. One day near the end of filming Buddha, like that dog in Racine's play, snatched some doughnuts from a table on the set. The ape was seized by his irate keeper, taken back his cage and beaten to death with an ax handle. Buddha's name was not listed in the film's credits.

Tyke the Elephant was captured in the savannahs of Zimbabwe and shipped to the United States to work in a traveling circus, where she was routinely disciplined with a sharp hook called an ankus. After 20 years of captivity and torture, Tyke reached her tipping point one day in Honolulu. During the elephant routine under the Big Top, Tyke made her break. She smashed through the railings of the ring and dashed for the exits. She chased after circus clowns and handlers, over-turned cars, busted through a gate and ran onto the streets of Honolulu. She was gunned down, while still wearing her rhinestone tiara.

Then there is the story of Tilikum the orca. When he was two, Tilikum was rudely seized from the frigid waters of the North Atlantic off the coast of Iceland. The young killer whale was shipped to Vancouver Island, where he was forced to perform tricks at an aquatic theme park called Sealand. Tilikum was also pressed into service as a stud, siring numerous calves for exploitation by his captors. Tilikum shared his small tank with two other orcas, Nootka and Haida. In February 1991, the whales' female trainer slipped and fell into the tank. The whales wasted no time. The woman was grabbed, submerged repeatedly, and tossed back and forth between the three whales until she drowned. At the time of the killing, Haida was pregnant with a calf sired by Tilikum.

Eight years later, a 27-year-old man broke into the aquatic park, stripped off his clothes and jumped into the tank with Tilikum. The orca seized the man, bit him sharply and flung him around. He was found floating dead in the pool the next morning. The authorities claimed the man died of hypothermia.

In 2010, Tilikum was a star attraction at Sea World in Orlando. During an event called "Dining With Shamu," Tilikum snatched his trainer, Dawn Brancheau, and dragged her into the pool, where, in front of horrified patrons, he pinned her to the bottom until she drowned to death. The whale had delivered his third urgent message.

Tilikum is the Nat Turner of the captives of Sea World. He has struck courageous blows against the enslavement of wild creatures. Now it is up to us to act on his thrust for liberation and build a global movement to smash forever these aquatic gulags from the face of the Earth.

— Oregon City.

Sources

Bierne, Piers, "The Law is an Ass," *Society and Animals,* Vol. 2 No. 1. (1994)

Boguet, Henri. *An Examen of Witches.* Trans. E.A. Ashwin. Portrayer Pub. (2002)

Cartmill, Matt. *A View to a Death in the Morning: Hunting and Nature.* Harvard. (1996)

Castillo, Hugo P. "Captive Marine Mammals in South America," *Whales Alive!,* Vol. 7, No. 1 (1998)

Coe, Sue and Cockburn, Alexander. *Dead Meat.* Running Press. (1996)

Cohen, Esther. "Law, Folklore and Animal Lore." *Past and Present* 110. (1986)

Davis, Susan. *Spectacular Nature: Corporate Culture and the Sea World Experience.* University of California. (1997)

Dubois-Desaulle, Gaston. *Bestiality: An Historical, Medical, Legal and Literary Study.* Panurge. (1933)

Evans, E. P. *The Criminal Prosecution and Capital Punishment of Animal.* Faber and Faber. (1987)

Ferrero, William. "Crime Among Animals." *Forum,* 20. (1895)

Finkelstein, J.J. "The Ox That Gored." *Transactions of the American Philosophical Society,* 71. (1981)

Frazer, James G. *Folklore in the Old Testament.* Tudor. (1923)

Girgen, Jen. "The Historical and Contemporary Prosecution of Animals." *Animal Law.* Vol. 9:97. (2003)

Humphrey, Nicholas. *The Mind Made Flesh.* Oxford University Press, (2002)

Hyde, W. W. "The Prosecution and Punishment of Animals and Lifeless Things in the Middle Ages and Modern Times." *University of Pennsylvania Law Review,* 64, 7, 690–730. (1914)

Peterson, Dale and Goodall, Jane. *Visions of Caliban: On Chimpanzees and Humans.* University of Georgia Press. (1993)

Salisbury, Joyce. *The Beast Within: Animals in the Middle Ages.* Routeledge. (1994)

Serpell, James. *In the Company of Animals.* Oxford University Press. (1986)

Singer, Peter. *Animal Liberation: A New Ethics for Our Treatment of Animals.* Random House. (1975)

—. "Heavy Petting." *Nerve.* (2001)

Tester, Keith. *Animals and Society: the Humanity of Animal Rights.* Routledge. (1991)

Thomas, Keith. *Man and the Natural World.* Oxford University Press. (1983)

—. *Religion and the Decline of Magic.* Oxford University Press. (1970)

A MESSAGE FROM TATIANA

It was on December 26, 2007, when people around the world would first hear about the shocking attack that had occurred at the San Francisco Zoo. One person had been killed and two others critically injured. Blood was splattered everywhere. The police had gunned down the perpetrator. It was, according to all reports, a scene of mass chaos. For not only had a murderous assault taken place on Christmas day, but the killer was not even human.

Tatiana was a four-and-a-half year old Siberian tiger. She had been born in Denver, Colorado, but she was transferred to San Francisco in 2005. She was, at the time, considered to be a sparkling new addition to the zoo's tiger exhibition. Such embracing attitudes did not last long, especially after Tatiana managed to scale the twelve-foot high wall of her enclosure and escape. There had been these teenagers. They were yelling obscenities, waving their arms, and possibly throwing stuff at her. One visitor described how these young men had been doing the same exact thing with the nearby lions, and that the lions were pissed off. The woman gathered up her family and promptly left the area. Angry lions are scary, even when they are tucked behind bars. Tigers can be even more frightening.

Tatiana went directly after the men who had been taunting her and ripped one of them to pieces. The other two ran. For twenty minutes, Tatiana roamed the zoo grounds. She was presented with many opportunities to attack park employees and emergency responders. She could easily have gone after other visitors. But Tatiana was singular in her purpose. She wanted to find those two remaining teenagers, and she would do just that at the Terrace Cafe. With a dismembering taking place, police encircled the spot and shined their lights onto the tiger. Tatiana turned and approached. They shot her dead.

Zoos and circuses have a standard operating procedure in dealing with the aftermath of such incidences of violence by captive animals. Step One is to claim that escapes and attacks are very rare. They almost never happen. The general public has nothing to worry about. Journalists have nothing to investigate. Yet, we have to ask, is this true? It was one year earlier when Tatiana attacked a trainer. With families watching from about four feet away, the tiger squeezed her paws through the narrow bars of the cage, clawed onto a keeper's arm, and pulled it in for a bite. "While we were heading out," a parent lamented, "I could still hear . . . screaming." San Francisco officials would state that it was "the only injury of its kind that has happened at the zoo." This was not true. Tinkerbelle the elephant had been involved in a series of dust ups with zoo employees. Then there was Fatima, a female Persian leopard. In 1990, she jumped onto the back of a trainer and bit his neck. "I thought the leopard was going to kill him," one onlooker noted. "He was screaming, 'Help me, help me; get him off, get him off.' I was scared. That was not the kind of thing I expected to see at the zoo." If only the visitor had known.

In the past two decades, in the United States alone, captive tigers have killed ten people and injured countless more. A partial list would include the 2008 attack on a trainer at the Hawthorn Corporation. Hawthorn is a leasing agency and training facility located outside of Chicago, Illinois. Its fifty tigers are loaned out throughout the year to various circuses and entertainment enterprises. In 2007, it was Berani, a Sumatran tiger, who chomped onto a trainer's head at the San Antonio Zoo. A year before that it was a tiger named Enshala at the Lowry Park Zoo in Tampa, Florida. Enshala escaped her enclosure and went after a veterinarian. Lowry's ten-member weapons team, trained by local police, assembled. Many zoos, in fact, have these armed squads whose sole purpose is to respond to escapes and attacks. As for Enshala's fate, she would die after being hit by four shotgun blasts.

In 2005, it would be back to Hawthorn—where a tiger attacked a touring visitor. In 2004, the Cole Brothers Circus had an escapee run into the Forest Hills neighborhood of Queens. His name was Apollo, a white Bengal tiger, and he would startle picnic-goers and cause a five car pile-up on the Jackie Robinson Parkway. In 2003, another white

Bengal made the news. It was during a Siegfried and Roy show in Las Vegas, when Montecore clamped down on the neck of Roy Horn and dragged him off stage. Roy barely survived the encounter. That same year a Sumatran tiger named Castro attacked his trainer at the Sacramento Zoo. The man would also survive, but not by much. In 2000, an Amur tiger escaped during a fundraiser at Zoo Boise in Idaho. "Feast for the Beast," as the party was publicized, was almost just that. The tiger chased down a patron and began chewing on her. Police ended up shooting the woman but missed the cat.

In 1998, it was Ringling Brothers and Barnum and Bailey Circus's turn for trouble. While stopped in St. Petersburg, Florida in January, several tigers were brought into the center of the ring for a photography session. Trainer Richard Chipperfield was in charge. At some point in the photo session Arnold, a four year-old tiger, decided to grab a hold of Chipperfield's head with his teeth. Only after being whipped and sprayed with a fire extinguisher did the tiger let go. But the damage had been done. Arnold was returned to his cage, and the trainer's brother, Graham, executed the tiger with five shots. Graham himself had been attacked several years earlier by a group of performing lions. As for Ringling Brothers, their problems would continue. In November of that same year, another tiger would escape and take a run at a trainer. It also ended violently.

Our list of confrontations could go on. We could add to those incidents that happened outside of the United States. There was, for example, a tiger attack in Moscow in February of 2006. Asked afterwards about whether the Russian circus was going to kill the tiger involved, the trainer responded with honesty. "If we were to shoot every tiger that attacks us, there wouldn't be any remaining." Not so lucky was the fugitive tiger from a Polish show. In March of 2000, this animal fled into the streets of Warsaw. A circus veterinarian tried to stop him and they tussled. Police opened fire and killed both man and tiger.

Also, we have not even begun to address the activities of other big cats: lions, jaguars, cougars and cheetahs. The latter, for instance, seems to be particularly adept at the art of escape. Olivia the cheetah climbed a fence, bounced off a tree, and cleared a wall to get out her San Antonio

Zoo enclosure. She roamed the visitor-filled park for twenty minutes. Halala scrambled over a twelve-foot wide moat and a twelve-foot high wall at the St. Louis Zoo. Keepers had no idea how she did it. At the Nashville Zoo, an unidentified male cheetah would spend ten hours on the loose before being captured. And who could forget what happened in October of 2008. Two cheetahs, while being transferred to the Memphis Zoo, escaped from their cages and strolled about the cargo hold of their Boeing 757 passenger flight. Indeed, such incidences occur far more often than the zoos and circuses would lead us to believe.

Step Two in the standard operating procedure is to deny agency. The key words to remember are "accident," "wild," and "instinct." The tiger injured her trainer by accident. She is, after all, a wild animal. She was just following her instinct. Repeat these lines enough and people will believe you. Yet, when we begin to explore these incidents more deeply, we discover that the zoos and circuses are deceiving us once again. Tatiana targeted a group of teasers. She could have escaped the enclosure anytime, but she needed motivation. She could have attacked others, but she wanted revenge. A frequent visitor to the zoo told a reporter of witnessing a similar attempt by another tiger in 1997. The unnamed female had just missed scaling over the wall. Evidently, she wanted at the nearby keeper. As the man would explain to those around him, "She always does that. She hates my guts." The veterinarian at Lowry Park admitted to the same thing after Enshala was killed. "This cat hates me." Remember the case of Fatima, the leopard who jumped onto the back of a San Francisco trainer. Schoolchildren told a newspaper reporter that only seconds before the attack the man washing out her cage had sprayed Fatima with water. Or how about Montecore. She had been performing for over six years at a clip of eight shows a week. The night of the attack she refused to obey a command and the trainer threatened her. She bit the man's arm. When the trainer hit her in the head with a microphone, she grabbed him by the throat. In each of these scenarios, the actions were neither accidental nor instinctual. These cats attacked for a reason.

Consider the case of captive elephants. These animals have the capability of inflicting large-scale fatalities. They are big, strong, and fast. Yet, when given the opportunity to plow through a crowd of visitors or stomp a row of spectators, they almost never do. Instead, they target specific individuals. There is the case of Janet, a Great American Circus elephant. During her rampage in 1992, she had a group of children riding on her back. She could have easily thrown them off and killed them. But she didn't. Janet, in point of fact, paused midway through the melee, let someone remove the children, and then continued her assault on circus employees. As to her primary motivation, that was revealed when Janet picked up a fallen object off the ground and smashed it repeatedly against a wall. The object turned out to be a bullhook.

The bullhook, or ankus, is a nasty device that the many zoos and circuses use to train their elephants. It looks like a crowbar but with a sharpened point on the curled end. Think of a large inverted fishhook and you would be on the right track. Trainers use the device as a weapon to strike, stab, and cause pain and fear. Ringling Brothers trainers were videotaped in 2009 viciously beating their elephants with these instruments of torture. The philosophy behind the bullhook is straightforward: violence equals discipline. It is with no understatement to say that the methods of training in this industry can be brutal.

Circuses, for example, have long preferred the use of the whip as their means to direct tigers and lions. The whip allows the trainer to maintain a safe distance and still deliver a good deal of pain and fear. Some circuses have updated to more modern devices: electrical prods and stun guns. Others have chosen to stick with the blunt instruments. Hawthorn's trainers, for example, like to use baseball bats. But no matter the instrument, the purpose of these weapons is control. The trainer wants the tiger to jump through a hoop of fire. The tiger does not want to. The trainer whips, shocks, or beats the animal until he or she performs the action. This is a learned response, and all captive animals have had to endure this violent education. Some of them have been taught with negative reinforcements. Others have been fortunate enough to train with positive reinforcements. In either case, here is where things can take an interesting turn.

Every captive animal knows, through learned response and direct experience, which behaviors are rewarded and which ones are punished. These animals understand that there will be consequences for incorrect actions. If they refuse to perform, if they attack a trainer, or if they escape their cage, they know that they will be beaten, have their food rations reduced, and be placed in solidarity confinement. Captive animals know all of this and yet they still carry out such actions—often with a profound sense of determination. This is why these behaviors can be understood as a true form of resistance. These animals, as will be shown throughout the book, are rebelling with knowledge and purpose. They have a conception of freedom and a desire for it. They have agency.

We have now officially reached dangerous ground, as the above claims will always be met with the accusation of anthropomorphism. According to many, only humans can be endowed with emotions, culture, intellect, and the ability to resist. But there is a retort. The main thing to understand about the idea of anthropomorphism is that, historically, it has no empiricism behind it. Rather, it is a loaded term: loaded with political, economic, social, and cultural meanings. The Catholic Church, in ancient times, used it to destroy paganism and thus increase the church's power and influence. Today, it is science and industry that wields the sword. Their methodology, though, is opposite to that of the church. Instead of uniting various sectors, they seek to divide and draw wide chasms between humans and other animals. This distance, they hope, will create a general public who neither knows nor cares about the lives and labors of tigers, elephants, or monkeys. It is a human centered and human dominated world, which science and industry seeks. This narrow perspective allows them to continue their exploitation of other animals in a completely unquestioned and unmolested fashion. The ultimate goal, of course, is to make the largest degree of profit possible.

As for those individuals who dare go against the idea, they will automatically be called out and publicly censured: "You are being anthropomorphic!" Sadly, this kind of reaction and labeling has led to self-censorship. There are lines of inquiry that a great many people are afraid to cross, as to do so can mean ridicule, castigation, and, yes, unemployment. The smart person will simply internalize the term. Nowhere has this behavior gained a stronger hold than within the university—home of the status quo. Yet, it should be remembered that it was not so long ago when, in universities across the country, the ideas of eugenics and

racism were also considered to be true, essential, and scientific catego-
ries of analysis. Professors loved them to no end. Today, the situation has
changed, and the university is embarrassed, even to the point of denial,
of its iniquitous past. Anthropomorphism awaits the same graveyard.

Step Three in the standard operating procedure is a public pledge to
prevent such incidences from ever happening again. If it was an escape
that occurred, then the zoo or circus will make design modifications.
San Francisco, for its part, extended the concrete wall and constructed a
glass partition, which raised the overall height of the tiger exhibition to
nineteen feet. Electrified hot wires were strung along the moat. The zoo
put up signs that forbid the harassment of animals. If it was an attack that
occurred then these institutions will change their protocol. The training
of employees will be made more extensive and intensive. Handlers may
no longer be allowed direct contact with the animals. Also, the animal
perpetrators themselves could undergo retraining or be placed under
an entirely new system of management. But, if the animal is a repeat
offender, then the zoo or circus might get rid of him or her altogether.
In the past, summary executions were used. Some of the more popular
methods included firing squads, poisonings, and hangings. These have
since become a political liability, so the industry has instead turned to
animal dealers for help.

This is how it works. Flagship institutions, such as the National
Zoo, the Lincoln Park Zoo, the San Diego Zoo, Six Flags, and Ringling
Brothers, will sell their unwanted animals to licensed auctioneers and
dealers. These individuals will then turn around and re-sell them to
unlicensed third parties. Alan Greene's *Animal Underworld* (1999) can
provide more detail on this subject, but suffice it to say that the key facet
in this relationship is the absence of a direct connection between the
original sellers and the final buyers. Thus, zoos and circuses can deny
involvement in such dirty business and hide their avarice. As for the
unwanted animals, they will end up in private collections, canned
hunting operations, research labs, and exotic-meat slaughtering facilities. Some of the animals, especially tigers, will be killed outright for
their organs, fur, and claws. According to Interpol, the international
trade in exotics is an eight billion dollar a year industry. And no animal

is safe. These flagship institutions will sell endangered and non-endangered species alike: leopards, camels, Bengal tigers, antelopes, gazelles, lions, white rhinos, gorillas, chimps, and orangutans. Perhaps you will remember Knut, the famed polar bear cub. In 2007, a kind of hysteria revolved around him, as visitors by the thousands flocked to Germany to catch a glimpse. Knut's owner, the Berlin Zoo, licensed his image and placed it everywhere. The zoo made $8.6 million off of the Knut craze. Nevertheless, by December of 2008, Berlin wanted to dump the bear. Knut had grown up, and he was no longer cute or marketable. It was only through a public uprising that the zoo relented and agreed to keep the polar bear—at least, until the fervor dies down.

Step Four in the standard operating procedure is to manage public relations. The American Zoological and Aquarium Association (AZA), governing body of the industry, provides workshops on the successful PR techniques. The central thesis of them is this: control the information. Every institution should have a designated spokesperson. When questioned, and regardless of the question, this person should state repeatedly that the zoo is an important resource for conservation and education. Reassurances must also be made that appropriate changes have been implemented and that the park is safe for the return of visitors. Again, rigorous control is foremost in importance—as damaging information can easily leak out. Such was case in aftermath of Tatiana's raid.

News came that the tiger was being fed ten pounds less meat per individual feeding in San Francisco then she had been during her confinement in Denver. This led some to speculate that the zoo was trying to get Tatiana to be more active for visitors. If the tiger was continually hungry, the thinking went, she might move around more and thus be more entertaining to paying visitors. Officials were forced to deny the claim. Next came news of a $48 million bond, which the zoo had received earlier, almost all of which was spent on enhancements for visitors. The animals, meanwhile, continued to reside in decrepit and cramped exhibits. Tigers can have a range of over 100 square miles in their habitats of Eurasia. In San Francisco, Tatiana barely had only 1000-square feet to roam around in. Such realities of captivity are known to cause psychological problems: unconscious swaying, incessant pacing, and self-mutilation. Zoo officials, again, had to defend themselves. The tiger, they affirmed, was not suffering from depression and her enclosure was more than adequate in size. The final piece of bad news for the zoo came when it was revealed that there were two near escapes by other animals just a week after Tatiana's rampage.

During one of them, a female polar bear named Ulu tried to scramble over a wall but was turned back with the stinging spray from a firehose. A keeper quietly confided that Ulu only did this because he and others had been "pelting" the bear with empty tranquilizer darts. In response to this incident, the zoo's director followed standard procedure. "That doesn't sound like an escape attempt to me," he began to explain. The bear was simply being a bear. Yes, the zoo is now planning to raise the walls of Ulu's exhibit, but not because of what Ulu did. In all seriousness, the zoo's PR flacks suggested, this kind of scrutiny and questioning is unnecessary if not vindictive. The zoo is the real victim.

There is an African proverb. "Until the lion has his historian, the hunter will always be a hero." For myself, the meaning behind the adage has long represented a challenge—one which I took up in 1998. I had just recently matriculated to the University of Toledo in order to study with the historian Peter Linebaugh. My purpose was singular: I wanted to understand history from below. That fall, I took a research seminar on the Gilded Age, and the topic I chose to write about was the Toledo Zoo. It could have ended up being a standard history: the zoo and its directors, their curatorial ideas and the evolution in exhibit design, and a list of animals. Yet, my work with Linebaugh led me to see the research material in a new light. Information that I would have previously missed or passed over now became evident. More specifically, I noticed that the captive animals were resisting and that resistance was having an effect. The zoo and the circus no longer remained the hero.

In late 2006, I decided to engage this topic once again, and, through my research, the resistance became ever more evident. Captive animals escaped their cages. They attacked their keepers. They demanded more food. They refused to perform. They refused to reproduce. The resistance itself could be organized. Indeed, not only did the animals have a history, they were making history. For their resistance led directly to historical change. In the case of Tatiana, her eyes were burning bright that Christmas day. She inspired others and brought about larger questions concerning captivity and agency. Concerned citizens, animal advocacy groups, and the City Board of Supervisors all got involved. Even the *Wall Street Journal* published an article exploring the incident. The San Francisco Zoo, for its part, still has not recovered. Yet, we must never forget from where this struggle begins and ends: with the animals themselves.

A note on the book's primary and secondary sources. The vast majority of information came directly from newspapers, both national and international. Federal, state and local governmental documents filled in some important details. Lawsuits and their trail of paperwork supplied a scant more. On-line databases were rich with biographical detail—in particular, the Orca Homepage at www.orcahome.de and the Elephants Encyclopedia at www.elephant.se. Writings by the various 19th and early 20th century animal collectors, such as Frank Buck, Carl Hagenbeck, and Charles Mayer, were certainly of use—as were the manuscript collections at the Local History Department at the Toledo/Lucas County Library and the Toledo Zoo. *Bandwagon*, journal of the Circus Historical Society, assisted with its long-reaching archives. A handful of contemporary books were also helpful: Susan Davis, *Spectacular Nature* (Berkeley, 1997). Alan Greene, *Animal Underworld* (NY: 1999). Erich Hoyt, *The Performing Orca* (Bath, 1992). Eugene Linden, *The Parrot's Lament* (New York, 1999). Dale Peterson and Jane Goodall, *Visions of Caliban* (Athens, 2000). Charles Price, *The Day They Hung the Elephant* (Johnson City, 1992). Don Reed, *Notes from an Underwater Zoo* (New York, 1981).

CHAPTER ONE

ELEPHANTS EXIT THE BIG TOP

WHEN HE ARRIVED AT REGENT'S PARK IN 1865, THE ELEPHANT WAS sickly and underweight. Zoo officials were, to say the least, disappointed in their newest acquisition. Sure, he was quite young. But he was a bull-male. Shouldn't he have been a little bit bigger? In any case, this runt of an elephant needed a name. Park directors set to thinking. The calf was taken, so they thought, from somewhere inside of the French Sudan, and the cultures there were known for worshipping an idol called Mumbo Jumbo. Why not just shorten this and call him "Jumbo." Indeed, they decided, this would be a fitting name. It would ultimately prove to be a most ironic choice.

In truth, Mumbo Jumbo was anything but a complimentary christening for an elephant or any other creature. For the word was derogatory and demeaning—originating, not from the African lexicon, but from the European imperialist imagination. Mumbo Jumbo was a "grotesque" idol, an object of unintelligent veneration. Today, the title continues to hold onto its negative ethnocentrism: referring to obscure meaningless talk and writing; nonsense; or an ignorant ritual. Yet the abbreviated version of the term, Jumbo, has not. Its history has actually flowed in the opposite direction. Jumbo has come to mean big and enormous. It connates success and skill. A jumboism is a preference for largeness. Jumbomania is the idolization of largeness. A century ago, the mere whisper of "Jumbo" could bring about smiles and cheers. Its mention could even cause tears, sorrow, and solemn remembrance. Jumbo remains a word of respect. How did this divergence between the longer and shorter versions of the term happen?

The story begins with the capture of an infant elephant in Eastern (not Western) Africa, some time around 1861–2. After a lengthy and arduous journey across the Sahara Desert, the elephant who would become

Jumbo ended up in the markets of Cairo, Egypt. There, he was spotted and purchased by the animal collector Johann Schmidt. Schmidt specialized in the trade of exotic creatures. He bought them from trappers for a low price and sold them to European zoos for a high price. Such were the beginnings for one young, little elephant.

Schmidt dispatched his precious cargo across the Mediterranean Sea. Arriving in continental Europe, the elephant was then transported overland to Paris. Jumbo's new home turned out to be none other than the famous *Jardin des Plantes*. He was soon introduced to his first cage-mate. This was Alice, a young African female elephant. The pair, though, did not remain in the City of Lights for long.

The managers of the French menagerie soon decided that they wanted to add an Indian rhinoceros to the collection. The London zoo happened to have one and was willing to make a trade for a pair of elephants. With the deal agreed upon, Jumbo and Alice were shipped across the English Channel. The two arrived in London in 1865. The male elephant made for a disappointing show. Sickly and thin, he looked as if he could die at any moment. But, over the next few weeks, he made a robust recovery.

For the next seventeen years, Jumbo remained in London. And he grew and grew and grew: in terms of both size and popularity. Reaching a height of eleven and a half feet, the elephant came to weigh-in at a hefty six-and-a-half tons. This sheer size earned him the title of the world's largest elephant. As for his popularity, everyone knew about Jumbo: from the thousands of yearly visitors who gazed their eyes upon him during his exhibitions to the countless number of schoolchildren who rode on his back in the *howdah* (or Indian carriage). Even Queen Victoria, Theodore Roosevelt, and P.T. Barnum once made that steep climb onto the broad back of this mighty pachyderm. Jumbo was almost as well known in the Americas as he was in England. Yet, not everything was quite as idyllic as it might seem. For the Regent's Park Zoo did have a serious problem on its hands—one which it zealously kept secret from the general public.

Jumbo had always been known for his mild temperament. He was friendly to visitors. He was gentle around children. But, as he entered into his teens, his mood and behavior began to change. Jumbo had his own personal handler, a man called Matthew Scott. Scott earned his reputation as a top rank animal trainer years earlier when attempting to trap an angry, adult hippopotamus. The animal had escaped his enclosure and was running amok in the park. When cornered by the keeper, the hippo charged him and took a ferocious snap. Scott only survived this attack with his life and limbs intact by nimbly hopping a fence at the last second. His new job, by contrast, looked at first to be far simpler: taking care of a gentle elephant. By the 1880s, however, Scott found this assignment to be ever more challenging. Jumbo had now entered into adolescence.

Modern zoologists call this developmental period: *musth* (Hindi word for madness). And they define it as a phase of glandular secretion, higher testosterone-levels, and heighten sexual arousal. In other words, this is a case of over-active and uncontrollable hormones; otherwise known as "heat." One would have hoped that the fields of natural science would have moved beyond the 17th century and biological determinism. But to no avail. Non-physiological factors—such as captivity, poor labor-conditions, brutal training methods, or the grind of the entertainment industry—do not matter. Intellectual maturity and independence of mind are not considered. Rebellious attitudes and vengeful emotions do not exist. Freedom, or the desire for autonomy, is something that an elephant could never imagine. Agency is a non-concept.

But Jumbo was no scientist, and he certainly did not see himself as a machine. Resistance was his new thought. He flew into terrible rages. He tried repeatedly to escape. He hurled his body against his enclosure. On one occasion, while attempting to ram his fearsome tusks through the iron-doors of his exhibition cage, Jumbo injured himself so severely that surgery was required. Matthew Scott oversaw the procedure and, as usual, was able to calm the giant beast. The keeper's most successful method to soothe the elephant's nerves actually involved supplying Jumbo with large quantities of beer. This even became a ritual between the two: drinking time. Once, when the trainer forgot to give Jumbo his share of the nightly brew, he was slammed to the floor by the thirsty giant. Scott never made that mistake again. Yet, there were times—increasing in number as the years wore on—when inebriation did not work to quiet the elephant. It reached a point where Regent Park directors lived in constant fear of what Jumbo might do next. So afraid did they become that the principle director purchased an elephant gun for the protection of the zoo and its employees. If a fight ever got completely out of hand, Jumbo would be shot dead. But just when the situation looked its worse, the London zoo received an amazing stroke of good fortune.

P.T. Barnum's American circus, promoted as the Greatest Show on Earth, was lacking a center piece—that truly grand figure among other great spectacles. Barnum's archrival, the Cooper and Bailey's Allied Show, had its star: the baby Columbia. She was the first elephant ever born in captivity in the United States, and Barnum had made many bids to purchase her. But the Allied Show refused to sell. So Barnum did the next best thing, luring James Bailey to his side, and then went right on searching for another big-time celebrity. He soon found what he was looking for in London. This was Jumbo, a true icon with enough star power to fill his big top every night of the week. Barnum offered the zoo $10,000 for the elephant.

The Regent Park directors were elated. This was a lot of money, and Jumbo had simply grown too dangerous to keep. He had to be sold. The zoo, however, was not prepared for the sheer scale of negative publicity that it would receive regarding this move. The British public was outraged at the idea of shipping Jumbo off to the States. Thousands of children wrote letters to the Queen in protest. Lawsuits were filed to block the sale. Newspapers openly vilified park administrators. Yet, the zoo would not be swayed from its decision.

In the spring of 1882, patrons funneled in to catch one last glimpse of Jumbo and wave good-bye. Crowds of this size had never before been seen at Regents Park, and the zoo itself profited handsomely from this planned farewell, pocketing $40,000 in ticket sales alone. But the final day did come, and the elephant was escorted from his exhibit area and led onto the main grounds. The original plan was to load Jumbo into a large container, which would then be paraded through the London streets. The journey would end at a Thames quay for shipping. This plan, though, proved to be a far more difficult to carry out than first imagined. For Jumbo declined to enter the container.

Matthew Scott, his trainer, tried every technique he could think of to coax the huge elephant into the crate. But each time, Jumbo would approach, stop short, and proceed to lie down on the ground. After that, there was no budging him. As the days passed and embarrassment mounted, the London press declared that this delay was a testament to the fact that the elephant did not want to leave England. Barnum was not amused, and his agent in London grew impatient. The circus's chief handler was sent for. William Neuman, otherwise known as Elephant Bill, was Barnum's most notorious and brutal trainer. Instead of offering pachyderms a gallon of pale ale, Elephant Bill opted for a spear-like lance as his primary motivational tool. After his trip across the Atlantic, Neuman set to work straightaway at the reconditioning of Jumbo.

At first, the trainer tried more gentle means of persuasion: verbal commands, pushing, prodding. But none of these were successful. Next, he fitted the elephant with leg chains and pulled on the beast. This method too failed. Jumbo just flatly refused to enter the container. Neuman then pulled out his trusty lance and began using the weapon, but the Royal Society for the Prevention of Cruelty to Animals intervened and put a stop to the stabbings. Neuman was furious: both at this level of oversight, which would have never happened in the States, and at his own inability to quell Jumbo's recalcitrance. It was rumored that the American trainer even threatened to shoot the elephant, if that was the only way to get the animal to Barnum. Ultimately the use of lethal force was not needed, as Scott was finally able to convince Jumbo to walk into the crate. Some speculated that Scott himself was partially responsible for this delay, as he wanted to demonstrate his own self-importance. Nevertheless, after chaining the elephant into place, the trainers found themselves in trouble once again. Jumbo had abruptly changed his mind about the move and began to struggle with all his might, straining the iron chains and quaking the thick bars of the wheeled enclosure. But it was of no use. Not even the world's largest elephant could break free this time. Jumbo was taken out of Regents Park and transported down the Thames to the coast. From there, the elephant was hoisted onboard the *HMS Assyrian Monarch* for his long awaited trip across the Atlantic.

Jumbo reached New York harbor on Easter Sunday. With great fanfare, he marched through Midtown Manhattan to Madison Square Garden. The circus season had just kicked off, and he was now a member of P.T. Barnum's extravaganza. For the next several years, Jumbo would toil for Barnum. He traversed the country, shuffling from town to town. He rode on what must have seemed to be an endless train, being loaded up in a boxcar every night and unloaded every morning.

Jumbo was paired with Tom Thumb, the world's smallest elephant. Together, the pair of contrasting pachyderms would parade around the arena at the close of afternoon and evening programs. Life in the circus was a grind. The typical season lasted eight months, from March to October. Performances occurred six days a week, twice a day.

By his twenty-fourth year, the greatest star on Earth had been worn out. Whereas Barnum and others had made millions of dollars from this elephant, Jumbo himself had little to show for it. His body was exhausted, his strength sapped, and his vitality drained. Jumbo could barely even lie down. When he did, it was a struggle to return upright. Scott thought privately that Jumbo might not make it through another year on the circuit. And yet, another circus season had just begun. Opening in New York, the Barnum and Bailey big top had already traveled through Pennsylvania, New England, and Maritime Canada. By September it was in Ontario.

There are several versions of events that unfolded on September 15, 1885: the night that Jumbo the elephant was killed. Each begins in a similar manner. The circus was in St. Thomas, a small town located in the southern region of the province. The final performance had just ended. Tom and Jumbo were in the process of being led back to their respective train cars by Matthew Scott. While all three were walking along the tracks, the sound of a fast approaching freight train could be heard in the distance. It is at this point where the stories diverge.

One version has Scott, heroically but unsuccessfully, attempting to lead the elephants to safety by guiding them down a shallow embankment that bordered one side of the tracks. Another has the trainer scrambling off on his own, leaving the pair of elephants to their own devices. In both scenarios, the first to be hit by the locomotive was tiny

Tom Thumb. Tossed into the air like a rag-doll, he crashed into a nearby pole and sustained serious, but not life-threatening, injuries. Tom, years later, would be sold to the Central Park Zoo in New York City, where he would spend the rest of his days.

Jumbo was the next to be struck. It happened in one of three ways. The first account has the elephant initially following Scott down the embankment. However, Jumbo got confused or scared by the on-coming train, raced back up onto the tracks, and was hit from behind. Another has Jumbo rushing along the tracks. He was apparently looking for a gap in the line of stationary train-cars, which bordered the opposite side. But he missed the opening, and, when he doubled back, the train smashed into him. A third version has Jumbo escaping from Scott and charging towards the train. He rammed the engine head-on.

As for how Jumbo ultimately died, that also depends on which version of the story you believe. Some said that the world's most famous elephant was killed almost immediately. While others stated that he suffered for at least three hours before dying. Barnum himself cooked up his own tall tale: claiming that Jumbo died instantly after sacrificing his own life to rescue little Tom Thumb from the speeding train.

In the end, none of these unknowns, discrepancies, or fabrications are important. Jumbo died that autumn day. He spent his life working for the Regents Park Zoo and the Barnum and Bailey Circus.

Before the days of radio, television, or motion pictures, he was one of the first international superstars of the entertainment world. Indeed, over the past two centuries, books have been written about him. Songs have been sung in his honor. Movies have been made depicting him. An Ohio town was once named after him. He has been used to advertise countless consumer products.

To this day, Jumbo remains firmly planted in the English lexicon. That little, sickly elephant—once mocked as Mumbo Jumbo—grew into a large, powerful, and resistant fellow-creature, one still worthy of our respect and veneration.

Mary

The circus train had arrived early that Tuesday morning. The sky was still dark, and the railyard was just beginning to awaken. The place was Kingsport, a dusty coal-mining town hidden amongst the rolling hills of eastern Tennessee. Given its isolated location, the town rarely saw much in the way of big-time popular entertainment. The local residents must have been excited for the day's forthcoming festivities.

The circus was owned and operated by Charlie Sparks. Based in the southern region of the United States, Sparks World Famous Show catered to those small out-of-the-way towns often ignored by larger companies like Barnum and Bailey. The show first opened in the late 1880s. Founded by John Sparks, Charlie's father, it was a dog and pony act. This meant, literally, that Sparks had a few dogs and a pony performing tricks for an audience. Yet, over the next twenty-five years, the show grew into a mid-sized operation. It would come to boast of ten train-cars and feature numerous trapeze artists, gymnasts, equestrians, and clowns. The Sparks Show also had a couple of lions and five elephants. One of those pachyderm performers was a female named Mary.

Odds are that this elephant had been sold or traded at least a few times before reaching Charlie Sparks and his show. There was, of course, her original sale. She had been born in the jungles of southeastern Asia sometime around 1886. But she was soon captured, traded, and shipped to the Americas. By 1889, this young, little elephant was already working for her first circus. After that, it is difficult to say what happened to her. Circuses and traveling menageries went bankrupt frequently. Elephants exchanged hands. They were often renamed, especially if an elephant had a reputation for unruliness. No company wanted to deal with a performer who continually refused commands, injured trainers, or escaped from confinement. This was a hassle and a liability that few owners could afford. So what would usually happen in these circumstances is that the circus would try to sell the animal to someone who specialized in retraining disobedient and dangerous creatures. If that failed, the circus would change the name of that particular elephant and try to pass him or her off to an unsuspecting or desperate prospect. Either way, this issue was solved from its end, as the rogue beast was now someone else's problem. There were, however, some cases where the elephant in question had become so notorious that no one in their right mind would dare acquire the creature. In these situations, the animal would be put to death.

By 1916 Mary the elephant was owned by the Sparks World Famous Show. Mary was the star attraction, and Charlie Sparks promoted her as the largest living land animal on Earth. She was, according to the show's billing, three inches taller than Jumbo and weighed in at over five tons. Of course, these were very dubious claims. But this was the circus business, a less than honest profession populated by owners who regularly exaggerated about anything and everything. Still, Charlie Sparks made a shrewd move in comparing Mary to Jumbo. For even the most skeptical tobacco farmer remembered the exploits of Jumbo, and they would often purchase a ticket for that reason alone. It would be a mistake to underestimate just how well-known and respected Jumbo was in the late 19th and early 20th centuries. As for Mary, she had not reached that the same level of fame. Nor was she, in measurement, larger or heavier than Jumbo. Yet, audiences thronged to see her in considerable numbers. Mary was in her own right a mighty elephant, and she would forcefully prove that point in Kingsport.

The morning of September 12th began as most mornings did at the Sparks Circus. The animals were awakened and led out of their boxcars. Some were then loaded into wagons and carriers. Others, namely horses and elephants, were put to work. For each of these wagons and carriers had to be towed and pushed to the circus grounds. Every piece of equipment had to be carried. The most extensive labor involved setting up the big top. Gigantic poles had to be moved into their correct place. The canvas itself had to be unfolded and positioned just right. Cables had to be pulled to raise the entire structure. Indeed, without the bulk and strength of the elephant, this final feat would have hardly been possible.

With the morning tasks now complete, the circus's five pachyderms received a short but well deserved break. Their ankles would, as always, be chained and tethered to deter any inclinations of escape. Water and hay would be provided as their standard fare. The animals really needed this rest and nourishment, for their day was just beginning. Soon there would be the noon-time parade. This meant a complete shift in tasks: from manual labor to public entertainment. The elephants had to change into their costumes and march through the streets. They had to mull around with the local residents, pose for photographs and sketches, and give a few rides. They had to be happy, at least in appearance.

Next, there would be the two performances under the big top: a matinee at 2 pm and an evening show at 8 pm. The elephants had perform choreographed routines and tricks for the audience. They had to kneel on command. They had to stand on their hind legs. They had to balance on stools. They had to form a large circle with each elephant resting his or her front legs upon the back of another. None of this was easy.

Elephants know nothing of such things, as circus performances are not part of their society or culture. Nor do elephants, as strong and formidable as they may seem, even have the proper muscle development to carry out such demanding stunts. It takes months of rigorous training to learn these routines. It takes months to develop the stamina and muscle strength needed to perform these tricks. Then there is the harsh discipline and brutal treatment that each elephant had to endure in the name of training. Verbal abuse, beatings, and whippings were the common pedagogical methods. For example, in order to teach a performer how to lie down on cue, Charles Mayer—the leading elephant coach of the early 20th century—would stab an animal in one particular spot over and over again. Sooner or later, the elephant would lie down to protect the wound. After this procedure was repeated enough times, an amazing trick would be born: as the mere threat of being stabbed caused the animal to obey the command.

Finally, the circus would be packed up to travel to the next town for the next show. The tent had to be taken down and disassembled. All the equipment had to be reloaded. The wagons and carriers had to be hauled back to the train. It was only then, well into the witching hour, that the long, exhaustive day would finally come to a close. Unfortunately, another morning was soon on its way.

There were times, however, when the elephants did obtain reprieves from this monotonous, tiresome schedule. The most common type were short recreational walks. With a handler guiding them along, the elephants might amble into to a nearby field, explore a neighboring wooded area, or walk down a dirt road. Maybe, if they were lucky, they would discover a pond or a nice patch of mud. The ultimate point of these ventures was simply to get away from the circus—so that the animals could take in the sights, breathe some fresh air, and have a little natural stimulus. Ironically, it was during just such a relaxing perambulation in Kingsport when Mary chose to rebel against her trainer. A witness later described the scene.

While walking through Kingsport, Mary espied some watermelon. This sighting must have spiked her curiosity, as she stopped and reached for the rind. The temporary pause perturbed her handler. At first, he slapped at the elephant with a long stick and shouted for her to move along. Mary ignored the request and just kept chewing away. Some of the people watching this disagreement found it to be most comical and they began laughing aloud. The trainer was now growing embarrassed. He yelled angrily and struck the elephant viciously across the side of her head. This impetuous act of violence was not a smart move.

Mary grabbed the man with her trunk, raised him high into the air, and pitched him against the side of a nearby shack. Such was the force of this throw that the trainer crashed through the building's wall. With the thump of the body, the snap of the wooden boards, and the crunch of bones, the crowd stood there in a state of shock. Was the man dead? Was he still alive? Would anyone dare attempt to help him? But Mary put to end to such thoughts, as she walked calmly over to her handler and promptly stepped on his head. The crowd scattered.

Perhaps it was the deliberateness of Mary's action or maybe it was coolness of her demeanor, but whatever the cause, by the time the situation had settled down, the good citizens of Kingsport wanted blood. It did not seem to matter that no one from the town knew the deceased man. An elephant had killed a human and that was a good enough reason for an execution. Mary must die. Charlie Sparks, however, was not going to let his prized performer, and chief breadwinner, to be taken away that easily. The elephant was worth several thousand dollars. Hence, Sparks did his best to quell the public anger and convince local residents to change their minds. Mary, for the moment, remained safe.

As news of the stomping spread across the county and state, the clamor for retributive violence only increased. One eastern Tennessee newspaper deemed the elephant: "Murderous Mary." Towns announced that forthcoming circus shows would be cancelled if the man-killing elephant performed. Rumors circulated of approaching lynch mobs, the utilization of police force, and the intervention of the state government—each group seeking its own version of summary execution. By the time the circus reached the town of Erwin on the morning of September 13th, the pressure for action had intensified. The owner was forced to make a tough decision. Mary was to be executed after the matinee. This would be "the day," the folklorist Charles Price wrote, "they hung the elephant."

It would not be the first time that an elephant was killed in such a manner. Only three decades previous, Carl Hagenbeck—the father of the modern zoo—signed a "death warrant" for one of his performers after the animal almost killed him. "The monster," he demanded, "must be executed." Hagenbeck first tried to make a deal with an English sportsman, who, in exchange for a handsome sum of money, would receive the pleasure of shooting an elephant. For whatever reason, this arrangement fell through. So Hagenbeck and his crew hung the creature. There was also Columbia, the first elephant ever born in captivity in the United States. She was the one whom P.T. Barnum so coveted. Instead, he settled for Jumbo and little Columbia remained the pride and joy of the Cooper and Bailey Circus. This amicable relationship, however, did not last long. According to Charles Mayer, this elephant had developed a "nasty disposition" by the age of two. She struck keepers at the age of seven. By the age of eight, she was "kept hobbled." A few years later, Columbia, too, was hung to death.

Then there was the case of Topsy. In 1903, this thirty-six year old Coney Island elephant was slated to be executed by hanging. Luna Park officials even built a large scaffold for the grisly event. Yet the Society for the Prevention of Cruelty to Animals intervened and demanded that a more humane method be used. So officials chose electrocution. Topsy had originally come to New York City via the circus, but after killing her third trainer in three years, the elephant was sold to the nearby Brooklyn Boardwalk. The change in venues did not improve her situation or demeanor. Her handler turned out to be a drunk who was, on two occasions, arrested for physically abusing the elephant. Thus Topsy had no choice but to continue to resist. Her final act was charging after a group of Italian construction workers. A week later, several "very matter-of-fact electricians of the Edison Company" arrived at the park and began setting up for the execution. Edison had, for some time, been using Alternative Current (AC) to kill as many animals as possible in order to drive his archrival, George Westinghouse, out of business. Westinghouse used AC as his method of electrical supply, Edison used Direct Current (DC), and bad publicly (i.e., the apparent danger of AC current) could ruin anyone's reputation. On the afternoon of January 4th, Mr. Edision's executioners attached electrodes to the elephant's feet. At 2:45 pm, they flipped the switch. "There was a bit of smoke for an instant," a *New York Times* reporter noted. "Topsy raised her trunk as if to protest, then shook, bent to her knees, fell, and rolled over on her right side motionless." Two minutes later, she was declared dead.

As to the events a decade later, on September 13, 1916, Mary the elephant was held out of the afternoon show. Afterwards, she and the other elephants were collected and led off together into the adjacent railyards. While only Mary was to be punished, the trainers knew that she would probably become suspicious of any effort to remove her alone. They preferred to be safe than sorry. Upon arrival at the site, Mary was separated from her fellow performers and secured in place. There, she waited.

No one is certain how the method of execution was chosen. Legend has it that several means were discussed: poisoning, electrocution, and even draw and quartering via two opposite pulling steam-engines. Yet we do know the final decision. It was to be death by hanging. This was the South and lynching was the common form of punishment for those who dared resist the power and privilege of the white man. In fact, a few witnesses later swore that one or two African-Americans were also hung that afternoon in the hamlet of Erwin. But for Mighty Mary, a rope and tree branch would not do. A much larger and sturdier device was required. A 100-ton industrial crane was ultimately commandeered for the task.

By the time Mary was put into position under the crane, 3000 men, women, and children had gathered around the train yard. This crowd swelled to a size far greater than tiny Erwin's entire population. Apparently, everyone in the surrounding Tennessee counties wanted to the see this infamous elephant be put to death by the hand of man. None of them were to be disappointed.

The derrick car started up and a winch lowered a heavy metal cable. At the end of the cable was a linked chain. A handler grabbed the device and fastened it around the elephant's neck. The steam-powered engine began to roar and tow upward. Mary, though, was not about to go without a fight. As the noose tightened and pulled, she began to struggle and twist her body. The cable was not strong enough to withstand both the weight and the strain. It broke and Mary came crashing down with a thunder. The spectators erupted in panic, for the killer elephant was now free. Would she stampede through the crowd? Would she target her trainers? Or would she attack the rig and tear it apart? In reality, Mary was in no condition to retaliate. The fall shattered her hip. Collapsed there in a heap, immobilized and in agonizing pain, Mary must have been a pitiful sight. But her handlers were unmoved. Instead, they refashioned the noose and slid it on once again. This time, Mary was unable to free herself. The happy spectators settled back in and watched as the elephant died of asphyxiation.

Janet

Janet was a female elephant born in 1965. She had been captured in the tropical forests of Asia. Stripped from her mother and extended family, she was ultimately shipped to the United States. After her arrival, Janet was put to work in the circus, and it was in the circus where she remained for the rest of her life. Her main job was giving rides to children and adults. And it was one day, while providing just such an amusement, that this elephant reached her breaking point.

In 1992, Janet was toiling for the Great American Circus, a medium-sized operation based out of Sarasota, Florida. She had been owned by this same outfit since reaching the states nearly twenty-five years earlier, and she had grown quite disenchanted both with the company and her job. It was in February, while performing in the town of Palm City, Florida, when everything went down.

On the main stage inside the big tent, Janet was giving a ride to a group of schoolchildren. A crowd of some 1000 people watched and marveled at the spectacular display. But that delight soon turned to dread after Janet began resisting her trainers' commands. The elephant started thrusting her full weight against the steel barrier separating the ring from the audience. She toppled the high-wire platforms, which collapsed with a loud crash. A handler tried to calm the elephant but was rudely pushed aside. A police officer suddenly appeared and entered into the fray. He confronted Janet, but was promptly picked up by her trunk and slammed hard onto the concrete floor. As the cop lay there dazed and bruised, she grabbed him again and placed the man directly under her foot. He was going to be stomped. Several circus handlers, though, pulled him to safety at the last second. Janet seized this opportunity to bust through the barrier. She smoothly maneuvered through the screaming crowd, and escaped the arena.

Once she got outside, Janet began targeting certain people. Elephants, bear in mind, rarely forget: whether it be a face or a trespass. She chased down one circus employee and flattened him. Amid the chaos and the sea of hysterical patrons, Janet spotted another one of her tormentors trying to get away. This employee too was caught, toppled over, and plowed under. Janet was angry, and she has not been the only one.

It was in May of 1993 when Axel Gautier, the world famous trainer for Ringling Brothers and Barnum and Bailey Circus, was stomped to death. Descended from six generations of circus performers, this thirty-five year veteran developed such elaborate tricks as coaxing elephants to walk sideways on their hind legs. Gautier was on sabbatical from the Greatest Show on Earth and decided to tour the company's private breeding operations in Williston, Florida. Significantly, this facility—like its zoological counterparts—was opened in response to the strict new laws and regulations that had recently been passed regulating the exportation of elephants from foreign countries. Circuses and zoos no longer had easy access to their labor pool. The enterprises needed a new source. Thus, breeding programs and "conservation centers" sprang up around the country. As for Gautier and his visit to the Ringling operation, he went alone into a corral that contained a group of elephants. He must have known or trained at least few of them. In any case, the elephants knocked him down and stepped on him repeatedly. Gautier died of internal injuries. The circus maintained that this was an unfortunate accident, but they kept mum on the specific details. Twelve years later, another longtime Barnum trainer paid a visit to the facility, and the elephants promptly stomped him too.

In 1994, two handlers for the Jordon Circus were beaten up by an elephant named Sue. She had two kids riding on her back when she decided to grab one trainer with her trunk and hurl him into the air. The man landed with a thump. Sue strolled and stomped him repeatedly, breaking his arm, shattering several ribs, and inflicting damage to internal organs. The elephant then turned her attention to the other employee. Sue ran down the woman and kicked the crap out of her. It was only two years after that incident when Sue violently confronted a different trainer, this time in central Wyoming. When questioned by a local newspaper, a circus spokesman denied that this was an attack. The elephant, while giving a ride to six children, became "spooked" at the sight of a horse and backed into her handler. Spectators provided a much different story. They described how the elephant charged directly towards the trainer and bashed into the woman. Sue then began kicking the handler over and over again. When the women tried to escape, the elephant just pulled her back for more punishment.

In February of 1995, after a Tarzan Zerbini show, a trainer was trampled while attempting to load a female elephant into a trailer. Circus officials assured the media that this was a freak mishap, as the handler simply slipped under the elephant. Yet, according to a later lawsuit, this mauling was no accident. The former employee detailed how the animal purposely knocked him to the ground and stomped on him not once but twice. The elephant, he testified, was trying to kill him. Ten years later, there would be second confrontation involving a Tarzan Zerbini handler and the insides of a trailer. Again, the circus pleaded innocence: the man fell and the elephant was only "stepping on him out of curiosity, not out of aggressiveness." In the end, no lawsuit was filed, as the man had died from the wounds.

In April of 1999, yet another handler for Tarzan Zerbini went down. This time, an elephant broke free from her leg shackles and ran after this particular person. Spinning the man onto his back, she proceeded to deliver swift blows to the trainer's face, chest, and pelvis. Why did this happen? The circus would say nothing. However, an ambulance crew member noted that the injured man reeked of booze. Another employee confided that the circus's pachyderm performers were "originally trained by drunks and were badly beaten in the past. "Now," he warned, "the elephants don't like the smell of alcohol on people." A lesson to remember.

In January of 2000, an associate of the Ramos Circus was crushed to death at the outfit's home base in Florida. Kenya, an eleven year old African elephant, had managed to snap her leg chain and wander free. Indeed, while some people may know rivers, elephants know chains: as they are often tethered for fifteen, sixteen, or even more hours per day. At any rate, this elephant was now on the loose, and she targeted a member of the Ramos family. First, Kenya thumped the woman and trampled over top of her. The elephant then watched as this former acrobat struggled to her feet, only to push her over again and continue to deliver the lethal strikes. Kenya, shortly thereafter, joined this same woman in the afterlife—as the elephant also died. County authorities suspected foul play. Someone had poisoned her.

Finally, in 2006, a pair of trainers at a fair in Marlborough, Massachusetts were smashed up against a wall by a thirty-seven year old Asian elephant named Minnie. Both handlers were critically injured. A spokesman explained that the elephant, while being burdened with a group of children, shifted her position and accidentally bumped into the handlers. Visitors, on the other hand, gave a stunningly different report. They said that a trainer jabbed Minnie near the eye with a bull-hook. "People think the animal got crazy, but it was provoked," a witness said. The elephant was just trying "to defend itself." Several years previous, at the New York State Fair, there was a similar altercation involving Minnie. It was at end of a long day of hauling passengers when she knocked her handler into the grass, kicked him, and then stepped on him. This last action not only left a large imprint of Minnie's foot on the man's body but also a lasting impression upon his mind.

Interestingly, while scientists think they have identified the root cause of this kind of behavior in male elephants (i.e. *musth*), many remained mystified as to why it happens in females. For many decades, most thought that female elephants did not have the ability to act in such an aggressive manner. Sexism, it seems, does not just affect the way biologists see each other, but also the way they see other animals. In other words, while individuals have inferred (most infamously the former president of Harvard University, Larry Summers) that the discipline of science is better suited to men than women because of discrepancies in innate intellectual levels, so has science itself viewed female animals as unequal to males ones in similar ways. This is particularly the case with acts of resistance. It was and still is believed that female animals, as a whole, are simply incapable of this characteristic—at least not in any meaningful fashion or on any effectual level. Females are instead seen as imbibed with qualities of gentleness, placidity, and obedience. This is their nature; this is their instinct. Perhaps, biologists will address this issue sometime in the future. Of course, they will probably return and tell us that such kinds of behavior in females are nothing more than a variation of PMS.

Let us to return to Janet and the town of Palm City, Florida. One visitor snapped a photograph capturing this elephant sprinting along the midway with a group of children still clinging to her back. Eventually, circus officials were able to surround her and retrieve the frighten youngsters. Two handlers were then put in charge of loading the rogue elephant into the back of a trailer. But Janet declined the offer.

She snatched one of them and threw the man twenty feet into the air. She grasped the other and gave him a similarly high and mighty toss. Finished with those two, Janet began to ram her broad body against the trailer that she had been locked in so many times. Next, according to an eyewitness, "the elephant grabbed the training stick [from a fallen handler] and was slinging it against the van. Then she threw it down and just took off running." That stick, otherwise known as an ankus or bull-hook, is the primary teaching tool for elephants. It is an instrument meant to inflict pain and submission. Terror is how elephants are ruled. And Janet hated both: the ankus and the ankus-wielder.

It was just two years earlier when a Great American Circus elephant, very possibly Janet herself, pummeled a trainer during a show in Pennsylvania. Audience members later detailed how the animal, only seconds before the attack, refused to obey a series of instructions. The handler, at that point, commenced hitting the performer in the left ear and eye with an ankus and then hooked the creature's mouth with the barbed point. This type of corrective violence towards elephants is usually kept well-hidden by circuses but, on rare occasions, it makes a public appearance for all to see.

This was the situation with Mickey the elephant in September of 1994. This fifteen-year-old elephant was working for the King Royal Circus. During a performance in Lebanon, Oregon, he refused to perform a trick. The trainer shouted and promptly gouged the elephant in the neck with the bull-hook, drawing blood and gasps of horror from the audience. A few people called the cops. After the show, the handler was arrested and dragged off to the city jail. Responding to the brutal act, the King Royal manager fumed that "these animals can become killers." "What I'd like to do with these protesters," she continued, "is take our nicest elephant and put it in their back yards for about an hour. Then they'd see just how much destruction one of these guys can really inflict."

As to the escalating situation on the Florida midway, the police—at the request of the owner of the Great American Circus—stepped in and drew their weapons. A crowd of spectators had already encircled the scene. "All the people were yelling," one bystander recalled. "They were saying you shouldn't shoot that animal." The audience had chosen a side in this struggle, and it was not with the circus. Alas, the police paid no mind to public opinion and began their fusillade: firing a total of forty-seven bullets into the elephant. Janet fell in the hail of gunfire. She lay prostrate on the ground, bleeding profusely but still alive. Fifteen minutes later, an officer arrived with larger caliber bullets and finished her off. Janet's bullet-ridden body was taken to the local garbage dump and unceremoniously discarded.

Debbie and Frieda

In just a two month span, Debbie and Frieda perpetrated a lifetime of trouble. The pair of elephants escaped twice. They caused tens of thousands of dollars worth of property damage. They engendered lawsuits and bad publicity. They frightened city officials and drove their employers, the Clyde-Beatty Circus, mad with frustration. In the end, Debbie and Frieda had worn out their welcome. They would, subsequently, lose their positions at the circus and be sold off to the infamous animal contracting firm, Hawthorn.

The turmoil began in May of 1995. The circus was in Hanover, Pennsylvania for the week and the trainers were already on edge. Apparently, they were worried about the elephants, who were in an agitated and irritable state. Some speculated that the beasts' bad mood was due to the surface of the North Hanover Mall parking lot on which the animals were being kept. The black-top was bothering the elephants' feet. Others thought that the handlers were being overly nervous, as these animals had worked on such surfaces before and without incident. In either case, circus administrators should have paid closer attention to the situation.

On Friday the 19th, the elephants were awaiting their entrance into the big tent when two of them broke away. Sprinting from their trainers and maneuvering through the protective fencing, Debbie and Frieda found themselves in the middle of the parking lot. Automobiles were their new obstacles; although, to an adult elephant, the cars did not prove much of a challenge. The escaped pair rammed their way through, stomping and smashing a total of six cars. When they reached a nearby shopping mall, Debbie and Frieda charged forward: crashing through the glass-plate window of a Sears Auto Center. It was only then, after having caused a sufficient amount of damage, that the elephants chose to leave the scene and wander into a wooded-area. Trainers eventually caught up with the pair and led them back to their trailers.

In attempting to explain the rampage to a questioning media, a Clyde-Beatty spokesman placed the blame on a motorist. It was a car horn, he explained, that started the ruckus. The automobile was too close to the tent, and, when the driver began honking, the animals became "spooked" and ran away. Witnesses, however, did not swallow this excuse. They agreed that a car horn did beep shortly before Debbie and Frieda fled, but that noise was not the rationale behind this escape. Rather, they described how trainers were driving the elephants towards the tent by beating them savagely with bull-hooks. This violence, the witnesses concluded, was the true reason why the animals became enraged and escaped.

Presented with the contradicting evidence, Clyde-Beatty chose to ignore it. Instead they reiterated that the elephants were scared off by the horn-happy motorist. The pair were simply spooked. This was an accident, nothing more. In fact, the circus went on to explain, such unfortunate episodes among elephants are very unusual. Breakouts like this almost never happen, they averred. The general public has nothing to worry about.

Little did the public know, however, that one of those elephants, Frieda, had a rich history of resistance. A decade earlier, she attacked a visitor in Atlantic City, New Jersey when the man blew into her trunk. Soon thereafter, she killed a drunken woman at a mall in New London, Connecticut. Trouble, it would seem, has a way of coming in twos. And so it did again in 1995.

On July 10th, only months after the incident in Hanover, the situation with Debbie and Frieda worsened. This time, the Clyde-Beatty Circus was in Forest Park, New York, and the pair made their escape during a performance. One minute audience members were marveling at a well-trained elephant routine. The next minute, the big tent had descended into madness. Debbie and Frieda charged for the exits. Families tried to do the same. Ironically, while the two elephants made it through with relative ease, the latter found the process to be considerably more difficult. People panicked. They pushed and shoved one another. Children were knocked to the ground. Numerous visitors were trampled under foot. There were many injuries sustained that day. As for Debbie and Frieda, they were already outside, exploring the borough of Queens.

While it is said that New Yorkers have seen it all, this pachyderm rampage was certainly a first for most. Indeed, in a city where a naked person preaching about the love of Jesus would barely illicit a glance, the sight of two giant elephants stampeding down the street deserved broader contemplation. Local residents stopped and gawked. Others pointed and let loose with expletives. There were even a couple motorists who, so mesmerized by the outrageous sight, took their eyes off the road and crashed their cars. But the excitement soon faded. The elephants were rounded up and led back to the circus grounds.

Responding to another round of media inquiries and public criticism, Clyde-Beatty decided to take a more forthright approach. It admitted that these breakouts were a serious problem and that this obstreperous pair of elephants was becoming increasingly difficult to control. "They did it once and we thought it was an isolated incident," a spokesman stated plainly. "But they did it a second time, and it's now a behavior pattern." The circus industry, some critics believed, was ripe for change. It needed to evolve, develop new ideas, and stop using elephant acts altogether. Clyde-Beatty, however, was not interested in such suggestions, and the circus industry as a whole remained firmly unmoved. It preferred to stick with the status quo. The result would be a series of additional high profile escapes in the coming years.

In 1999, for instance, Luna the elephant broke loose from her trainers during a Royal Hanneford show. This fifteen year old Asian elephant was performing in Poughkeepsie, New York, when she, according to one audience member, "went crazy." Luna fled from the ring and busted through the perimeter barriers. She then proceeded to climb up into the second tier of circus seating. Amazingly, not only did the terrace hold under her enormous weight but no one was seriously injured that afternoon.

A few months later, Kamba the elephant walked out during a performance at the Texas State Fair. Leased from Elephant Encounters, a Dallas-based contracting service, this twenty-one year old African elephant managed to find her way out of the fairgrounds and into the city streets. At first the trainers tried to lure her back with food. But Kamba was not interested. Next they tried to cajole her. Trainers pushed and pulled. Trainers hit and stabbed. But Kamba would still not budge. Finally, they chained her to a large truck and literally dragged her back to the fairgrounds. Yet, the circus's problems were not over, for the elephant now refused to enter her trailer. The trainers, once again, tried everything, but Kamba stubbornly ignored them. She preferred to snack on a pile of leaves and take a leisurely stroll around the fair. Only Kamba was going to decide when it was time to call it a night.

In 2000, it was Barbara and Connie's turn. These two veteran performers worked for the Culpepper and Merriweather Circus, and they escaped from their trailer. Connie led the way with Barbara following close behind. One handler got in Barbara's way and yelled halt. He was plowed over. Afterwards, circus officials tried to assure the media that the Barbara was merely "spooked" and that the trainer just fell down. Yet witnesses told the newspapers that the man was most definitely "trampled." In either case, these two elephants made good use of their free time and explored the desert town of Yucca Valley, California.

Two years later, another pair would escape from a circus. This was Mary and Tory, two disgruntled employees of the George Carden show. It was in front of a packed house in Stout, Wisconsin that these two Asian elephants decided to sprint out of the ring and march right through the tent door. While Tory was caught before she could make it off the circus grounds, Mary got away. She ended up walking two miles. Along the route, this elephant got to see Stout and the local university campus. Authorities, though, did not appreciate this unplanned excursion. They finally trapped Mary with a blockade of municipal fire-trucks.

Then there was Tonya. By March of 2002, this elephant had escaped four times in the last six years. The first breakout happened in York, Maine at a wildlife park. The second occurred while working for a circus in Mentor, Ohio. The third took place while she was in Washington, Pennsylvania. In the final getaway, the elephant was in Easley, South Carolina. It was there, while being loaded into her trailer after a show, that Tonya made a run for the nearby woods. Only after some considerable effort were local authorities able to track the elephant down and corner her. Tonya, however, was "reluctant to surrender."

As for our original pair, the twenty-four year old Debbie and the twenty-nine year old Frieda, they were placed into isolation until further notice. The owners of Clyde-Beatty had gotten sick and tired of dealing with them and decided that the best solution was to remove the source of the problem altogether. The two troublemakers must be sold. All Clyde-Beatty needed to do now was to find a willing buyer, a task sometimes easier said than done. But in due course the circus tracked down someone who was eager to take the elephants off its hands: the Hawthorn Corporation.

Operating out of Richmond, Illinois, a small town located in the northeastern corner of the state, Hawthorn is a contracting firm owned by John Cuneo, Jr. The company's principle services are leasing, obedience training, and performance training. Its clients include circuses, zoos, and other businesses that deal in live animal entertainment. As for Hawthorn's contractors, they are the animals themselves. In the mid-1990s, the company employed nineteen elephants, one lion, and eighty-four tigers—each available for lease on a weekly, monthly, or yearly basis. The amusement industry very much prefers and benefits from this type of contractual, temporary arrangement. Circuses no longer carry the expense of training the animals or caring for them during the off-season. Zoos no longer shoulder the primary responsibility for the animals in terms of physical and psychological care. Smaller fairs have more flexibility with their exhibitions and scheduling by shuffling animals in and out at a moment's notice.

This arrangement is equally beneficial to Hawthorn. The animals are kept on the road as much as possible. Oversight is always nominal. At its private facilities, costs are slashed to the bare minimum. The elephants, for example, are chained twenty-four hours a day inside spartan barns, and they receive little in the way of quality food, adequate sanitation, or proper health care. All of this maximizes the company's profits.

It was into this world of contract labor that Debbie and Frieda arrived in early 1996. Cuneo, for his part, did not waste any time wringing a profit from his new acquisitions. He immediately put the two elephants through re-obedience training and then sent them back on the road, albeit separately. Cuneo was no dummy. In the coming years, Frieda would remain quiet, but Debbie would once again appear in the news. In October of 2001, she and another performer, Judy, busted through a show in Charlotte, North Carolina. This time, it was with the Vasquez Circus, and the performance was actually taking place inside of a church. Sacrilegious or not, those two elephants tore that place apart.

Tyke

On the 20th of August 1994, the city of Honolulu hosted its final circus. It was an unforgettable event. For that was the day Tyke the elephant came to town. This twenty-one year old performer had evidently enough of her employer, the Hawthorn Corporation. Tyke was tired of being leased out to circuses and carnivals. She was sick of the dismal and dangerous working conditions. She was finished with the abusive training and routine beatings. She was through with the untreated injuries and wounds and the lack of basic healthcare. Most of all, Tyke was through with the constant travel and having to perform—day in, day out.

Tyke was born in Africa in 1973. She was, as with most of the other elephants in this chapter, just a baby when she was captured and sent to North America to work in the entertainment industry. Where once this little elephant had a mother, she now had none. Where once she had a family, Tyke now was confined among complete strangers. John Cuneo was her new owner, and this elephant now had a job. Tyke was to spend the rest of her life performing the circus. That life came to a tragic end in Honolulu, Hawai'i.

Tyke was being leased out to Circus America, a company that she had worked for in the past. During this particular tour, the show had traveled all the way to the Pacific islands of Hawai'i. The trip from the mainland must have been a difficult one, and the animals could not have been pleased with the arrangement. Indeed, this leg of the tour only served to exacerbate a tension that had been building between the circus pachyderms and their trainers.

It was soon after crossing the Pacific that an elephant named Elaine went out of control and injured a family of visitors during the middle of a show. According to witnesses, the elephant had been performing inside of the ring, when she appeared to ignore a command. Her trainer became visibly upset. "He was yelling in an angry voice, very mean," one person explained. "Right after that – wham!" Elaine ran from the man and slammed into the protective fencing that separated the audience from the animals. A section of the guardrail buckled and collapsed under her weight, falling on top of a family of ten. There, the father, mother, and eight children remained trapped, until Elaine could be calmed and the heavy fencing removed. This must have been a frightening experience, with the entire family only steps away from being crushed to death by an elephant. Yet, Elaine chose not to hurt them and they sustained only minor injuries. But this incident was only a prelude to the frenzy that would break out five days later.

The Saturday matinee was already in full swing. The stands overflowed with parents and their children, each with his or her own personal bag of popcorn and tuft of cotton-candy held tightly in hand. Sounds of chatter and glees of excitement filled the arena. A growing charge of anticipation could be felt circulating throughout the arena, for the crowd could now see five enormous beasts waiting to make their entrance into the center ring. The elephant show was about to begin.

Oddly, it was a groom—the person in charge of caring for, feeding, and cleaning up after the animals—who first came into the ring. Even more strange was the fact that this person seemed as if he was running for his life. What was happening here, the audience must have wondered? And who exactly was chasing this man? They soon found out, as one of the elephants sprinted into the ring and knocked the groom to the floor. This was Tyke, and she was mad as hell. The elephant kicked the man. She picked him up and threw him down. She was in the process of stomping him, when a trainer came into the ring. Tyke stiffened, turned around, and charged—killing the handler under the weight of her body.

By this point, the audience was in an uproar. Some remained frozen their seats, paralyzed by fear. Others rushed for the exits. Tyke decided to follow the example of the fleeing patrons. She busted through the railings of the ring, found a doorway large enough to accommodate her bulky size, and fled the arena. Roaming outside in a parking lot, she spotted a clown and chased after him. But when she noticed someone trying to close the main gate, thereby trapping her inside in the lot, she flatten him instead. The angry performer then made her way into the streets of central Honolulu. One driver, noticing an approaching elephant in his rear view mirror, wisely pulled off to the side and let the animal pass. Tyke ran wild for several blocks before the police finally cornered her. Wasting little time, they opened fire—riddling the escaped elephant with eighty-six bullets. One witness captured the bloodbath on video. Tyke, with her star-emblazoned headdress still on and blood streaming down her legs, collapsed in the road. Laying there motionless, she remained alive. Officials called the city zoo. Its employees soon arrived and gave the elephant a lethal injection. The problem was that it did not work. So the police stepped in again and placed three more bullets into Tyke's body. This was not the first time an elephant had been shot dead in Honolulu.

Back in March of 1933, Daisy had just killed her handler. This African elephant was a resident of the city's Kapiolani Zoo. She was bought in 1916 with money raised by local schoolchildren. After her arrival, Daisy was housed in a small wooden shed. She remained in this primitive hovel for the next seventeen years. In fact, the fatal attack occurred while the handler was trying to stuff Daisy back into her cramped, little home. The elephant, apparently not liking the idea, refused to enter, and the man began to apply pressure and force to further stress his demand that she move into her hut. This was when Daisy decided to retaliate. She grasped the handler with her trunk and pitched him high into the air. When he landed, Daisy gored and crushed her keeper. Minutes later the police arrived. They located the elephant, surrounded her, and gunned Daisy down.

Attempting to explain why this happened, the handler's wife said that "she [Daisy] was never mean before." It was the park's visitors who were the real culprits behind Daisy's lethal tantrum. They teased the creature, burnt her with cigarettes, and purposefully fed her noxious items. The visitors, the widow said, were the ones who turned this gentle giant into a killer. It was just a couple of years earlier, when a visitor had his arm broken by Daisy. Undoubtedly, many believed this individual had teased the animal and got what was coming to him. Yet the city's board did not care about what may have provoked Daisy to violence, and it demanded that the elephant be summarily executed. Only a last minute "Save Daisy" campaign was able to gain her a reprieve from the sentence. But after the second incident, Honolulu's only elephant was not so fortunate. Daisy's dead body was taken out to sea and dumped into the depths of the Pacific.

As for Tyke and his 1994 attack, the people of Honolulu once again sought answers as to why something like this would ever happen. The first to be questioned was John Cuneo, the owner of the now deceased elephant. From the outset, Cuneo emphasized that occurrences of this nature were very rare. Elephants were, in his experience, well-behaved and obedient. To prove this point, Cuneo explained to the press that before the melee began Tyke had been "spooked" by a strange noise or the sight of something unusual. Hence her actions that day lacked any real intention. The entire incident was a sad but freakish accident. Yet, Cuneo could not have been more off the mark. You see, there was a hidden history here.

In April of 1993, Tyke was working a show in Altoona, Pennsylvania for the Great American Circus. During a special performance for a group of some 3000 children, she busted out of the ring and rumbled into the aisles. Ramming through a doorway, Tyke made her way up onto the balcony-level. Police wanted to shoot her immediately, but circus employees assured the local authorities that the elephant could be safely retrieved. This proved to be a far more difficult task than imagined. First, handlers commanded that Tyke come down from the balcony. She ignored them. Next, they tempted her with a bounty of carrots and apples. Still she would not move. Finally, they brought in another elephant in order to lure Tyke from the balcony. This trick worked and the disgruntled performer came down the stairs.

Two months later, a similar episode took place involving Tyke. This time, it occurred at the state fairgrounds in Minot, North Dakota. The elephants had just finished rehearsal and were being led back to their holding pens, when Tyke broke away and attacked a groom. "She just spun around," the man later recalled, "put her head down and charged me." "The elephant was definitely trying to kill me." Trainers were able to rescue the man and he escaped with his life and only few broken ribs. But Tyke was not finished. She sprinted out of the tent and made her way onto the midway. For twenty-five minutes, circus employees chased her around. Each time they thought they had her trapped, the elephant gave them the slip. Eventually, Tyke gave herself up on her own terms. The events that transpired one year later, however, would conclude in a much different manner.

News of Tyke's death in Hawai'i made the international wires. Videos of her rampaging inside of the arena and being gunned down in the streets by police were broadcast world-wide. Many people, who had never before thought about the plight of circus elephants, now voiced their concerns. Others, who knew some facts, endeavored to learn more. As the interest in this subject grew, so too did the sympathy for Tyke and her fellow performers. The outrage over the shooting had just begun.

Then there were those individuals who were pushed into activism. Many joined or gave donations to well-known animal-rights organizations, while others chartered new advocacy groups. Two people, in fact, decided to establish a retirement community for older circus and zoo elephants. "Tyke," co-founder Carol Buckley explained, "was the catalyst to do it." Here, elephants were going to be able to roam unchained and unsupervised. They could hang out with friends or be alone. They would sleep in a state-of-the-art facility and have the very best in medical attention. They no longer had to work or live in fear. The Hohenwald Elephant Sanctuary, located in central Tennessee, opened in 1995.

In the months following Tyke's death, the global campaign against the use of elephants in the entertainment industry intensified greatly. Protests now met circuses everywhere they went. Boycotts against circus sponsors became more successful. Lawsuits against Hawthorn, Circus America, and the city of Honolulu were filed. The United States Department of Agriculture (USDA), which oversees the industry, was spurred into increased vigilance, enforcement, and prosecution.

In 1996, the federal government penalized Hawthorn a total of $12,500 for the earlier events in Hawai'i. In 1998, the USDA slapped the company an additional $60,000 fine and suspended its license for forty-five days, owing to charges related to the mistreatment and premature deaths of two of the company's other elephants. Tunga and Hattie had each died of tuberculosis and a general lack of basic veterinary care. In 2003, the USDA filed forty-seven new charges against Hawthorn, several of its employees, and the Walker Brothers Circus, which was then leasing the company's animal performers. These violations included physical abuse during training, causing physical harm and discomfort, and failing to provide adequate veterinary care. In March of 2004, Hawthorn's owner, John Cuneo, copped to nineteen of the charges and paid a fine of $200,000. More significantly, Cuneo was required to relinquish all of his elephants.

The first two elephants liberated from Cuneo's operation were Misty and Lota. They arrived at the Hohenwald Sanctuary nine months later. Sadly, Lota showed up emaciated and dying of TB. She had spent thirty-six years at the Milwaukee County Zoo in Wisconsin. But due to her continued misbehavior and resistance, Lota was ungraciously sold to Cuneo in 1990 as a punishment.

Interestingly, when responding to concerns about this sale, the zoo director, Charles Wikenhauser, mocked them as foolish and sentimental, adding with a wagging finger that people should really focus their attention on human issues. Lota was, after all, just an animal.

In 2006, another eight of Hawthorn's elephants were released to Hohenwald: Minnie, Lottie, Queenie, Liz, Debbie, Ronnie, Billie, and Frieda. Sue should have accompanied them, but she had died days before. Finally, in 2007, the two males, Nicholas and Gypsy, began their long awaited trip to the Performing Animal Welfare Society Sanctuary (PAWS) in Galt, California.

Tyke, the elephant, may have died that autumn day in 1994, but her actions proved far from futile. She was part of a larger struggle against oppression and exploitation: Jumbo, Mary, Janet, Debbie, Frieda. Indeed, her resistance that day altered the course of history. Humans were inspired into action. The city of Honolulu never again hosted a circus.

Hawthorn has never again touched an elephant. Tyke's adopted sisters and brothers are now living out their lives in peace. The legacy of Tyke remains engraved in the memories of animal lovers around the world.

CHAPTER TWO

PACHYDERMS PREFER TO FORGET ABOUT THE ZOO

WHILE JUMBO IS ARGUABLY THE WORLD'S MOST FAMOUS HISTORICAL animal, he was not London's first star pachyderm attraction. That honor went to Chunee. Born in Bengal, this male elephant arrived to the isle in 1810 and, for the next sixteen years, entertained the people of England. Princess Victoria, before she became Queen and paraded on the back of Jumbo, first marveled at the mighty Chunee. English writers, it seems, had a particular fascination with the creature. Charles Dickens, William Wordsworth, and Robert Browning each paid Chunee regular visits. Lord Bryon might have been his biggest fan of all. But it was not just the privileged and intelligentsia who were attracted to this elephant. Everyone wanted to see the famous Chunee: rich or poor, man or woman, adult or child. Even those living in rural England would make the occasional long pilgrimage into the city, in order to cast their eyes upon this giant beast.

Chunee resided at the Royal Menagerie. Opening in 1773 as a seasonal rest stop for circus animals, the Menagerie would eventually develop into a full-time zoo and remain in business for the next six decades, until closing in 1829. Over the course of these many years, a series of individuals and families owned the small zoo. First, it was owned by the Pidcock family. Then it was acquired by the Italian Polito brothers, Stephen followed by John. The final owner was Edward Cross, who was himself a former employee. Yet, throughout all of these changes, the function and operations of the zoo remained essentially the same. The menagerie was, from the outset, a private enterprise designed to produce a profit. It provided entertainment at a low cost, and its audience was the general public. At the end of Cross's tenure, for instance, he charged an admissions fee of one or two shillings, depending on what attractions the individual visitor wanted to see. Moreover, as opposed to the Regent Park Zoo, which was at the time exclusive in its admittance policy and elitist in its mission, Cross carried on the tradition of catering to all people, regardless of class. Anyone who could afford the cost of a ticket was welcome through its gates.

The menagerie was housed inside of a large commercial structure. Known as the Exeter Exchange, the building was situated in the central part of the city on the Strand. This was London at its busiest and most congested with pedestrians, horses, carts, and carriages all competing for limited space. It was undoubtedly an odd spot for a zoo. One has to wonder just how many unsuspecting by-passers were frightened out of their wits, after hearing the roar of a lion or the trumpet of an elephant, in this dense, teeming commercial district.

Even more bizarre was the fact that the menagerie did not sit on the ground floor of the building. Instead it occupied an upper story. This must have made for an awkward, if not precarious, arrangement, as accommodating a group of animals in the upper section of any structure, let alone one constructed in the 17th century, was probably not the wisest of decisions. This was especially the case with an adult, male elephant. For not only must it have been difficult to deal with the logistics of holding or moving a creature that weighed several tons and had several yards of girth, but what would happen if he ever got mad and started charging around the place? The Menagerie, for its part, recognized the danger involved and it tried to resolve these issues by having an enclosure specifically designed and built with the grown-up Chunee in mind. This new cage, management hoped, would be strong enough to both support the elephant's weight and withstand any struggles.

As for the rest of the captive animals, they were exhibited alongside the walls in small, cramped cages. These cages were stacked on top of one another in a building-block arrangement. Tigers sat atop lions. New-world monkeys perched over old-world monkeys. All were camouflaged behind a maze of iron bars. None of this was particularly aesthetic, as the place had the feel and look of a warehouse more than anything. Yet, to be fair, space was limited. The zoo itself only occupied two rooms. Furthermore, these types of displays were typical for the era. Museums and menageries often had large collections and very little concern for interpretation. Hence they would cram as many objects and specimens as they could into a singular exhibition. This arrangement, as overwhelming and unintelligible as it would appear to modern eyes, did not seem to bother 19th century visitors. Regardless, such an environment could not have been a pleasant experience for the animals who had to live inside the cramped enclosures. There was no room to move, let alone to run, swing, or fly. Air circulation and proper sanitation were not concerns of the zoo. And external simulation, with the exception of looking at the audience, was something that was never going to be realized by the captives of the Royal Menagerie.

Despite all of this, Chunee appeared, at least on the surface, to be remarkably well-adjusted. Many a visitor commented on his mellow disposition. He was an amicable, if not particularly affectionate, elephant. Chunee even performed a few tricks. There was one in particular that everyone loved. It involved him reaching out with his trunk and taking off a man's hat, which he would then pull back into his enclosure. Was the purloined going to be kept there? Would Chunee destroy it? Alas, after a brief minute, he returned the cap and placed it gently atop the gentleman's head. Well-done!

Sometimes, however, the trick did not go quite as planned. Chunee would smash an occasional hat. He would cover others with his dung and place them back on unsuspecting owners. He could be rough in the return process, leaving the visitor with a bruised head. Or he could just plain refuse to do the trick—no matter how hard his handler tried to make him perform. Indeed, Chunee could certainly be disobedient when he wanted to. He could even be deadly.

The first serious incident happened in 1815 when Chunee attempted to kill his handler, Alfred Copps. Copps was, at time, inside of the enclosure. He might have been training the elephant or just cleaning the cage; we do not know. But something set Chunee off, and Copps bore the brunt of his fury. Backing the man into a corner, Chunee rushed straight ahead with his tusks pointing outward. Remarkably, when the dust settled, the elephant saw that he had missed his target. The man remained alive, pinned against the wall with a tusk resting on either side of his body. Copps must have breathed a sigh of relief; that is, until he saw Chunee's trunk coming down fast upon him. In between the blows, the handler must have been cursing himself for ever taking that job. In the end, he survived the beating but only because Edward Cross intervened at the last second and created a diversion with a well-placed thrust of a pitchfork into Chunee's backside. Copps chose never to return to the Menagerie.

The next man in line for the job was George Dyer. By all accounts, Dyer was a particularly wicked trainer, who enjoyed using a twelve foot spear as his vicious method of encouragement. Yet Chunee was never without recourse. If Dyer stuck him in the side, he could always respond with a spray of dirty water or a strike of his trunk. Once Chunee hit the handler square across the face, breaking Dyer's nose. So powerful was the blow that physicians were unable to set the nose in a proper manner, thus leaving the man permanently disfigured. Fights between Chunee and Dyer became so bad that the owner was forced to hire an assistant. Cross wisely selected someone with experience.

This was John Taylor, and he definitely knew a thing or two about the animal business. Not only had Taylor spent much of his adult life working with captive animals, but he paid a steep price in gaining this experience by having an arm chewed off years earlier by a circus lion. Despite this gruesome injury, Taylor returned to the profession and remained congenial towards other creatures. In fact, Taylor was a strong advocate of non-physical training methods. No animal, he believed, should be abused. This enlightened philosophy differed markedly from Dyer's brutal way of thinking, and Taylor often complained to Edward Cross about these differences. So bitter did the infighting become between the two men that Cross got sick of hearing about it and fired both of them.

Chunee's next handler was Richard Carter. He, like Dyer, preferred an aggressive, violent approach to elephant management. Using a long, razor-sharp spear, Carter was determined to keep the elephant in line and retain his job. But Cross was not so confident. He believed that, in addition to physical force, a new means of control was needed. Cross ordered the staff to begin the drugging of Chunee. These experimental psychiatric dosages, in combination with large qualities of ale, would, Cross hoped, keep the menagerie's prized exhibit in a calm, malleable state. But the daily doses of booze and drugs didn't sedate the embittered elephant.

By late 1825, Chunee was out of control and literally tearing the place to pieces. He rammed against the walls. He butted against the beams. He pounded the ceiling, sending pieces of it flying everywhere. The specially-engineered enclosure was failing, and Cross thought that the entire building itself might collapse. The final straw came when Chunee gored an assistant, killing the man. Cross decided that the elephant must be put to the death.

At first, the staff tried using poison. They mixed it in the elephant's daily feed and waited for the inevitable. But Chunee just stood there, refusing to eat. Next, they bought several of his favorite treats, hot buns, and injected one of them with the deadly toxin. Chunee, as always, greeted the perquisite with a cursory sniff before commencing with the snack. He ate them all. All, that is, except the poisoned one. The would-be assassins then tried to trick the elephant by having an inno-cent-looking visitor present the buns. But Chunee did not buy that either. The Menagerie was forced to devise another method of execution. Cross enlisted the help of the Metropolitan police.

The following day, three constables arrived to the Exeter Exchange with their rifles. Cross led the men upstairs and lined them in front of Chunee's gated enclosure. The men aimed and opened fire. "I expected to see him fall," one witness later wrote. "Instead of which he made a sharp hissing noise, and struck heavily at us with his trunk and tried to make after us, and would have but for the formidable double-edged spear blades of the keepers." Chunee was tougher than anyone had expected. This was going to take some time, and Cross needed advice. Besides a hunter, he wondered, who would best know how to kill such an animal? Cross settled on a physician and sent an employee to gather one. When the medical doctor showed up, he directed as to where best to shoot the beast in order to quicken the kill. Yet Chunee refused to be a stationary target. As the constables fired, the elephant kept moving from side to side and front to back, and avoided being hit in the vital areas.

Growing increasingly desperate, Cross sent another employee to Somerset House. Perhaps, he thought, professional soldiers would have better aim. With fourteen of them standing at the gates of the enclosure, they too opened fire. But Chunee still would not fall. Indeed, the scene itself had descended into a kind of nightmare, with blood in the cage rising to an almost ankle-deep level. This execution, Cross bristled, had to come to an end, and he ordered for more powerful rifles and ammunition. The soldiers, once re-armed, began shooting again. When this appeared to fail, Cross called in for a canon. It was not to be needed. The 152nd musket ball finished the deed, and Chunee died.

While death may have a dignity all to its own, the field of zoo management does not. Those vultures had descended before the elephant was even dead, and they set to work at once. Chunee's trunk was pitilessly hacked off and sold to the highest bidder. His eyes were gouged out and kept as a scientific prize. His body was dissected by physicians. His skin stripped off by biologists. His intestinal tract and muscular tissue extracted for study. Ultimately only his skeleton remained at the menagerie. Cross had it mounted for a very profitable and unproblematic display.

Babe

The Toledo Zoo was in desperate straits. Its elephant, Josie, had recently died from choking on a piece of food. While the death was sad and regrettable, the zoo had to move forward. It simply did not have the time to investigate the death or mourn her loss. Rather, all of the focus had to be put on finding a replacement. The zoo, which had opened a few years earlier in 1900, needed a new leading attraction. Today, zoological parks call such creatures a flagship species. They are the larger-than-life animals: the elephants, tigers, hippos, gorillas, and panda bears. They are the ones that heighten the reputation of a zoo and boost its image. They provide an easy focus for the marketing department to lure a larger audience. Most importantly, they afford assurances to the parks and their employees that the external funding will continue to flow. Prestige, then as now, is essential for the survival of these institutions, and elephants play a central role in creating this impression. Indeed, if the young Toledo Zoo had any hopes of growing and prospering, it had to obtain another pachyderm. This was an absolute must. One significant obstacle, however, stood in its way. Elephants did not come cheap. For help, the zoo turned to the children of northwest Ohio.

Throughout this era, zoos around the country relied upon local youth for financial support. In truth, most parks would not have survived their early years without these tot-driven campaigns. Those pennies from heaven did not so much fall from the sky as they were pried from the mouths of babes. It was schoolchildren who were asked to scrimp together everything they had in order to fund the purchase of a new captive animal. It was schoolchildren who were asked to save up for years in order to support the construction of a new exhibit. They were the ones who had to make the sacrifices. The same cannot be said for those who collected the donations. Members of zoological societies were, almost exclusively, very wealthy individuals. Many were captains of industry. Some owned banks. Others sprang from old money. All were capable of fully funding these institutions by themselves. But they chose not to. Instead, society members siphoned tens of thousands of dollars from those who could least afford it. This was, for better or worse, the arrangement of the time, and the children of Toledo and its neighboring counties would perform their role admirably. By 1912, the kids had amassed enough pennies to purchase a new elephant. Now it was up to the zoo to find one.

In the late 19th and early 20th centuries, if you needed a pachyderm, you went to see William Hall. Based out of Lancaster, Missouri, Hall was the foremost animal dealer in the United States. He was an early transnational entrepreneur. His operations extended world wide in their reach with buying and selling facilities located as far away as Cape Town, South Africa. His particular skill was in the art of trans-Atlantic shipping. No one, it was said, could get more animals across the ocean alive and healthy than Hall. Even today, mortality rates can be quite high with up to 50 percent or more of the cargo dying in route. Dehydration, heat exhaustion, suffocation, and starvation are the usual causes. This is especially the case in smuggling operations, which, sadly enough, is how much of the trade is carried out. The business of commerce in exotic species has never been considered an ethical enterprise. Regardless, this was Hall's chosen profession, and one in which zoos dealt with on an almost daily basis.

Hall began his operations dealing, not in pachyderms, but in equines. He would go on to supply the American Express Company and the municipalities of Philadelphia and Chicago—all of whom relied heavily upon horse-power for their transportation needs. Hall was also a shrewd defense contractor, servicing entire countries with horses during periods of war, such as the British in the Boer War or the Allies in World War I. At any one time, his Missouri farm had up to 2000 horses living on site, awaiting shipment. It was not until 1904 that Hall first purchased an exotic species: two camels. But from that point on, his stock in such animals would only increase, eventually including a large selection of tigers, lions, and elephants. In 1912, one very conspicuous member of Hall's inventory was sold and sent via boxcar to the state of Ohio. The Toledo Zoo was finally about to get its elephant.

Born on the Indian subcontinent, York was a strong male elephant with a reputation for being difficult. Just a few years previous, while working for the MacKay Circus, York had stomped a trainer to death. Zoo officials knew of this and they were certainly wary. For not only were they going to have to keep this elephant under control for the next couple decades, officials also had to try to prevent outsiders from learning about York's rap sheet. It would not be good for public relations. What parent would want to take their kid to see a dangerous killer? Consequently, the zoo decided that the best course of action would be to preempt any difficulties and simply change the elephant's name. Thus, York was rechristened to Babe.

From the beginning, the Toleo Zoo used Babe to advertise its image. Look, there's Babe marching in a parade. How amazing! Look, there's Babe posing in front of a piano, as if he is trying to play. How cute! We should all go to the zoo. Barely a week went by that one of the area's newspapers did not mention the elephant by name, show a photo of

Babe, or run a sketch of him. Babe was big news and would remain so for the next thirty years. Yet, as popular as he was, not everything about him could be spun in such a positive way.

Babe's frequent escapes became something of legend in the Walbridge neighborhood. Here, he could often be found eating geraniums, knocking down laundry lines, and demolishing porches. So routine did his escapes become that the newspapers treated them as a running joke. Babe outsmarted his keepers once again, they would smirk. The zoo, for its part, tried to be as matter of fact as possible. "The present house is not regarded as having the proper safeguards when Babe is in his ugly moods," an official would clarify. "Although the big elephant has both forelegs chained, the former being anchored by another chain to the concrete floor, the big pachyderm manages at times to unhook one or both chains. With his trunk he is able to open the big double doors of the house." Their elephant, it seemed, could not be stopped, and the zoo admitted as much. A new, stronger enclosure was needed.

Babe could also be violent with employees. In 1915, he killed his then trainer, goring the man right through. The zoo first responded by sawing the elephant's tusks off, thereby lessen the danger involved. Next, it assigned a new keeper to Babe. Hopefully, this one would work out better. The last thing the zoo needed was another fatality. How would it explain that to the public? Some officials began wondering privately if this elephant was more trouble than he was really worth. Maybe, some speculated, William Hall was not the best source of pachyderms.

Hall specialized in taking in rogue elephants. But his operation was no sanctuary or retirement community. Nor was it a rehabilitation center, tending to physical injuries and wounds, or counseling service, treating psychology trauma and scars. Rather this was a place to dump the unwanted. If a circus or zoo could no longer handle a particular performer or if it simply wanted to rid itself of an animal, it could always find a willing purchaser in Missouri. As one of Hall's men described it, the company "would buy the outlaws nobody else would have. Then we'd work over them and kind of straighten them out. In the summers we'd rent them out to circuses and carnivals." Hall's operation was, essentially, a labor camp—a place where elephants would be whipped, beaten, terrorized, and sent back on the road. This arrangement, however, could have its drawbacks. We can identify three of them by name: Hero, Black Diamond, and "Old" Major.

In the 1916 season, Hero was leased to the Orton Brothers Circus. He was an Asian elephant, large and male. Hall had purchased him six years earlier, just another rogue that nobody wanted. And, while Hall's men might have straightened Hero out for the short term, they were not able to eradicate all of the resistant behavior from him. At a show in Elkton, South Dakota, Hero escaped from his intoxicated trainer and made a break for freedom. It is notable how many alcoholic handlers there have been over the years. Circuses seem to be full of them. Perhaps, this is a sign of how lax the industry is in its hiring practices. Or, possibly, all of the drunkards are a symptom of a larger problem—elephant training itself was and is a morally corrupt enterprise. In either case, our elephant Hero was now on the run. Who knows how long it had been since he was able to be out on his own, free to roam wherever he wanted. Although not the jungles of southeastern Asia, the vast northern grasslands of Dakota must have seemed extraordinary. It was a full five hours before the armed posse caught up with him. Hero was shot dead.

Wherever Black Diamond went, he was kept in a complex system of restraints. Chains draped over his body. One pair stretched from his back legs to the trunk, another circled around his torso. A thick iron bar stood in the center, mounted between his two enormous tusks. No chances could be taken with this animal. Black Diamond was a dangerous elephant, unpredictable and recalcitrant. His movements needed to be limited and his speed slowed. And at no time should he allowed to raise his trunk—hence the insertion of the iron bar. In fact, when circuses marched Black Diamond in a parade, he was—in addition to the regular security measures—chained to two other, more obedient elephants. Only the fictional Hannibal Lector garnered as much concern and technological ingenuity as that imposed on Diamond. Ironically, like Lector, this elephant too would get his revenge.

In October of 1929, while employed with the Al Barnes Circus, this thirty-one year old elephant was in the middle of performing in yet another street parade. But what set this one apart from the rest was that his old trainer, Homer Pritchett, showed up to the event. Black Diamond spotted the man through the crowd and began to thrash about. Breaking away from the other elephants and snapping his own chains, he ran forward. "It put its tusks into a car on his right and pushed it over into another car," a witness remembered. "People were screaming and running away, and you couldn't get anywhere because it was such a big jam-up." Corsicana, Texas had never seen anything like this before. Although, oddly enough, there was an elephant named Texas—also owned by William Hall—who had rampaged in a similar manner while working for the Atterbury Circus. As for Black Diamond, when he reached his target, he grabbed Pritchett with his trunk and tossed the man to the ground. Pritchett scrambled away with a broken arm, far better off than the trainer Black Diamond had killed a few years earlier. Not so lucky, however, was Pritchett's companion, who was left standing there alone. Black Diamond smashed her.

Four days later, local authorities led the elephant to a stand of trees and chained him into place. With a firing squad at the ready, the order was given and the shooting commenced. Black Diamond struggled and tried to free himself. But he could not get away, and the gunfire continued. The mighty Black Diamond soon collapsed. A photographer captured a final image: the elephant lay motionless; his body tangled in a mess of blood-stained chains.

Then, there was "Old" Major. The elder of the group, Major had well over thirty years of experience in the entertainment industry. Season after season, Major traveled across the country—from one end to the other and back again. In 1935 Hall sold the veteran performer off for good. The recipients were the Cole Brothers Circus, and they were quite happy with their purchase. A circus could always use another well-trained act. The self-congratulations did not last long.

Major had only been with them a couple months when he attacked a trainer. The Cole Brothers were perturbed. Not only had they lost a valuable employee to an injury, they knew that more trouble loomed on the horizon. Within weeks, the elephant went after another handler. It happened inside the ring while practicing a routine. A trainer had barked out an order and Major lashed out, bringing down the full weight of his trunk down upon the man's head and shoulders. Tumbling to the floor, the handler scrambled to his feet and ran for safety. The elephant, though, was close on his tail. Major wanted him dead. It took an army of employees and much concerted effort to bring the disgruntled performer under control. The circus thought it best if the aging beast was "chained securely and left to cool off." Yet, by the next day, Major was still in a fury. Whenever anyone approached, the visitor was met with a violent swing of the trunk or swipe of the tusks. The owner of the Cole Brothers Circus called an emergency meeting to discuss the issue. Could Major ever be calmed? Would he work again as before? Or was this it, an elephant who had been pushed beyond the breaking point? The meeting concluded by issuing a death warrant for Major.

For whatever reason, circus officials decided not to kill Major inside the barn, where he was being held. Instead they wanted to bring him out into the yard and shoot him there. Thus, they gathered an array of handlers, grooms, ticket-takers, and anyone else they could find. Each man was armed with a gaff and the crew was set to its task. In time, Major was cajoled out of the barn—although, once outside, the elephant stopped short and refused to move any further. This spot, officials resolved, would have to do. A local reporter described what happened next. A marksman advanced, "stepped off fifteen paces and took his stance, rifle to shoulder . . . Major eyed him contemptuously, the heavy trunk raised as if he were ready to charge. The rifle cracked. Witnesses saw the huge frame quiver, the trunk laid supinely over the head, there was a fast derisive snort, and the tons of flesh sank slowly to the ground." "Major," the reporter concluded, "had closed his 70 years of life as he had lived them with a challenge to mankind." Cole Brothers kept to its tradition and hacked off the "old" performer's tusks, so that they could be put on display. The circus maintained a morbid collection of ivory trophies sawed from executed elephants.

As for Babe at the Toledo Zoo, his fate seemed destined to be the same as those who came before and after him. The year 1922, in particular, lent heft to this conclusion. The relations had disintegrated between the elephant and zoo. Struggles became an almost daily affair. "Five-hour battle[s]" were not unusual. "Babe, for weeks, has been in bad humor," the zoo would have to repeat. "The call of Spring is in his blood and he resents his confinement." The situation would only worsen, when the elephant's personal handler was sent to the hospital because of injuries sustained from a fight with an escaped baboon. In his absence, the zoological society enlisted city police to help keep watch over Babe. Officers were stationed twenty-four hours a day, both inside and outside of the barn. With their high-powered rifles, the cops stood at the ready, scared as hell. Equally as frightened were the zoo managers. For the question was not if their prize elephant would rampage but rather when. Officials began drawing up plans to kill the animal.

As news of this lethal plot leaked out in the newspapers, the general public took notice and reacted angrily. The good people of Toledo did not want to see Babe put to death. They demanded that the zoo come up with a new strategy of management. Zoo officials bowed to the pressure and soon announced that construction on a new elephant house would soon begin. The zoo, however, had a problem—as it first had to develop a design that specifically addressed Babe's resistant behavior. Otherwise, what would be the purpose of spending all that money? The new exhibit must (a) prevent escapes, (b) withstand violent rages, and (c) allow for minimal contact between the handlers and the elephant. Ultimately, engineers decided that the best way to accomplish these goals was to dig below ground level. This sunken pit could then be poured with concrete and reinforced with steel rebar. When completed, not even Babe would be able to escape from here. They turned out to be correct. Babe would remain at the zoo for next two decades and continue to be its most popular attraction. He would die in 1943. His final obituary read: "Animal which became killer and outlaw executed following Paralytic Stroke."

Tillie

Tillie began her life of captivity known as Chocolate. But unlike the dessert, which denotes images of sweetness and experiences of delight, Chocolate the elephant could be anything but. She did, if truth be told, resemble the food's more controversial side—its stimulant side. For

Chocolate was high-spririted, independently-minded, and stubbornly resistant. If somebody pushed her, she would push right back. If somebody hit her with a bull-hook, she would make that person regret ever doing so. This was one elephant not to be underestimated or messed with. In the end, Chocolate would be kicked out of two zoos for misbehavior and placed in a specialized detention facility.

Born in southeastern Asia, Chocolate was brought to Europe in 1965. Her new home was the regional zoo in Kolmarden, Sweden. It was, most would say, an odd place for an elephant to live. Located on Lake Mälaren, this park sat less than 100 miles from the Baltic Sea. Here, winters could last four to five months. The skies would remain overcast, as the sun kept hidden behind the clouds. The temperatures during this season rarely rose beyond the freezing mark. All of this meant that the elephants had to spend nearly half of the year indoors, living in small, cramped quarters. When they ventured outside for any extended period, they were exposed to the cold, damp air. This could easily get into their lungs, joints, and feet, making for sick, arthritic animals. Overall, this sub-Arctic climate is horrible for elephants. They do not get to walk or even get much of a good stretch for months at a time. There is no physical or mental stimulation. There is little sunlight. These conditions lead to depression and despair. This was especially the case for Maggie, an elephant confined in the Alaska state zoo.

In 1983, this South African native arrived to the city of Anchorage. Maggie was the sole survivor of a family that had been "culled" only months earlier, and the event must have been traumatizing. At the zoo, there was one other pachyderm, Annabelle, who had been living there alone for the past seventeen years. Annabelle would die of a foot infection in 1997. Maggie, in turn, spent the next decade by herself. Prolonged isolation is very hard on female elephants. They are highly social creatures and need each other for companionship. In Africa or Asia, their families are extended to include a matriarch, six to twenty related females, and an assortment of calves. Even the dead are long remembered in elephant societies. Furthermore, elephants enjoy interacting with fellow animals. Humans conveniently tend to think of other species as being segregated or divorced from those around them. But this is demonstrably not the case. They, like humans, need to create and develop these kinds of holistic relationships. Animals have a culture all to their own.

Maggie, unfortunately, had none of this social interaction. In fact, the best that the Alaskan zoo could come up with to ease her discomfort and alienation was a giant treadmill. On this $100,000 machine, the elephant could, the zoo keepers fantasized, exercise her way to good physical and mental health. Ironically, this was not a new idea. The 18th century policy wonk, Jeremy Bentham, advocated just such a device in his essay on the Panopticon. Here, the Queen's elephants would be put to work: spending eighteen out of twenty-four hours a day treading a wheel. Not only would this project be advantageous for the health of the animals, but it would also produce mechanical power and revenue for the mill's owner. Maggie, however, was not convinced. She refused to use her machine. In 2007, under growing pressure by citizen groups, park administrators agreed to send Maggie to the PAWS sanctuary in Galt, California. Our elephant Chocolate could only have imagined such joys.

For fifteen years, Chocolate remained at her Swedish zoo—enduring many frigid winters and appreciating, the best that a tropical animal could, the mild Scandinavian summers. She watched as Kolmarden became the country's leading zoological institution, a feat which Chocolate herself played not a small part in accomplishing. Yet, behind the scenes, the situation was not so rosy. The elephant was maturing and becoming more self-aware. She would no longer acquiesce to any order or demand. Her attitude began to shift from "to go along, to get along" to open defiance. It came to a point where Chocolate became so contrary that the zoo could no longer handle her safely. She was simply too aggressive and too dangerous. Chocolate had already injured several keepers, and zoo officials knew that it was just a matter of time before she killed someone. Kolmarden threw up its hands. Chocolate had won the battle of wills.

By 1980, the elephant had been sold and shipped off to the States. Her new home was in the more temperate Tampa, Florida. For a while, the association between Chocolate and her new zoo remained amicable. Perhaps it was the return to the heat and humidity which calmed her. This climate change put the elephant at ease. Or maybe it took awhile for Chocolate to figure out that, when the Tampa handlers screamed out "Tillie," they were referring, not to another elephant, but to her. Apparently, she had a new name. The years went by. Tillie became a mother. The Lowry Park Zoo filled its pockets with money made from displaying Tillie and her calf. It made cash on the side by featuring the elephant in local television commercials. In time, though, Tillie became less tolerant of this life.

Troubles first flared in June of 1993. Tillie and another pachyderm were being led on their daily walk, when, suddenly, they sprinted away from their handler. Tillie plowed through a gate, and, together, the two wandered outside of the grounds. Elephants remain, despite all of the efforts by zoological parks, opposed to a sedentary life of endless sequestration. Whether in Asia or Africa, these animals will cover many miles per day. Their typical home range can be anywhere from nine to thirty-one square miles. And this expansive use of open space is not merely about finding food or water. Elephants love to walk and to roam on their own accord. They enjoy being constantly on the go, seeing new sights, and interacting with fellow creatures. They are highly social travelers. In zoos, indoor facilities are measured in feet (not miles), and outdoor sites might, at most, reach two or three acres. Indeed, the escapade in Tampa was not the first occasion, or the last, that an elephant or two escaped from a zoo.

A decade previous, Misty fled her Irvine, California facility. Running over her trainer and busting through a security fence, she strolled by a nearby swap-meet, caused a traffic-jam on a freeway, and nimbly avoided capture for over three hours. In 1997, Cally and Tonya took off from a Maine zoo. A gate was either left open by accident or it was opened by the elephants themselves—officials could not determine which. The pair exploited this fortunate opportunity to do some exploring. Tonya was the first to be caught. But Cally was nowhere to be found. She had simply disappeared. It was not until hours later that employees stumbled upon her in a wooded area. Cally was in the process of taking a much deserved mud-bath—a pleasure that the elephant never had in captivity. As for Tillie and her partner, they would also be located and brought back to their enclosure. Yet this was just a foreshadowing of more dramatic events to come.

One early July day, while Tillie was in the middle of a training exercise, she paused and refused to continue. When shoved by her handler, she pushed back and sent the woman tumbling into an adjacent pool of water. There was no doubt that this was an intentional act, and the trainer, while not hurt physically, was emotionally shaken. For their part, Lowry Park administrators chose to view this action not as a second warning by the elephant but rather as an isolated incident. At the very least, they believed, it was Tillie having some fun at the expense of another. At most, it was normal interplay between a handler and an animal—each striving for dominance over the other.

Significantly, zoos and circuses will on occasion admit to this fact: that the relations between animal handlers and elephants are primarily antagonistic, coercive, and, often, violent. This is a question of domination and resistance; the answer of which is played out every day behind the doors of these institutions. In other words, we can think of these relations as a dynamic, whose outcomes are determined through a process of negotiation. On the one side, there are the zoos and circuses. They attempt to impose control by using everything from repetitive action, to physical abuse, to gastronomic bribes, to verbal intimidation: the goal of which is to instill obedience, servility, and profitability among the captive animals. Theirs is a management of exploitation. On the other side of the equation are the elephants. They seek to survive this predicament, and, if possible, obtain some influence over it. Theirs is a struggle against exploitation, and it can take many forms: ignoring commands, slowing down, refusing to work without adequate food and water, taking unofficial breaks, breaking equipment, damaging enclosures, fighting back, or escaping. Much of the time, it is the institutions who ultimately win out in these negotiations. But, occasionally, the elephants succeed in their rebellion. The victory may be ephemeral: extra hay or carrots. It could be partial: long-term change in training techniques. Or it might be historic: release to a sanctuary. In the case of Tillie and her latest outburst, the Tampa zoo quickly sought to regain dominance. The elephant was taken to "the privacy of the barn," chained, and disciplined. After being tortured, Tillie was put through a set of commands to see if she would obey. She did and was placed back on display. The relative calm, however, did not last long.

During a final day in July, as Tillie was being led towards the barn, she was told to pause and to hold "steady." The elephant, instead, marched directly towards the trainer—the same woman who had been pushed down only weeks before. The command, "move over," was given and cued with a strike of a bull-hook. The elephant responded with some slaps and kicks of her own. When the handler tried to flee the scene, Tillie pulled the woman back for more punishment. There was an assistant on hand, who tugged on and beat the elephant. But Tillie ignored the person and the pain. She would not stop kicking until the target of her rage was dead.

Tillie's lethal act of resistance followed a pattern common in many zoo elephants: trouble comes in stages. There was, for instance, JoJo at the Lion Country Safari in West Palm Beach, Florida. She charged her keeper twice in the same year. The third time, in March of 1990, JoJo gored the man, crushing five ribs, inflicting liver damage, and requiring a transfusion of twenty-three pints of blood. "I told her to back up," the trainer later explained to a newspaper reporter, "and I saw it come into her eyes." This was the look of anger, and it was not to be forgotten. Then there was Tamba at the Washington Park Zoo in Portland, Oregon. She slammed her handler against a wall in 1991. Administrators dismissed this as an accident. 'Don't worry about it,' was their attitude. Seven months later, Tamba fractured the man's skull. After this, the press demanded a better accounting. A park curator gave them one. Tamba, the official stated plainly, "just didn't like him." Finally, there was the case of Misha at Six Flags in Vallejo, California. She "took advantage" of an employee in 2001 by shoving the unsuspecting person into a bush. A year later, she tried to hit another with her trunk. Misha missed but her message was sent. Unfortunately, no one at the park was paying attention. In 2004, she gored a third employee in the abdomen. The tusks, a fireman explained in graphic fashion, went "all the way through."

As for Tillie, she was sold immediately after the killing. It was her third strike, and she was, quite literally, out of the Tampa zoo. As with her previous owner in Sweden, this park also came to realize that it could no longer hold or control the elephant. Tillie would kill again and officials knew it. Her message, it seems, had been received. In actuality, if it had been only two decades earlier, Tillie would have been executed—as this had been, for over a century, standard procedure for habitual offenders. Resist beyond a certain point, and you would be put to death. Yet, with the reburgeoning of the animal rights movement in the 1970s, these institutions no longer operated with impunity, and this ultimate method of punishment had become all but unacceptable. Hence, Lowry Park ended up placing the elephant in a "better equipped" facility: the Two Tails Ranch.

Opened in 1984 and located in Williston, Florida, Two Tails is a working ranch with a broad mission. First, in partnership with Ringling Brothers, it serves as a breeding program for the reproduction of circus elephants. These "conservation" centers were started in response to stricter laws and regulations regarding the exportation of elephants from foreign countries. Zoos and circuses simply needed a new, more reliable source of free labor. Second, the ranch is a training facility. In fact, its current owner and operator is Patricia Zerbini—one of the foremost pachyderm trainers in the world. If anyone could keep Tillie in line, it would be Zerbini. Finally, Two Tails is home to a number of older elephants. But this is no retirement community. Under the guise of "education," these animals are used to entertain visitors, furnish rides, pose for photographs, and give demonstrations and clinics. Moreover, they are required to travel and perform at fairs, exhibitions, and special events. For most captive elephants, work is something that is never finished.

In 2000, we would hear from Tillie again, but the news was not so encouraging. She had become the subject of a USDA investigation. The federal department discovered that the elephant was ill and suffering. Evidently, Tillie had contracted tuberculosis and was receiving no veterinary care for the disease. Tillie remains at the ranch.

Moja

Newspapers referred to her simply as "M." Was this a key anonymous source? An unknown serial killer? Or, maybe, a protected crime victim? In actuality, the answer was none of the above. M. was an elephant, who lived at the Pittsburgh Zoo. An eight-year resident, she had just days earlier injured a handler. Yet, when questioned by the local media, representatives for the park—who on normal occasions are quite verbose if not braggart when discussing their operations—became strangely tight-lipped and would provide only the first initial of the involved animal. Why all of this mystery?

M. stood for Moja. She was born at the San Diego Zoo in May of 1982. Her mother was Wankie, a twenty-three year old who had spent most of her life in Southern California. It was her first calf, and the birth was considered a triumph. For Moja was a rarity, one of the few African elephants to have been bred successfully in captivity. The zoological profession could not have been more pleased, and it touted the news far and wide. But for Wankie and her calf, the celebration was to be short-lived—as Moja was shipped in October of the following year to the city zoo in Tacoma, Washington. If some readers are thinking that this does not sound like much time for a mother and daughter to spend together, they would be correct. Elephants are affected acutely by such an abrupt separation.

In pachyderm society, family is everything. Females, for instance, are never alone. Daughters will spend most of their lives with their mothers. These intense bonds are nearly unbreakable, and extend beyond the material world and into the spiritual. Elephants are known to have their own graveyards and complex rituals regarding the treatment of the dead. Visits are made often to these funerary grounds, and the bones of relatives are touched, caressed, and even carried around. As for male elephants, the maternal bond is equally as strong for the first segment of their lives. But, upon reaching adolescents, males become more independent and begin to venture out from the herd for extended periods of time. Eventually, males separate and remain solitary—although maintaining friendships with other males is important. Zoos and circuses, however, do not recognize or value the significance of these relations: familial or otherwise. The majority of calves are removed from their mothers by the age of two, if not sooner.

Wankie, for her part, never again saw her calf. She died in 2005, somewhere in the middle of Nebraska on Interstate 80. The Chicago Lincoln Park Zoo, who then owned the elephant, had sold her to Salt Lake City. Evidently, Chicago's two other elephants, Tatima and Peaches, had just died of mycobacteriosis (a disease causing lameness). Wankie was also infected and dying. Local citizens wanted her taken to the sanctuary in Hohenwald, Tennessee. Park officials, however, denied the request. Instead, they sent Wankie on a 1400 mile trip in the back of an unheated semi-trailer. With temperatures dipping below freezing and attendants bickering about whether to place a tarp over her crate, Wankie collapsed. She did not get up. Was Moja in her final thoughts?

At the Tacoma Point Defiance Zoo, Moja stayed until her sixth birthday, when she was sold to a private contractor. Thus began her pitiful life in the circus industry. Interestingly, she spent at least one season working alongside Tyke and Elaine for Circus International. She was, in fact, backstage during the infamous 1994 Honolulu performance, wherein Tyke killed her trainer, escaped into the city streets, and was shot to death by police. That trainer was none other than Moja's current owner: Allen Campbell. Following the fatal incident, the Pittsburgh Zoo stepped forward and offered to purchase the performer. The proposal was accepted, and Moja was shipped to Pennsylvania.

We would not hear from Moja again until the turn of the millennium. In late 2000, Moja, who had given birth to a calf eleven months previous, and Victoria, as she was named, was preparing to observe her first birthday. She was, in fact, the first US-born African elephant to survive beyond the age of one since 1985. The next time Moja made the news was in November of 2002. She and Victoria were being led on an early morning walk, when they decided to make an unscheduled stop outside of a zoo cafe. Their handlers did not approve, for any pauses or alterations in the routine were not allowed. One of the trainers shouted commands in a harsh voice and threatened with an ankus that the two elephants better move along. Moja and Victoria refused. At some point in the escalating argument, the mother asserted herself. She knocked the handler down and crushed him. She and her calf then walked away from the scene. Panicking, the zoo alerted city police. Officers arrived and encircled the park, and the Special Weapons and Tactics team fortified the main entrance. In the end, this show of force was not needed—as Moja and Victoria were soon boxed in by an assembly of vans and trucks and led back to their enclosure.

The zoo seemed to be at a loss about the attack. Such events, it claimed, were "relatively rare" and "largely unexplained." The head of the AZA's elephant advisory committee added, "I can't say what would cause the elephant in Pittsburgh to do what it did. It's very unlike females to behave like that." One park administrator even pointed out that M. was the zoo's most docile elephant and a model of subordinate behavior. "She's never threatened anybody. She's never postured to anybody." This last statement, however, was almost immediately proven to be false—as M.'s confidential dossier was leaked to the press. Ten months previous, M. had injured another trainer during a similar morning stroll.

When confronted with this apparent contradiction, the zoo confirmed that such an incident did occur but that it was "nonaggressive." M., a spokeswoman explained, got into a wrestling match with another elephant, and her trainer was knocked over in the process. This was inadvertent, and the man suffered nothing more than a bruised leg. Was the zoo finally telling the truth? No. For the melee not only left the employee with a severe leg injury and collapsed lung, but this former elephant trainer for the Ringling Brothers Circus was unable to work for the next three months. Moreover, when the man returned to the job, he refused to ever handle another elephant again. The accident was, in his mind, no accident. It did not matter what the zoo said. He knew differently. Moja had injured him on purpose, and the smart move was to avoid all future contact with these animals. Precedent, it seems, was on his side.

Consider, for instance, the example of Shanti at the Lincoln Park Zoo. In February of 1994, this three year-old, captive-born elephant was being moved out of her enclosure when she and her handler both slipped simultaneously on a slick surface. Shanti's leg fell upon the trainer and the woman received some moderate trauma. "At no time did the animal appear to be aggressive towards the keeper." This was an unfortunate accident. Well, that was Lincoln Park's story and officials stuck to it. But, according to a later lawsuit, events transpired in a far different manner. The young elephant, it was described, had snapped her chains and the trainer was trying to re-secure them. When the woman slipped to the ground, she was deliberately stepped on and gored. The trainer suffered several broken ribs, a broken sternum, a collapsed lung, and a deep puncture wound. The zoo, not without retort, argued that these injuries were caused, not by Shanti, but by a pair of pliers that the woman was carrying in her back pocket at the time. The handler, nevertheless, won the suit and affirmed to the press that Shanti was quite the "unruly" elephant. Lincoln Park evidently came to the same conclusion, as Shanti was sold the following year to a private contractor.

Then there was the case of Alice and Cha Cha at the San Diego Zoo. In 1991, a keeper was killed at the park when struck in the head by an elephant. Zoo biologists quickly determined that a fight had broken out between two elephants, Alice and Cha Cha, and this woman had somehow gotten in the way. She was quite simply in the wrong place at the wrong time, and her death, while tragic, was accidental. The Occupational Safety and Health Administration (OSHA), however, performed its own investigation. It found out that the experienced handler was actually in the process of training one of the elephants when another approached and struck her. Was this a gaffe? Was the one elephant trying to hit the other but missed the target? Perhaps a similar incident, which occurred the same year at the Houston Zoological Garden, provided a clue. Two pachyderms, Indu and Methai, had engaged in a tussle, when a handler stepped in and yelled at the pair to stop. Indu turned around and, "like a bolt of lighting," charged. She slammed the man into a fence and proceeded to butt him repeatedly with her head. The zoo, after the fact, minced no words. Indu, "depressed and aggressive since watching her newborn calf die two months ago," assaulted the man. Indeed, OSHA came to the same conclusion about the incident in San Diego: "animal trainer killed when attacked by elephant."

But let us return to Moja and her fate. She was put into isolation immediately following the attack and kept there until further notice.

Pittsburg, like other zoos facing similar circumstances, needed to make a choice. Would it transfer Moja to another institution? Would it sell her to a contractor? Would it place her in a sanctuary? Or would it take a chance and keep her? Ultimately, the Pittsburg zoo opted to keep the elephant. Its reasoning was coldly straightforward. "This is," a spokeswoman explained, "a breeding female African elephant. This is an endangered species." Moja had already given birth to one calf (who survived), and she might give birth to another (and she did in July of 2008). Yet park administrators still faced several unresolved problems—all of them involving their elephant and her recalcitrant behavior. As one employee summarized, "She may have learned that she can push a human out of her way, and might do so again when irritated." So what was the zoo's solution? The answer lay in protected contact.

Known as PC for short, protected contact is an alternative system of management that is based upon the principles of (a) positive reinforcement (not social dominance) and (b) prohibition of physical punishment. Its mission is to keep a physical barrier between the trainer and the elephant at all times. This not only diminishes the chance of attack and injury but also allows the elephants themselves to have choices and control over their own environment. Walls, fences, wire, and bars—not bull hooks and sticks—provide the means of protection under this system. Significantly, the initial development of PC has two distinct parts.

The first occurred in San Diego, California. It was 1988 and Dunda, an African elephant, was being punished for her continued disobedience at the city zoo. Trainers had chained each of her legs and pulled them taut. The trainers then went to work on Dunda with ax-handles and clubs, beating her for two straight days. When a video of this was shown on a local television station, the viewers reacted with disbelief and rage. Stung by the intense response, the San Diego Zoological Society brought in two outside consultants, Gail Laule and Tim Desmond, to commence the implementation of a new program of elephant management. This would be the beginning of PC. The consultant's contract lasted nine months and was meant to be renewed. But it was not and the project remained unfinished. The zoological society was placing its bet on the hope that there would be no more attacks. Three years later, after Alice killed her San Diego trainer, the zoo was forced to save face and restart the program.

The second part to the development of PC happened in Oakland, California. It can be traced to the actions of three individual elephants. The first took place in 1988 at the Brookfield Zoo in Chicago, Illinois, when Patience knocked a female trainer to the ground, butted against her, and hurled her into a stone wall. The next transpired in 1990 at the Knowland Park Zoo. This time, it was Lisa who confronted the same trainer (who had since relocated to Oakland) and ripped the woman's finger off. The final event occured in February of 1991, when another Knowland elephant, Smokey, attacked and killed a handler. Cumulatively, these actions forced Oakland administrators into making a radical change in their training methods. That June, Knowland Park would come to adopt PC. Other zoos would follow suit. Remember Indu? Her institution took up this new system of management and quickly. Likewise, at the Pittsburg Zoo, Moja's second act of resistance prompted administrators to make a startling announcement. All park elephants, henceforth, would be placed under protected contact. This was a victory for Moja—however short-lived it might have turned out to be. In the coming months, administrators would renege on their promises, and PC was not installed. Today, the bull-hook, the stick, and the club remain in use at the Pittsburg Zoo—that is, until Moja decides differently.

Flora

The Miami Metro Zoo had been forewarned about its newest acquisition. For while Flora appeared to most people to be gentle and good-willed, she could be quite the opposite in both mood and action. This elephant was, according to her former employer, "extremely intelligent and would push the envelope." Flora had never taken a particular liking to captivity or imposed tasks, and she would, on occasion, become dangerous, even deadly. Any dealings with her called for, nay demanded, intense caution and a "constant eye." Miami officials, whether they fully understood it or not, had taken on quite the challenge with this elephant—a challenge they would ultimately lose.

Flora was born in Zimbabwe in 1982. Two years later her mother was killed by ivory poachers. Flora was captured and sold. She reemerged in St. Louis, Missouri as the proud possession of Circus Flora, her namesake. Over the next decade and a half, this elephant labored for this small, one-ring outfit. She performed at town festivals. She made appearances in elementary schools. She gave rides at birthday parties. These festivities were Flora's specialty. In her wintering home of Bethune, South Carolina, a generation of children grew up riding on her back and cheering around her feet. Season after season, Flora duly entertained the masses and created a sense of goodwill among young and old alike. Everyone respected Flora and her gentle soul. This jolly mood would last up until her fifteenth year.

The first altercation occurred with a visiting handler. The woman had been brought in from Arizona to help train Flora. Whether the circus was beginning to have trouble with the elephant or whether this was just a matter of Flora learning new techniques, we do not know. After finishing a new exercise, the woman trainer was dismounting the animal from a ladder when she fell off. Flora then stepped on the handler's leg, crushing it. News of the stomping spread quickly, as did the speculation. Was this an accident? Was this an attack? Was Flora plotting an escape? County police, regional media, and even a television helicopter descended on the rural municipality. "When we got the call," the sheriff commented, "they said an elephant was running wild through the town and two people were already injured." But "when we got there, poor old Flora was just sitting in her pen." Circus officials said afterwards that the situation had gotten overblown. A few months later, Flora struck again.

This time it happened during a circus stop in South Carolina. Flora was giving rides to patrons. A trainer was on hand. The audience was, as always, filled with a mixture of awe and apprehension. Everything seemed to going well. Then Flora suddenly grabbed an adult visitor, who was in the process of dismounting, and hurled her against an adjacent tree. After crashing back onto the grass, the woman was picked up and thrown twice more. Flora was done giving rides. In 2001, the circus sold the elephant to the Miami Zoo.

One of the first things that Miami did upon obtaining Flora was to stop allowing elephant rides at the park. This was not an unusual move. The San Antonio Zoo had prohibited rides back in 1992, after Ginny, a now deceased Asian elephant, killed a handler. A decade later, officials at the Indianapolis Zoo would be forced to do the same, after two attacks by their African females, Cita and Ivory. For Miami administrators, it was the judicious decision. Flora had a well-earned reputation, and the park did want to take any chances of her injuring its patrons. The subsequent lawsuits would have been financially calamitous.

Next the Miami Zoo initiated a new training program. Given Flora's recalcitrant demeanor, the zoo knew it had to keep the control measures as tight as possible. Anything less and the situation could easily get out of hand. For that first year, the program worked well, and the elephant kept quiet. But, by the beginning of the second year, Miami began to experience problems. During a special group training session, Flora knocked a keeper to the ground and began kicking him. As the blows were delivered again and again, the man tumbled along like a tin-can in the street. His trip ended in a pile of rocks: with a broken arm, bruised spleen, and damage to the brain. "It was pretty ironic," a spokesman admitted candidly, "because they were in the middle of a speech about how, in order to handle elephants, you have to dominate, and they were saying how the junior handler was trying to dominate the big elephant, and then this happened. It was kind of like a battle of wills." Well, Flora had won this battle, and Miami had only to look at the history of three other contemporary elephants, Sissy, Callie, and Winkie, to see what was going to happen next.

Sissy had been at the El Paso Zoo for only six months, but, as far as officials were concerned, this was six months too long. At her previous park in Houston, she did not even make it a full year. The trouble really started back in 1997 at the Frank Buck Zoo in Gainesville, Texas, when the elephant crushed the park supervisor to death. After that, Sissy was all but ungovernable, and no one wanted to risk having her around for any extended period of time. So, what was El Paso to do? In one word, Hohenwald. This Tennessee sanctuary has always been ready, willing, and able to take in any female elephant, regardless of her reputation. Yet, there was a significant obstacle standing in the way of this move. Namely, zoos will do almost anything to avoid confessing that they might not be able to adequately care for or tend to an animal. And they certainly do not want to admit that an animal can, by his or her own actions, force a zoo into a counteraction—that is, to actually force a zoo into releasing him or her to a sanctuary. This is why the governing body of the industry, the AZA, refuses to concede that Hohenwald exists. For true sanctuaries, in its mind, cannot be an alternative. To acknowledge them would be a fatal admission that an animal might be happier and healthier while living in another location or place. This arrogant stance on the part of the AZA suffered a recent blow, when an extensive study was released in the journal *Science* in 2008 that showed captive elephants as having half the life span as their counterparts living free in Asia and Africa. But the zoo industry is very stubborn. It has chosen to ignore the data altogether and remained firm in its position. This is, without a doubt, what happened in the case of the Los Angeles Zoo and Callie.

Callie was an aging elephant with many problems. She had a chronic leg injury, due to a trailer accident. She had degenerative joint disease, caused by years of standing on cement and concrete. She had tuberculosis, resulting from poor living conditions and lack of veterinarian care. Callie also had a record of being resistant. In 1996, in front of a crowd of visitors, she charged a keeper, butted him to the ground, and tried to trample him. Publicly, the zoo claimed that this was an "extremely rare" accident and that Callie merely "slipped." Privately, in an OSHA report, it was disclosed that she was "known to be difficult to handle" and "the least tractable of the zoo's six female elephants." For all of these reasons and more, Los Angeles wanted to rid itself of this multi-ton headache. Hearing of the plan, Southern California citizens asked that Callie be sent to a sanctuary to spend the rest of her days. The zoo ignored the pleas and instead shipped the elephant up the Pacific coast to the San Francisco Zoo—an institution with arguably even worse facilities than Los Angeles. Tinkerbelle had been living there since the 1960s, and she had the same ailments as Callie. Chained for fifteen to sixteen hours a day to a cement slab, she had developed joint disease and debilitating foot pain. Tinkerbelle also had her recalcitrant side: attacking a veterinarian in 1988 and, two years later, purposely pushing a trainer off a ten foot ledge. Regardless, this is where Callie was sent. She would be euthanized in 2004. As for the decision in El Paso, administrators chose to eschew such controversy altogether and truck Sissy off to Tennessee without a whisper to the local press or public. She would just disappear from the official record. It would be the same for Winkie.

At the Vilas Park Zoo in Madison, Wisconsin, this thirty-two year old elephant had made a mess of things. Always known for her bad temper, Winkie would within a two-year period become too much for the zoo to handle. First, in 1998, she intentionally swept a trainer off his feet— immediately after which another elephant, Penny, knelt her full weight down upon the man. This same trainer had been injured twice before by Winkie. Then in 1999, while having her feet examined, she seized a vet with her mouth in an aggressive manner. The zoo director stated plainly that this was an attack. "It seems like Winkie doesn't react well to strangers. That seems to be her history." Fearful of what she might do next, Vilas Park packed up the elephant as quietly as it could and shipped her to Hohenwald. It was like she had never been there.

What happened to our original elephant, Flora? The Miami Metro Zoo had to finally come to accept the hard truth. As the rider who Flora attacked in 1999 explained: "I just think elephants are not meant to be captive. As they mature, they get to a point where they aren't going to take it any more. It's not her fault, she's just becoming more and more unhappy." Following the example of El Paso and Vilas Park, the Miami Zoo decided to send the elephant to live in the tree-covered hills of Tennessee. In February of 2004, she arrived. Flora, Sissy, and Winkie remain there: alive, well, and in good-spirits.

CHAPTER THREE

MONKEYS GONE WILD

THE RESIDENTS OF BELLAIRE WERE ACCUSTOMED TO MANY DIFFERENT sights, but monkeys were not one of them. So when a Japanese macaque turned up on the outskirts of this southeastern Ohio town in 1988, people took notice. At first, no one was quite sure what to think. Was there really a monkey living in the woods? Or were people just seeing things? These doubts were partially cleared when word came that an animal, fitting that same description, was missing from the Pittsburgh Zoo. Yet this news only led to further questions. This particular monkey had escaped more than six months ago, and Pittsburg, Pennsylvania was over sixty miles away. Could a macaque really pull off such an extraordinary feat?

Alphie was born in Texas. He was brought to Pittsburg as a young macaque to work in the children's section of the city's zoological park. Over the subsequent years, Alphie grew into adulthood and sired several children of his own. He was, by all reports, a popular figure at the zoo— among both visitors and keepers. His fame would grow even further on July 23, 1987. The previous night, a severe thunderstorm had struck the region bringing heavy rains and high winds. The zoo received some moderate damage with overturned objects and fallen tree limbs. One of those limbs happened to fall within the Japanese macaque exhibit. Alphie and two others fashioned the branch into a bridge and escaped.

Early the next morning, trainers noticed that a few of their monkeys had gone missing. The search was on. However, with nearly seventy-seven acres to cover, the hunt was not going to be an easy task. The three macaques could be anywhere. Making matters worse, the monkeys themselves are not very big and are adept at hiding. Employees and volunteers fanned out, searching high and low. By mid-afternoon, two of the little rascals were rounded up. Alphie proved to be more elusive.

Not only did he make it off the park grounds and into the surrounding Highland Park neighborhood, but he headed north and crossed an Allegheny River bridge during rush hour traffic. Pittsburg administrators were dismayed but not defeated.

Over the coming days, city police, zoo employees, and numerous volunteers laid down a dragnet and scoured the region. They tried traps. They put out drugged food. No luck. Residents called in to report sightings: "He's in my backyard!" Officials would soon arrive, spot their prey, and take quick aim with a tranquilizer gun. Alphie, however, was always one step faster. He would dodge the dart and disappear back into the trees. The zoo assured the media that these were only temporary set backs. Alphie was born in captivity. He could not survive on his own. Anyways, Alphie liked the zoo and enjoyed being cared for by others. Why wouldn't he want to return? But as the days turned to weeks, the zoo's confidence waned. Alphie, administrators believed, would not make it back alive. He was surely starving to death. He might have already died.

This presumption was proved wrong, as news soon emerged that the zoo's macaque had been spotted again. The monkey was alive and well, and heading towards the border of West Virginia. Alphie must have looped around after the initial search and crossed the Ohio River. The media was stunned. Could a monkey really do this? The answer is a firm yes, and Alphie has not been alone in accomplishing such feats.

At Tupelo Buffalo Park and Zoo, located in northeastern Mississippi, a white-face capuchin named Oliver escaped twice in a four day period in the fall of 2007. The first time, after picking his cage lock, Oliver remained on the lam for six days. The zoo tried to lure him back with chips, candy, and Fruit Loops cereal. Eventually, a local businessman offered a cash reward. Oliver was ratted out while dining in someone's backyard vegetable garden. The zoo spent $300 on more secure locks and put the monkey back into his cage. "I know he wasn't happy when we caught him," the park manager explained. Indeed, Oliver quickly figured out those new locks and escaped once again. "They see a lot of things and they can mimic things," the zoo demurred about capuchins. Oliver "might have a piece of wire hidden in his cage or something."

At the San Francisco Zoo in November of 1994, a group of five Patas monkeys fled their enclosure. They, also, used a fallen tree limb as a bridge. One female made it over the zoo's exterior wall into the Lake Merced neighborhood. Another soon followed. The zoo could find neither and turned to the general public for help: "Please call if you have any information." No word on whether either turned up. Interestingly, monkeys have been found living autonomously in many parts of the United States.

During the summer of 1992, for instance, the Miami area was literally overrun with monkeys. They were spotted in trees, yards, streets, and strip malls. They were popping up all over the city and the suburbs. "For some reason," a Fish and Game officer wondered, "we've had an unbelievable rise in macaques in south Florida in the last two months." One of them attacked a child and another went after a cop. "They're like little escaped convicts when they get loose. They're causing quite a disturbance," said the owner of an animal trapping service. Business for him had never been so good. He caught three in little under a month. The fourth he ended up shooting to death. Now he was after number five: the parking lot bandit. "He was acting like a little crook," a delivery driver told of the macaque. "If the car was empty, he'd try to open the door. I told him 'No,' and he charged me."

In May of 1996, a monkey was spotted near the Staten Island Mall in New York City. Four emergency service officers tried for over forty-five minutes to catch the animal. He fled into the woods. "We never got closer than twenty-five feet from him," one of the men admitted. "He was traveling really fast. He probably climbed a tree and we'll never see him again." They did not. In April of 1999, a rhesus monkey was shot to death by Sarasota, Florida police. Residents said that the animal had been living in the area for several months. One year later, three monkeys were spotted in Sussex County, Virginia. The first report came from a motorist driving on I-95: "two monkeys just threw a banana at my car." When a state trooper went to investigate, he was greeted with a barrage of crab apples. The monkeys slipped away. In all of these cases, no one knew where the animals came from. Most pet owners report their missing monkeys. Zoos do the same. Some speculated that the monkeys might have escaped from an exotic animal dealer or traveling circus, but that was just a guess. There was, however, another sinister possibility. They were fugitives from laboratories.

The Tulane National Primate Research Center (TNPRC) has had more than its fair share of mass escapes. Founded in 1964 and located in Covington, Louisiana across the causeway from New Orleans, the TNPRC performs biomedical research with viruses, bacteria, and parasites. It houses over 5000 monkeys of eleven different species. The first big escape happened in 1987. One hundred rhesuses broke out of their corral and fled into the swamps. The second occurred in 1994, when twenty-eight pigtail macaques made it off the grounds. Each time, the capturing process was lengthy and not always successful.

Carl Hagenbeck, the prolific 18th century exotic animal trader, wrote about a comparable expedition in northern Africa. He was rounding up baboons, which labs then and now (including the TNPRC) use in their research. The start was usually easy. Set the traps and wait. It was when the animals were captured that the drama began. First, you had to move fast, "for baboons are endowed with great strength, and would soon break through the wall of their cage." Using a forked stick, the younger animals were held down and muzzled. Their hands and feet tied, and their bodies swaddled in cloth to immobilize them. As for the parents or any older baboons, they were shot straight away—too difficult to deal with. Next, you needed to leave the area and get as far away as possible. For the baboons, who were not originally caught in the traps, would return and fight to rescue their friends and family members. Hagenbeck described several such "battles." "One little baboon, who had been injured by a blow from a cudgel," he remembered, "was picked up and safely carried off by a great male in the very midst of the enemy . . . In another instance, a female who already had one infant on her back, picked up and went off with another whose mother had been shot." Sometimes hunters could fend off these advances. Other times the baboons won out and opened a few cages. Making matters even more complicated was the fact that caravans of captive baboons would be frequently attacked along the way to the port. Hagenbeck writes about being great distances from the original trapping sites but baboons were still showing up and making formidable attempts at rescue. Were these the same animals as before, following the caravan from behind? Or were they new ones, who heard the muffled cries and came to the aid of their brethren? He did not know.

The third mass escape at Tulane occurred in 1998. Twenty-four rhesus monkeys broke through the main gate. Apparently, they had figured out how to pick the lock of their outside holding cell. All but one was recaptured in the coming days. The rhesuses were part of a larger shipment that had come from the Henry Vilas Zoo in Madison, Wisconsin. A scandal had broken out there and the University of Wisconsin, which technically owned the monkeys, was desperate to rid itself of the evidence.

The trouble began in August of 1997. The UW Primate Research Center had been exposed by the city newspaper of experimenting on and killing monkeys. This was in clear violation of a prior written agreement between the school and the Vilas Zoo. According to the contract, the rhesus monkeys could be utilized but were not to be harmed in any way. There was to be no invasive experimentation. The university, for its part, played dumb on the preliminary accusations. But as evidence mounted, administrators came to admit their deceitful actions. Sixty-five rhesuses had been used in AIDS research. Twenty-six were killed for their tissue and organs. Another 110 were sold to other research facilities—Hazleton (now Covance), Ciba-Giegy, Baxter-Travenol, and a variety of universities. The primate center had made between $1800 to $2500 per monkey sold. Responding to the public outcry, UW Graduate School dean, Virginia Hinshaw (now chancellor of the University of Hawai'i), admitted that she had known about the violations for over a year but did nothing. She promised that from this point forward the monkeys would be taken care of and long-term homes would be found for them. Local schoolchildren once again raised money for the cause. A sanctuary in Texas offered housing and to pay transport costs. Hinshaw, though, reneged on her promise. The University of Wisconsin made its first shipment of 100 rhesuses to the TNPRC in March. No lab wanted the last fifty. They, ironically, were sent to the Texas sanctuary.

The fourth mass escape from Tulane was in 2003. Two dozen rhesuses made it into the swamps. Eight remained on the loose. In 2005, an additional fifty fled the facility grounds. Lab executives assured the public that there were no real dangers involved as these primates came from the center's breeder colony and were not used directly in research. The sight of lab workers searching in protective suits, however, did not inspire confidence. By the next day, six rhesuses were still unaccounted for.

An escaped macaque from the Oregon National Primate Research Center made it three days before being recaptured. A fugitive squirrel monkey from the New England Primate Research Center managed seventeen days and covered a distance of over ten miles before being hit by a car on the highway. At the University of Florida, a rhesus fled while being transferred from his cage. He dodged handlers, rammed through a steel mesh door, and tore out a window screen to gain his freedom. "We'll have to trick him," a representative said. "Hopefully we're smarter than the monkey." Officials from the National Primate Center in Davis, California were not. In February of 2003, a female rhesus vanished while her cage was being cleaned. Two weeks later, there were no clues to her whereabouts. The center assumed that the animal must have climbed down a drainage pipe and drowned in the sewers. Her body was never found.

Yet it has not just been monkeys who have frustrated laboratories. In March of 2008, at the Keeling Center for Comparative Medicine and Research in Bastrop, Texas, an eighteen year old chimpanzee named Tony leapt fifteen feet in the air, grabbed the top of a wall, and scaled over. When confronted by a guard, he wrestled the man to the ground and snatched away the tranquilizer gun. Tony was shot to death by police. "A chimpanzee escape," a spokesperson assured afterwards, "is an extraordinarily rare event in most circumstances." Not true. Just one year earlier, three chimps had fled from Keeling Center. One of them, Jake, was able to avoid capture for several hours before being sedated and put back into his enclosure. Jake would escape again—in April of 2008.

But let's return to our original macaque, Alphie. He would make it out of the state of Pennsylvania and into neighboring West Virginia. From there on, there would be occasional glimpses of Alphie. People began putting out food in their backyards in the hopes of gaining a closer look at the AWOL macaque. The Pittsburg Zoo would, in turn, send someone into the area to lay traps. Alphie, though, always seemed to be one step ahead of the authorities, as if he knew to keep moving. Sometime around the New Year, the macaque crossed into Ohio.

The citizens of Bellaire seemed especially enthralled with the visitor. Crowds of folks with cameras in hand, flocked to the small town to try to capture an image. Alphie was a celebrity. The Pittsburg Zoo did not see it that way. Administrators wanted their monkey back, and they hired a specialized bounty hunter to accomplish the task. In Bridgeport, a few miles north of Bellaire, Alphie's luck finally ran out and he was caught. This was January 27th, six months after his initial escape. The macaque had traveled over sixty miles. The Pittsburgh Zoo spared no expense and flew its famous escapee back in a helicopter.

When he arrived, Alphie was met by a medical team. He was given a full physical examination. This is where things took an odd turn. For the zoo not only discovered its monkey had gained weight on his extended adventure, it learned that Alphie had the Herpes B virus. Did the macaque contract the virus along his travels? Doubtful. The more likely answer was that the park's entire macaque clan had long since been infected. The zoo thought it prudent to keep the news secret.

The Herpes B virus is widespread among macaques, but it is non-lethal for their species. Humans, however, can contract the virus and it is deadly with a fatality rate of 70 percent. Scratches and bites are the most common means of transfer. The Pittsburg Zoo understood these risks. Nonetheless, it felt that, because Alphie had never been known to be aggressive, the macaque should be returned to the children's section of the park and his newly constructed "escape-proof" enclosure. Yet, not every monkey is so passive in dealing with handlers or visitors.

In December of 2008, for example, three macaques in the Guangdong Province of China attacked their owners. They were street performers by trade, skilled in bicycle riding. Such work is hard and the discipline can be severe. During one performance, one of the monkeys refused to carry out a command and was beaten with a large stick in response. The two others saw this and turned upon their owner: pulling his hair, twisting his ears, and biting his neck. The injured macaque then picked up the fallen stick and hit the man in the head with it until it broke. "They were once wild and these performances don't always come naturally to them," the owner confessed. "They may have built up some feelings of hatred towards me."

At the Portland, Oregon Police Association's Circus, two monkeys turned on their handler. They beat him severely and dragged him into stands. There, they began to lay into audience members. It was a crazy scene, one that undoubtedly led to many lawsuits. Yet such attacks are not nearly as frightening as those that occur inside of research laboratories. In 1991, an employee at National Center for Toxicological Research in Jefferson, Arkansas was scratched by a monkey and infected with Herpes Virus B. He would survive and sued the federal government for 100 million dollars. A scientist at the Yerkes Regional Primate Center in Atlanta, Georgia was not as fortuitous. In December of 1997, she was hit in the eye by fluids thrown from a macaque. The monkey was confined within a resistance-proof cage. "There's no way you can get bitten or scratched doing what she was doing," the Center said afterwards. But the macaque had either spit or threw urine through the cage's mesh covering. The scientist would die six weeks later from Herpes B. In response, the Center for Disease Control took a blood-survey from 231 lab workers. It found that four workers had been unknowingly infected with different viruses. "All of them reported being injured by these monkeys, like bites, and some of them had severe bites or scratches," the report concluded.

It was just a couple of years earlier when the Ebola outbreak happened in Reston, Virginia. Six out of 178 employees at Hazleton Research lab had contracted the deadly virus. All had been previously attacked by a macaque. As the public would find out, the monkeys themselves were infected with Ebola even before arriving at the Reston facility. Macaques came from a place called Ferlite, a breeding farm located in the Philippines. What the public did not know, however, was that Hazleton continued to do business with the Ferlite farm after the Ebola scare. Two more shipments, in January of 1990 and March of 1996, contained infected macaques.

As for the Pittsburg Zoo, it kept Alphie on display for the next three years. When public disclosure finally came that he and eight other macaques had Herpes B, people were shocked. Why had this information been hidden for so long? What were the risks involved to past visitors? What was going to be done? The zoo director responded first that the nondisclosure was a serious error in judgment by the past administration. Second, the dangers involved, while real, were minimal. Third, the macaques had already been placed into quarantine and would have limited interaction with park employees. Alphie and the others remained in lockdown until July of 1994, when they were shipped off to a new destination. Their home was to be the Ashby Acres Wildlife Park in New Smyrna, Florida.

Little Joe

Electrified wires were the answer. There was simply no way that Little Joe, a 300-pound adolescent gorilla, could ever figure out how to get around these. Sure, the gorilla had just escaped over a twelve foot wide and twelve-foot-deep moat, a feat which no ape should have ever been able to do. But these shock-inducing wires, the Franklin Park Zoo assured itself and the general public, would certainly do the trick and prevent any further escapes. Right? Well, no. Only one month later, in September of 2003, Little Joe out-smarted his captors once again and made it out of his exhibit. And this time, he made the national news.

Responding to the barrage of questions that followed, the best that the Boston, Massachusetts zoo could come up with was a collective shrug of the shoulders. How did the gorilla get over the moat? We don't know. How did he get by the electrified wires? We don't know. Is a teenage ape really smarter than a medley of experienced keepers, curators, and engineers? No comment. The zoo's spokesman kept repeating, "There's a lot we have to find out, and we'll be reviewing what happened." When pressed further for a better answer, one employee slipped off the scripted response and offered his honest take on the situation. Gorillas "go through a stage where, physically and psychologically, they're growing much stronger, and become much more lean and long, and containment can be an increasing challenge at the age." Gorillas, he hinted, can resist their captivity. Indeed, whether this employee fully grasped the potency of his acknowledgement or not, the fact is that these animals do have a long history outmaneuvering and overcoming the very best of ideas and designs deployed by zoological parks.

At the Los Angeles Zoo, a gorilla named Evelyn escaped seven times over a twenty year period. Born in 1976, she had been the offspring of the only two surviving lowland gorillas at the facility—that is, the only two who lived long enough to tell the tale of their transfer from the western jungles of Africa to the urban center of southern California. The other four apes had died almost immediately upon arrival from a combination of negligence and sheer stupidity on the part of the staff. Nevertheless, this is the place where Evelyn was brought into the world, and it was here where she would grow—both in terms of her size and her resourcefulness.

The gorilla's most infamous escape occurred in October of 2000: for not only did Evelyn get out of the gorilla enclosure, but she wandered the park grounds for over one hour. Visitors had to be evacuated. Television helicopters criss-crossed the sky with their cameras aimed down upon the scene, each in a desperate search for the elusive ape. When keepers finally tracked her down, they shot her with a tranquilizer dart. The gorilla pulled it out and stumbled into a nearby bathroom. There, she was cornered, hit with another dart, and "subdued." Park officials were not quite certain how Evelyn got out of her exhibit. There was that time when she scaled a high wall after getting a boost from another gorilla. But cooperation did not appear to be the answer here. Instead, keepers guessed that she probably used some overgrown vines to pull her way out. Whatever the case, Evelyn was not the only troublemaker at the California zoo.

In July of 2000, Jim, a thirteen year old gorilla, escaped. Approaching a group of school children, he was fire-hosed back by a keeper. "Jim started running," the man exclaimed, "and then soared across the twelve foot wide moat. He landed without a wobble." In another incident, Jim made it out after noticing that someone had forgot to lock his cage. Gorillas constantly keep a close watch on this sort of thing. They know the comings and goings of employees and volunteers and whether or not all doors have been securely fastened. In the summer of 2004, seven Columbus, Ohio gorillas did just that and fled their cage. They never were able to get out of the main primate building and onto the grounds, but, at least for a few hours, they were able to do some exploring. Then there was Mema, the San Diego gorilla. In the summer of 1992, she made it from her unlocked exhibit and roamed the park for two and half hours, frightening visitors, running from handlers, and dodging two tranquilizer darts. That same year at the Miami Metro Zoo, a gorilla named Jimmy decided to take matters into his own hands and picked his cage lock. Officials noted that for some time Jimmy had been working on this particular skill but, as of yet, had failed in his attempts. The zoo was confident that the gorilla would never be able to understand the complex locking mechanism. They were wrong.

Of course, patience is a virtue that not all primates share. Waiting for a keeper to slip up or months spent learning the art of lock-picking might be okay for some gorillas but not all. There have always been those, who like Little Joe or Evelyn, have been more active or immediate in their approach to resistance. Some have tried to batter down the doors with brute strength. Jim used this method once in Los Angeles, and succeeded. Togo, a gorilla at the Toledo Zoo, once ripped off the entire roof of his exhibit. He also, on several occasions, bent the bars of his cage and attempted to slip out between the gaps. But, perhaps, his craftiest idea came when the zoo placed him behind a thick layer of shatter-resistant glass. "Let's see the gorilla get out of this one," his overseers must have laughed. Never without a retort, Togo studied the new structure for a moment and then began removing the putty that held the window in place.

Other gorillas have used their keen athletic abilities to flee. An unidentified female gorilla at the Pittsburg Zoo, for example, leapt across a sixteen foot moat, grabbing a stalk of bamboo along the way, and pole-vaulted herself to the other side. After the chaos had settled and each question had been answered, the media still stood in disbelief. Gorillas look so big and slow, like some sort of lumbering, lethargic giant. They cannot possibly be so agile and acrobatic. Or can they? Yes, a spokesperson assured, gorillas can. And, while Pittsburg administrators might have been surprised by the manner in which the escape was executed, they were not caught entirely unprepared for it. These types of breakouts were the precise reason why the park developed its "Animal Escape Procedure Team for Primates" in the first place: to strategize and prepare for the inevitable. These animals know what freedom is and they want it. At the end of the day, the Pittsburgh zoo assured visitors that the bamboo would be trimmed to a lower height whereby no gorilla could repeat the same action. These primates would have to discover a new means to get out of their enclosure.

Then there was the limber Jabari of the Dallas Zoo. In 2004, this thirteen year old climbed out an exhibit that was, according to the facility director, "among the best in the country." It was only a few years earlier when the entire structure had been redesigned. This happened because of another gorilla. His name was Hercules, and, after his November of 1998 escape, the zoo was fined $25,000 by the United States Department of the Agriculture. Zoo executives vowed it would never happen again. Consultants were brought in. Gorilla habitats from around the country were surveyed. The answer appeared to lie in a specially engineered wall: sixteen feet in height and concave in shape. It would be, experts guaranteed, escape-proof. No gorilla could ever master this barrier. Yet, Jabari accomplished the impossible. As the Dallas director later admitted, the gorilla "had to have scaled the wall . . . This blows our minds."

And who could forget about Bokito at the Diergaarde Blijdorp Zoo in Rotterdam. During his escape in 2007, this gorilla scaled several supposedly unscalable stone walls. Then he somehow managed to get himself across a water-filled moat. This latter feat, a zoo spokesman explained, was most remarkable "because gorillas can't swim." Significantly, there is still some debate about this, as to whether gorillas can actually swim or not. Some biologists say no. These creatures sink like stones. Others say maybe. Big apes could theoretically paddle around a little bit before drowning. Either way, everyone agrees on one particular point: gorillas are deathly afraid of water. They do not like it and do not want to wade into it. Nor are they alone. Many primates and monkeys are frightened by bodies of water, whether a steam, a river, or a lake. Zoos know this, and they use the fear to their advantage. A water-filled moat makes for a most effective border and deterrent. It is Alcatraz for primates. Nevertheless, there will always be those individuals held in captivity for whom no cage could ever be strong enough and no body of water wide enough to contain their zeal for freedom. Bokito was one of those defiant spirits. Another was a gibbon named Archie. At his Minnesota zoo, he would regularly escape from his water-enclosed island. Each time, Archie would be netted, tranquilized, and dragged back. And each time, he would stick a figurative middle finger up in the air, overcome his fears, and cross the water again. Why did he continue to do it? A park administrator spoke candidly: Archie enjoys beating up on visitors. Indeed, for zoos, escapes are often just the start of their problems.

When Little Joe broke out from his Franklin Park exhibit for the second time, he ended up attacking two people. One of them was a teenage girl. The other was a young child. The gorilla threw them both onto their backs. He dragged them about. He bit the teenager several times. After that outburst of violence, Little Joe made his way out of the zoo and into the Boston streets. The surprise of a lifetime awaited the people at one neighborhood bus stop, as standing beside them was a gorilla. Little Joe, though, decided to skip the bus and ran off again. It took two hours, over fifty cops and zoo workers, and more than a few tranquilizer darts to bring Little Joe into custody. Franklin Park could breathe a sigh of relief—but only momentarily. Soon, the AZA would be calling. USDA inspectors would be on their way. Local and state law enforcement would want to talk. Lawyers were undoubtedly racing each other to the park. Lawsuits would follow. The media was already everywhere.

A similar frenzy attended Jabari's escape at the Dallas Zoo. He had attacked a group of parents and children. Keepers tried to tranquilize him, but they missed. Jabari was too quick. After an extended chase, the gorilla was finally cornered and shot to death by police. It was an ugly sight, and one soon not forgotten. At the press conference that followed, one particular line of questioning weighed on people's minds. Why did the gorilla do this? Why did he attack this particular group of people? Why did he attack innocent children?

Such occurrences are easier to rationalize and explain if they involve zoo employees. We can imagine that a trainer probably tried to prevent the animal from escaping and thus got injured in the process. Or, maybe, the animals were extracting a little revenge for being held in capitivity or for being mistreated. The first thing Jimmy did in Miami after unlocking his cage was to assault his trainer. The same can be said for Hercules in 1998. He knocked his handler down and bit the woman repeatedly on the arm and side. The injuries proved to be quite serious. Or there was the case of Kongo, a twenty-seven year old from the Bronx Zoo. This gorilla actually made his slip while being transferred from one cage to another. When confronted by his keepers, Kongo did not hesitate. He ran straight at the two men. "The scene was chaos," one witness observed. Yet, when we insert visitors into this question of attacks, it becomes more problematic. Was Jabari or Little Joe making a random choice? Were these visitors in the wrong place at the wrong time? Or was there intent behind the assaults?

The Dallas Zoo favored the first explanation: the attack was random. Similar was Franklin Park's explanation. Little Joe, the director stated for the record, could not be blamed for acting like an animal. He meant no harm. His actions were an aberration. But a deeper investigation into these incidences suggests other possibilities. For instance, witnesses at the Dallas Zoo reported that a group of children had been teasing Jabari immediately prior to his escape and attack. The gorilla, they believed, had been provoked.

Significantly, the zoological industry has always had trouble in dealing with cruel and sadistic behavior on behalf of visitors. Some parks have attempted to tackle the issue by posting warning signs and hiring more security guards. Others have chosen to ignore it. Few have ever admitted publicly how frequently captive animals are tormented by zoo visitors.

The hard truth is that teasing is endemic at zoos, and it is perpetrated by both children and adults. The sight of visitors yelling, screaming, and banging on windows and fences is normal. People hurl rocks, coins, bottles, cans, and other objects at animals. Cigarettes butts have been found in cages for as long as there have been cigarettes. Sometimes, even needles, pins, nails, razorblades, and shards of glass find their way into exhibits. Every year an undetermined number of animals die, or become ill, due to the accidental ingestion of foreign items tossed into enclosures by visitors. Can visitor behavior possibly get worse? Yes, it can. Animals have been poisoned at zoos. They have had acid thrown on them. They have been punched and kicked. They have been stabbed and shot. Pellet-guns seem to be a particularly favorite weapon among visitors.

But let's return to the matter of intent in escaped animal attacks. We know that Jabari had been teased and thus had motivation for his attack. Whether he chose the right group of children to take his frustrations out on is another issue. Neither the Dallas Zoo nor the parents involved have been forthcoming with such information. As to Little Joe, no reports about taunting surfaced in the days that followed the incident. His attack, however, was anything but random. The teenager involved turned out to be an off-duty zoo volunteer. Little Joe could have chosen any number of visitors to beat up on. Yet he chased down this particular person. He obviously had his reasons. And while Franklin Park administrators chose not to acknowledge this fact, they still had to deal with it. In the end, there were four separate investigations. The AZA threatened to pull accreditation. The zoo itself "refused to rule out putting the restless primate to death in order to protect the public." Little Joe had caused a public-relations nightmare.

At the Los Angeles Zoo, Evelyn and Jim's escapes in 2000 caused similar unwanted attention. Stories began to emerge about the decrepit conditions of the gorilla house. Reporters wanted to know more about escapes. When they were told that the zoo did not keep records of such things, they started their own investigation. The results were shocking: thirty-five break outs in the past five years. In November 2000, the USDA demanded that the park secure its exhibit. "Every time a gorilla escapes," a handler admitted, "we raise the walls a little higher—and we're about to do it again ... We really need a better, more secure enclosure. It would make it a lot easier for me to sleep at night." In 2003, the zoo shipped its entire gorilla population to Colorado until an entirely new, more secure enclosure could be constructed. Ironically, one year later, Evelyn would escape from her Denver Zoo habitat. Along the way, she assaulted a keeper, roamed the primate building for nearly an hour, and caused a "code red" alert. The event prompted an independent investigation, and the findings made the national wire. There had been forty-five separate incidents in the past five years where a Denver zoo employee had been injured by an animal.

Back in Boston, Franklin Park officials decided ultimately not to execute Little Joe. Instead, they placed him into solidarity confinement where he would remain until a new enclosure could be designed and built. Years ticked by and Little Joe stayed out of the public view. Rumors surfaced that the gorilla was being drugged by keepers in order to keep him under control. These stories were denied. In 2007, the exhibit was unveiled. With triple-layered glass walls, a woven-steel cap, and twenty-four hour video surveillance, the place made for quite a spectacle. Franklin Park, though, was not nearly as excited as the media or visitors. It just prayed that there would be no more escapes. Stay tuned.

Ken Allen and Kumang

While bread and circuses might work to pacify the human species, orangutans require a different combination of incentives. Their control lies in bananas and sex. Orangutans are almost helpless amid such temptations. It's instinct, don't you know. Surely, if San Diego Zoo officials could just discover the correct instinctual cocktail, they could solve their orangutan problem before it got any worse. All they needed was a lot of bananas, some willing female participants, and time.

Efforts on this project began in earnest in the summer of 1985. The new Heart of the Zoo exhibit had opened three years earlier, and day-to-day operations could not have been going better. But then that darn Ken Allen started acting up. Ken was born in February of 1971 to the San Diego Zoo's Maggie and Bob. He was, officially speaking, a Bornean orangutan—although he never stepped foot on the island nor knew anything about arboreal culture. It might be more correct to classify him as a zoo orangutan. Institutional life was the only one that Ken had ever experienced. The zoo is where he was born, and the zoo is where he died of lymphoma in 2000. In between, Ken had to deal with captivity on a daily basis. Interestingly, the San Diego Zoo understood from the very beginning that he was going to be more difficult to handle than the facility's other orangutans.

In his nursery, Ken would unscrew every nut that he could find and remove the bolts. Keepers would no sooner put them back when he would be at it again. Nor could Ken ever be kept in his room. One of his favorite schemes, a trainer described, was to "grab someone's hand who was waving at him, and swing himself up." Good luck trying to catch the little red devil after that. Yet, for the zoo, the ape's later life would represent a much greater challenge. In fact, when Ken was first moved into the Heart of the Zoo exhibit, he was caught throwing rocks at a television crew that was filming the neighboring gorillas. When he ran out of rocks, Ken threw his own shit. The crew scattered. In an ironic twist, there would be a similar problem at the zoo several years down the road. Large glass windows had been installed in the exhibit, and the orangutans took to pitching rocks at them. San Diego officials, thinking quickly, instituted an exchange program. One non-thrown stone would get you a banana. But the orangutans were not interested and kept trying to break the windows. The park finally had to bring in a contractor to dig up the entire ground floor of the exhibit in order to remove all of the rocks, as each shattered window cost the zoo $900 to replace. What happened next? The orangutans began to tear the ceramic insulators off of the wall and threw them instead. Evidently, these animals really wanted out.

Ken Allen would make his first successful escape on June 13, 1985. Keepers found him mingling among visitors outside of his exhibit. After he was placed into isolation, officials set to work trying to figure out exactly how he did it. A few years previous, Ken had constructed a ladder out of some fallen branches. "He was very methodical about it," one employee noted. "He would carefully put the foot of the ladder on the ground, and pound it with his hand to be sure it was solid, and then he would climb to the top of the wall and climb back down." But there was no ladder to be seen this time. So that was ruled out. It might have been human error: a door left ajar or something. But that didn't appear to be the case either. The zoo was stumped. But it was not going take any more chances. Cinderblocks were stacked to raise the height of the retaining wall, and several portions were smoothed over to prevent any handholds. These alterations, the zoo anticipated, would do the trick. They didn't.

Ken escaped again on July 29th and then again in early August. Each time, San Diego zookeepers made additional changes. The walls were built taller. The surfaces were made smoother. Electrified wires were added to guard the perimeter. Keepers brought new females into the exhibit. The hope here was that one of young ladies might attract Ken's attention. "We want," the trainers' stated bluntly, "to turn his wanderlust into just lust." San Diego even started using spies. Zoo employees would disguise themselves as visitors. They would dress up in blue jeans, sunglasses, and Hawai'ian shirts, and watch from afar to see if they could spot anything unusual happening. The zoo eventually began using two spies at the once, as officials were certain that Ken recognized its informants. This belief would be affirmed.

Less than an hour after being released from solidarity confinement on August 13th, Ken was spotted standing with a small crowbar. Undercover trainers figured that someone must have forgotten it during the last round of construction, and they were alarmed. What would Ken do with it? Should they clear the area just to be safe? Those worries were put to ease when the orangutan casually tossed the tool aside. Ken did not appear to be interested in it—although the trainers should have known better. As one noted expert warned, if a tool like a screwdriver is ever accidentally left in a cage, an orangutan will "notice it immediately but ignore it lest a keeper discover the mistake. That night, he'd use it to dismantle his cage and escape." Strangely enough, the crowbar itself landed only feet from a fellow inmate, Vicki, but this did not ring any alarms either. The keepers' focus was on Ken, and they followed him as he meandered across the exhibit to the far side. Within minutes, a loud noise disturbed their concentration. Vicki had been hard at work in a secluded spot, attempting to pry open the molding between two glass panels. The glass cracked but held in place. "I'm having a lot of trouble staying one step ahead of this group," the head trainer admitted afterwards. Some at the San Diego Zoo believed that the two orangutans were in on this escapade together with Ken supplying the distraction and Vicki the muscle. To err on the side of caution, administrators placed both animals into isolation.

It was not long after being released, now for the fourth time, that Ken made yet another attempt at escape. On this occasion, the zoo's spies were finally able to catch him in the act. He was hip deep in the shallow end of the moat when he pressed his feet against one wall and his hands against the other. Slowly, he inched his way up. The keepers were amazed for two reasons. First, orangutans are supposed to be intensely hydrophobic. That's why zoos use water-filled moats as a deterrent. Second, they had no idea that an orangutan could climb in that manner. Such feats, though, are not unheard of. At the Houston Zoo, for instance, Mango once escaped by pressing his fingers against a glass edge, toes against another nearby edge, and scaling his way upwards. "It's incredible," said the curator of primates. "There wasn't even enough to grasp. It was all finger pressure." Houston ordered an angled window.

As for Ken, his trip was brought to an abrupt end after he touched the newly installed electrified wires. The shock sent him running back into the exhibit, and the zoo was marginally pleased with itself. "We have discovered his way out," a spokesman explained with a measured tone. "But once he realizes we've blocked that exit and turns his wits to the rest of the enclosure, we may wind up chasing him again."

As the months ticked by, Ken seemed to quiet down. The structural modifications, in all appearances, must have been working, and San Diego breathed a sigh of relief. Everything had returned to normal. In April of 1987, this relative calm came to an abrupt end, as the orangutan was spotted outside of his exhibit. Repairs were being made to the moat's water pump that particular day, and the orangutan used this opportunity to flee. Ken was just biding his time until the electricity was shut off. How he came to understand that fact, we do not know. Perhaps he was watching carefully. Or maybe he performed random checks on the wiring and just got lucky that day.

Significantly, a similar case occurred at the National Zoo in Washington DC. Keepers there discovered that one of their orangutans had learned to recognize the very slight buzzing noise emitted by an electronic gate when it opened and closed. On those rare occasions when the door malfunctioned, this animal would head straight for it and walk out. But at the San Diego Zoo, its exhibit gate had remained locked.

Moreover, the zoo had widened the moat after Ken's last attempt. So even if the electrical wires were shut off and the orangutan noticed it, he still should not have been able to scale the wall. "It really surprised us," a spokesman chirped. "We honestly felt that we had him contained." But Ken had escaped and he was now on the loose.

During his previous getaways, keepers were able to coax Ken back into his enclosure with little difficulty. A few bananas usually did the trick. But this time, it was different. Ken had no interest in complying with anyone. He was on the run, and the zoo knew it. Facility personnel armed themselves with darts and live ammunition, and went in pursuit. They were, according the subsequent reports, prepared to shoot Ken if necessary. The guards at the San Diego Zoo are trained for lethal action. "If he were to have attacked somebody, we would have had to kill him because a tranquilizer takes time to take effect." In the end, Ken chose to avoid using any means of violent resistance. Some orangutans, however, have gone in another direction.

Frank Buck had considerable experience in dealing with the red ape, as he was one of most prolific animal collectors of the modern era. It is with a combination of amazement and horror that one reads his travel journals. The sheer numbers of animals that he killed and captured is staggering. Indeed, after scrolling through the writings of Buck, Carl Hagenbeck, Alfred Wallace, Henry Ward, and the rest of the 19th and 20th century collectors, one can argue with strong confidence that the natural history museum and zoological park have been a driving force in the diminution and extinction of animal species on our planet. Buck would usually kill the mother orangutans and seize the children. Adults were too difficult to control - plus museums would buy their cadavers for taxidermy. The young ones were much easier to deal with, although even then there certainly could be problems. "Put your hand too close to the bars of these tree-dwellers that resents his captivity," he warned others, "and there's a good chance that you'll get only part of it back; or, if you get it all back, it won't be in working order." Buck's favorite method to discipline these apes was to use a crowbar, as a blow to the head was better than a gunshot to the body. The key was to bring them back alive, so that the animals could be sold in one piece.

Zoos, in fact, have very strict protocol when it comes to dealing with orangutans. All locks must be double checked, because the animals watch everything you do. Weapons must be kept nearby but must remain "OUT OF SIGHT of the animal." Orangutans know what guns are, and they don't like them. Employees must never cross the lines painted in front of the cages, because the orangutans will grab you. This is what happened at the Miami Metro Zoo in 2003, when a veterinarian got too close to Thelma. The twenty-year-old ape reached through the bars and pulled the employee's arm in for a bite. Zoos must also practice yearly drills, preparing for the inevitability of escapes. Each facility must have a command center. Each must have warning codes. The color red means danger and all visitors must exit the zoo or be placed into secure positions. The color green means that an incident is taking place, but that the zoo will try to keep it confidential from the press and public. When an escape does arise, a keeper must never engage the animal without assistance. Orangutans "may act VERY differently" when free. Furthermore, after the response team has been assembled, only those individuals that have "a positive relationship" with the animal should advance. Orangutans "may become dangerously aggressive if confronted by people whom they dislike." Even with these precautions, attacks still occur.

There was the case of Sara at the Gulf Breeze Zoo in Pensacola, Florida. She had fled from an unlocked cage in September of 2000 as it was being cleaned. A trainer tried to lure her back. "If she had seemed the slightest bit unsettled or crazy, I would never have approached," the woman remembered. "But she was perfectly calm." Despite this, Sara jumped on top of the trainer and bit her repeatedly. The orangutan evidently did not like the woman. "Sara was born in quarantine," the head zoo administrator deadpanned, "and will remain in quarantine."

More recently, there was the rampage at the Shaoshan Zoo in Taiwan. A local television station happened to be filming at the park that day and caught the entire incident on tape. An unidentified male orangutan was running loose. As he overturned motorbikes and smashed picnic tables, visitors screamed and hid inside of buildings. Police arrived, chased after the ape, and then were themselves chased by the ape. For two hours, the standoff continued. It concluded with a shot to the chest by a stun gun.

The zoo used a small bulldozer to move the orangutan's unconscious body back to the cage.

As for Ken Allen in San Diego, his standoff may have concluded more peacefully but that did not mean he was happy about being captured. "He was very, very agitated and upset and wound up because this time it had been a real chase," a keeper commented. It ended up taking the zoo over three hours to get the orangutan downstairs and into his basement holding cell. The struggle was considerable. At least the zoo could now rest easy in the knowledge that, if the electricity stayed on, Ken Allen should remain enclosed. But what San Diego did not count on was the fact that another orangutan was about to make her own brand of trouble.

In late August of 1987, Kumang made her first escape from the Heart of the Zoo exhibit. Visitors stumbled upon her and alerted officials. This nine-year-old orangutan had been exploring the park for about half an hour. Unsure of how she fled, San Diego turned to professional rock-climbers for consultation. "The keepers don't feel real secure; they think its just a matter of time before the orangutans get out again." As the climbers inspected the walls looking for hidden crevices, each of the animals was tucked away in the basement. It was better not to take any chances on them witnessing this activity. In the battle of wits, the orang-utans were clearly winning.

Eight months later, Kumang would make another successful escape. This time she enlisted the help of her sister, Sara. Zoo keepers quickly discovered the orangutans' means. It was a mop handle: a device which, in order to be used effectively, required cooperation between two con-spirators. One of animals had to hold the stick in place while the other climbed. There is a paradox involved in this. Organization and mutual aid are essential aspects in many animal cultures, including elephants, gorillas, and chimpanzees. Zoos, however, are places wherein that culture is restricted, altered, or even destroyed. This is done, whether intentionally or not, through the removal of autonomy, the break up of the family unit, restrictions on corporeal movement, continuous transfer of animals from one facility to next, and in the alteration of other living patterns. Psychologists call this a process of alienation and institution-alization. Hence, within these species, what we tend to see in zoos is a much more individualistic-based community. Yet, orangutans are a highly solitary creatures. They spend much of their time living alone in the trees and rarely have much contact with each other. But in captivity, this world is turned upside down. Orangutans are now thrust together in very confined circumstances. They have to learn how to live together in groups. Thus, in a unique twist, not only have orangutans come to adapt to this particular environment, they have developed organized means to overcome it. Maybe this is what the Russian chess master Tartakower was thinking that day at the Moscow Zoo, when he developed the Orangutan Opening. These creatures can observe, experiment, and evolve. Kumang and Sara certainly did, when they used cooperation as a tool to enhance their resistance. They have not been the only ones.

In October of 1991, a mass escape took place at the Woodland Park Zoo in Seattle, Washington. Here, five orangutans were able to slip through several security doors and scale a high wall. The zoo's response team initially tried to entice the group back to their enclosure with bananas. The tactic failed. Woodland Park then turned fire-hoses upon the orangutans. But this method failed. The group, holding together as one, simply would not budge. It was only after each of the five was tranquilized that the altercation was brought to a close. "Our first relief was that we were able to dart the large male, Towan," a general curator esplained. "He can be very dangerous. Ironically, we just recently had an emergency escape drill and the animal I chose was Towan." The zoo was certain that he was the ringleader, and it needed to be extra careful with him from now on. The best way to accomplish this, administrators decided, was to purchase a brand new security system. Two years later, though, Towan would beat that system and broke out once more. We don't know if he had help.

Then there was Siabu, Sara, and Busar at the Chaffee Zoo in Fresno, California. In 2004, they spent weeks, maybe months, unraveling a small section of the nylon netting that surrounded their enclosure. On October 14th, one of them was finally able to push his body through the hole and make it outside. "They're very, very smart," an official confided. "They may have been hiding it from us what they've been working on."

All three animals were placed into special holding pens for the immediate future.

As for Kumang, she would escape two additional times from her San Diego exhibit. The first was on June 9th, when she was found sitting among the flowers in a nearby orchid garden. Refusing to be taken on her own accord, Kumang was shot with a tranquilizer dart. Significantly, a trainer later commented that these orangutans know full well that, if they choose to escape, there will be severe consequences. "Good, bad or indifferent," every action leads to a counteraction, and these creatures understand this. Kumang evidently believed that some risks were worth taking.

The second escape happened the very next day. Kumang was spotted standing outside of the douc langur monkey enclosure. When confronted, she climbed atop the bird sanctuary and awaited her captors' response. They shot her with another dart. It was soon thereafter that the zoo discovered Kumang's method of escape. "She has learned how to ground the hot wire," a trainer explained to the local reporters. "She'll take sticks and pieces of wood and lean them up against the wire so that it is grounded. Then she pulls herself up by using the porcelain insulators on the wire as hand-holds…I'm not sure I would have been able to figure it out," the employee finished.

Over the years, zoo orangutans have developed a variety of creative means to overcome detention technologies and their captors. Some, like Kumang, figured out the basic principles of electricity, and thus have used a piece of wood or a rubber tire to ground wires. Others came to learn the engineering of locking mechanisms. The writer Eugene Linden explored two such orangutans in his book *The Parrot's Lament* (1999). Fu Manchu at the Omaha Zoo used a thin piece of metal wiring, which he kept hidden in his mouth, to pick open his cage lock. Jonathan at the Topeka Zoo crafted a device out of a slab of cardboard in order to release himself through a complex guillotine door. Both of the apes would eventually be found out, but that did not diminish their accomplishments or their hope for future escapes.

The San Diego Zoo, for its part, decided that the best way to deal with its own orangutan Houdinis was to confine them into their basement holding cells until the exhibit could be completely redesigned. This time around, the facility was going to take an "aggressive" approach to the problem, and it budgeted $45,000 for the task. "The escapes have been a source of frustration for everybody involved," a spokesman bristled. The orangutans had to be stopped. Construction began immediately.

For the next three months, the remodeling continued. The walls were made taller and smoother. Every corner was rounded. The existing hot-wiring was ripped out and replaced with a more advanced system. New, stronger doors were installed. In the meantime, Kumang, Ken, and the others sat in their dank, underground quarters. One employee spoke candidly about the situation. "People might think this is horrible, but at zoos back East or in the Midwest, this is where their animals live all winter long. Every year. We're real fortunate with our climate. It certainly is not ideal by any means, but it could be worse."

In February of 1989, the exhibit was at long last completed. Administrators, though, took one more precaution before the animals were released. They paid a contractor to sweep the entire enclosure with a high-powered magnet. No way were these little red apes going to get their hands on anything of use. With that done, the grand opening took place. What a great day for the city of San Diego and its tourist trade, the zoo boasted. The orangutan exhibit was back in business. Yet, behind the scenes, zookeeper confidence was not so high. "You never guarantee anything with these guys," one person grumbled of the orang-utans, "because their nature is very manipulative, very observant, hard workers…We won't really know if it's been successful from an escape standpoint until maybe two, three, four years down the road, until these guys have had time to scrutinize our repairs." Indeed, four years later, an orangutan named Indah finished her examinations and escaped from the exhibit. It was back to the drawing board for the San Diego Zoo.

Moe

What would begin in Tanzania would come to an end in the San Bernardino Mountains of southern California. The former marked a transfer into the world of domestication, and the latter witnessed a conclusion to it. In between, the life of Moe the chimpanzee was a complicated one. He was a pet. He worked as a commercial spokesman and actor. He became a criminal and served time. Moe, ultimately, gained an understanding of something that few among us ever have: the realities of Hollywood and the entertainment industry.

When he arrived at Los Angeles in 1967, Moe was nothing more than an infant, and he must have been scared out of his wits. It was only several weeks earlier that his mother was killed right before his eyes, shot dead by poachers. And that flight from eastern Africa to LAX could not have been pleasant or soothing. In any case, Moe now had a new home. It was deep in the valley, West Covina to be specific. His owner was James Davis.

In his early years, Moe did what many young, captive chimps do: he worked the circuit. Everyone loves a cute chimpanzee and most are willing to pay for the pleasure to see one up close. Moe attended birthday parties and entertained children. He held scissors at ribbon cuttings for local businesses. He rang doorbells and sold Girl Scout cookies. He rode in parades and waved to the people. He posed for photo-ops with city officials. Eventually, Moe got into acting. He was a chimp for the television show *BJ and the Bear*, and he performed in a number of movies. The Davis family must have made a fair amount of money from all of these activities.

This was, for a long time, Moe's life. It was off to a gig in one part of town, maybe to another somewhere else, and then back home to West Covina and his ten-by-twelve-foot steel cage. Yet, Moe reached a point in age where domestication was no longer tolerable. He simply refused to work any further, and all attempts to force him to do so led violent confrontations. Moe had grown big and strong, and the Davises decided that it would be best to lock him in his cage and leave him there. Moe would have a great many days and nights left ahead to ponder his captivity. In August of 1998, at the age of thirty-two, Moe made his first escape.

No one was quite sure how Moe got out of his cage, but he did. He also made it out of the house and into the neighborhood streets. Local residents barricaded themselves inside of their homes and called the authorities. When the police made it to the scene, everyone breathed a sigh of relief. Moe would soon be captured, or shot, and that would be that. But before the cop could even make it out of his car, the chimp seized him. As the city prosecutor later explained, the monkey "beat the . . . out of a police officer." When animal control arrived, the results were not much better. One of their officers was wrestled to the ground and bit to the bone. For three hours, the stand off continued. Moe would bite a total of four people and punch one police car, before being felled by two tranquilizer darts. The owner James Davis admitted candidly to the press that the chimp had "been locked up so long he wanted a stroll." Moe certainly got that and then some.

There have been other chimpanzees who have made similar escapes. In August of 1992, for instance, Rosie fled from the Hollywild Animal Park in Inman, South Carolina. It was detailed afterward that she was able to pry open the trap door of her cage just enough to squeeze her hand through the slim hole and twist the lock from the other side. A woman hanging her clothes was the first to spot the chimp. Rosie tumbled her to the ground and took off running. "I tell you," the woman sighed, "it's a dangerous thing living beside a zoo."

Five years later and one state north, another chimp made his get away. His name was Sydney and he lived at the Metro Zoo, a privately owned facility located in rural Rowan County, North Carolina. One day, Sydney bent the steel bars of his cage and slipped through. An entire week passed before the chimp was captured via a tranquilizer dart. Yet, even under heavy sedation, Sydney continued to put up a fight. This point was made most emphatically, when authorities attempted to place him back into his cage. A local TV reporter filming the scene caught the worst of the chimp's blows. His camera went from being aimed towards Sydney to having it thrust back violently into his own face.

Perhaps most infamous chimp escape artist was Gracie of the Los Angeles Zoo. From the years 1997 to 2004, she managed to escape five times. The first occurred after Gracie was able to open a guillotine door from the inside (a feat that keepers could never replicate) and lead a mass exodus. When a veterinarian tried to block the group's way, Gracie ripped an exit sign off the wall and hurled it at the doctor. The next escape happened one year later in August of 1998. The zoo had just finished the grand opening gala of its new five million dollar Mahale Mountain exhibition. The following day, Gracie scaled a supposedly unscalable wall—twice. Each time keepers had to turn the fire-hose on her. Los Angeles officials decided that it would be smart to shut down the exhibit for two weeks. They installed an electric fence around the perimeter, and constructed an outcrop of fake boulders to inhibit climbing. The moment Gracie was allowed back in, she headed straight for the wall but the countermeasures worked. She could not get out. In the end, it took her a little over a year to develop a new method. All she needed was a running start and proper positioning. In September of 1999, over the wall she went again. Administrators spent an additional $35,000 building a large overhang. There was no way Gracie could get around this, they assumed. Five years later, she found a way. "She managed," a spokesman described, "to bounce from one wall to another, and she got a handhold over one of the walls." For forty-five minutes, Gracie roamed the park. All 9000 visitors had to be evacuated. The zoo ended up putting Gracie into a special, secure enclosure till it could figure out what to do next.

After Moe's escape, the Davis family put him back into his cage. The city of West Covina tried to impound him. Citing a 1960 municipal code, the city argued that an individual could only own a "wild" animal so long as this creature was "not dangerous." The chimpanzee, having attacked four people, was a public hazard. Nonetheless, a judge allowed the Davises to keep Moe for the time being. This arrangement came to a swift end in September of the following year, when Moe chomped down on the finger of a visiting woman and she filed a complaint. Animal control officers arrived the next day and took Moe into custody. He was placed in a state-run quarantine facility.

We would not hear from Moe again until March of 2005. The chimp had been transferred to the Animal Haven Ranch in rural Kern County, north of Los Angeles. This official sounding facility was really just a private home with some small enclosures built in the backyard. The occupying family owned six chimps and one spider monkey. This is not an unusual arrangement. There are currently over 250,000 exotic animals licensed to private owners in the state of California alone. The number of unlicensed is undeterminable. The creatures themselves can be held outdoors or indoors. They may be penned, caged, chained, or just locked in a room. They can be kept as pets, used in canned hunts, or killed for their skin and organs. The Fish and Game Department is responsible for the oversight, but there is little true regulation. In most states, anyone can own an exotic animal. There are almost no qualifications for licensing, and even those few can easily be circumvented.

At Animal Haven, the chimps were all rejects. There was Susie, a fifty-nine year old who had somehow lost an arm along the way. She spent most of her life as a breeder, laboring to reproduce chimpanzees for use in the laboratories. There was another female, Bones, who came from an abusive home. Again, this is not unusual. There was, for example, the recent case of Sueko of Kansas City, Missouri. She lived for years in a home, wherein her owner made her wear an electrical shock collar. It was only after Sueko's escape that her severely scarred neck came to the attention of authorities. Animal Haven also had Buddy and Ollie. They were both former actors, owned by Bob Dunn's Animal Services. The entertainment industry uses chimpanzees when they are young and easy to control. But when they get older and more resistant, the chimps are sold for little to no cost to the buyer. "Just take them off our hands and do what you will," is Hollywood's attitude.

The Davis family knew about Moe's move to Animal Haven and they came on March 10th to pay a visit. It was a bad day to choose. For soon after they arrived, Susie, Bones, Buddy, and Ollie broke out of their cage. The female chimps made for the woods. Buddy and Ollie menacingly advanced towards the visitors. Mrs. Davis had her thumb ripped off. Mr. Davis had his hand, groin, and most of his face chewed off. Ironically, a group of schoolchildren was scheduled for a field trip later that day. They were lucky. The police in their subsequent investigation wanted to know how the chimps got out in the first place. "That's the million dollar question, isn't it?" one commented. As it turned out, the chimpanzees had discovered how to jimmy their lock using a stick. The news did not disturb the Fish and Game Department. It renewed the license for Animal Haven. As for the chimps involved, Susie and Bones were both captured. Buddy and Ollie did not survive. The ranch owners shot them dead.

The history of chimpanzee shootings is a long and extensive one. Stuffie and Ellie were killed in a hail of bullets in 1987 while leading a mass escape from the Toledo Zoo. Stuffie was the first chimp ever to be produced from artificial insemination in the United States and she had a notorious reputation at the Ohio institution. She would do things like hold milk in her mouth for hours until it turned sour and, when the head trainer came close enough, would aim and spit. "She intentionally hit the back of my neck, it would go down my shirt," the person grumbled. The trainer started wearing a raincoat and face-shield for all subsequent visits. Yet Stuffie kept at it for months. The Toledo Zoo definitely had a love/hate relationship with its chimps. It loved them for their popularity and cash receipts that this fame brought in. It hated them for their resistance. Whether it was the chimps' "very inelegant habit of tearing things to pieces" or their "savage and unmanageable" behavior, zoo officials always had their hands full. As one keeper snarled, "they are psychos." CoCo, for instance, enjoyed throwing his shit at visitors. "Scatological humor," trainers call it. Ultimately, CoCo was not even allowed outside of his singular cage—ever. Toledo considered him to be too dangerous.

Chip and Happy were shotgunned in 1999 at the Hogle Zoo in Salt Lake City, Utah. They, along with Tammy, had just escaped their base-ment-holding cell. While Tammy went one direction, Chip and Happy went another. The latter pair had a target in mind: a particular volun-teer whom they both hated. When they found him, they attacked. One former employee detailed how the zoo had been warned, several times, not to allow this person to "perform as a volunteer in the Ape House, as it agitated the chimpanzees … There's a lot going on in that building, and the animals—particularly chimpanzees—will bait keepers into making mistakes." The one-time famous animal collector Ellis Joseph found this out the hard way in 1921, when he went to greet one of his former chimps. The animal, "which seemed to be overjoyed to see him … bit him on the face and back."

Reuben, Jimmy, and Tyler were shot dead in 2005 at a roadside zoo in Royal, Nebraska. Reuben, twenty-two, was born at the St. Louis Zoo. At the age of one, he was taken from his mother and sold to Folsom Children's Zoo, and, when the cute infant stage wore off, he was sent to

Royal. Jimmy was somebody's pet before being abandoned. Tyler was a one-time Hollywood actor. None of the three deserved their fate at Zoo Nebraska. Like the vast majority of roadside zoos, this place was a dump. Between 2000 and 2005, the park received no less than 100 citations: general disrepair, no sewage drainage, no veterinarian care, no drinking water, no heat during the winter. Ken Schlueter, the park's then-director, ran an auto-parts store before taking the position. Was it at all surprising then that the chimps would make a run for it? Unfortunately for them, they ran into a group of heavily armed individuals. Visitors reported hearing extended rounds of gunfire from every end of the park. Reuben ended up being shot in the back with three different types of ammunition.

Jonnie was gunned down in 2007 at the Whipsnade Zoo in Bedfordshire, England. It was early in the morning when he and Coco fled their exhibit. Authorities later discovered that the two had dug a tunnel to freedom. Both chimps were recent transfers from Regent's Park in London. There, they had lived with Cherry, Coco's mother, since 1998. Interestingly, Coco and Cherry had been separated for twenty-five years before being reunited in London. On that special day, they recognized each other immediately and embraced. Coco, though, had a reputation for being difficult with keepers and visitors. Above her cage in Whipsnade read a sign: "Beware: Coco spits and throws poo at people." Jonnie, for his part, was liked even less. Keepers called him a "thug" and, during the escape, shot him straight away. Coco made it into a nearby field before being surrounded. She gave herself up.

As for Moe, he sat passively during the entire melee at Animal Haven. The facility would transfer him soon afterwards. His new home was to be Jungle Exotics, an animal leasing agency located on the eastern outskirts of Los Angeles. It provided tigers, lions, bears, chimpanzees, pigs, and other creatures for work in motion pictures and television. The site also housed Amazing Animal Productions, a direct-to-video company owned by Sid Yost. Yost, who liked to call himself Ranger Rick, had been sued multiple times for physically striking his chimps. He was even banned by a judge from having any further contact with primates, but he did so anyways. In fairness to Yost, the entire industry is guilty of such actions. It is standard practice to beat animals into submission and force them to perform. Steel pipes, cans of mace, blackjacks, and rubber hoses are some of the more favored devices. On the set of *Project X* (1987), to illustrate, trainers regularly beat the chimpanzee actors—all while a movie was being filmed that depicted the United States Air Force's use of monkeys in radiation experiments and directly questioned the ethics of that practice. And who could ever forget about everyone's favorite orangutan, Clyde, from *Every Which Way But Loose* (1978) and *Every Which Way You Can* (1981). One of the ape actors who played the role was bludgeoned to death during production. His name was Buddha and the axe handle that killed him was affectionately called, by his Gentle Jungle owners, the "Buddha club."

We do not know what happened to Moe while he was living at Jungle Exotics. He was retired from the acting business, but he still had to live in a hostile and unhealthy environment. Indeed, it is little wonder then that on June 27, 2008 Moe escaped for the final time. "We can't figure out how he broke those welds and got out," the leasing company puzzled. "That cage should have been able to hold a gorilla." The last people to see him were a group of construction workers. Moe, they pointed, was headed straight into the San Bernardino National Forest. The search went on through early August but it turned up empty. Neither volunteers, helicopters, nor bloodhounds could find him. Everyone involved presumed that the chimpanzee was dead. We, however, can be more optimistic in our hope. Moe might be up in the mountains, living free.

CHAPTER FOUR

SLIPPERY WHEN WET: SEA MAMMALS DREAM OF FREEDOM

SINCE ITS OPENING AT THE TURN OF THE 20TH CENTURY, THE TOLEDO Zoo has seen more than its far share of marine mammals come and go. Yet, within the lore of this northwest Ohio institution, few among these animals have stood out so much as two notorious sea lions. Their names were Lilly and Cyril. Lilly was infamous for escaping from the zoo, while Cyril grabbed headlines when he was discovered swimming freely in the Maumee River, which borders the zoo. Both animals led their captors on wild, extended, and ultimately humiliating chases.

Lilly was a female sea lion. She was born, in all likelihood, somewhere along the coast of southern California or northern Mexico. She would have been captured while she was very young. "As so often happens among wild animals, the older individuals are very morose and unmanageable," collector Carl Hagenbeck explained about the species. "They think of nothing but regaining their liberty, and cannot be persuaded to take any food." It was the same way with other sea mammals. "The commonest way of catching young walruses is to kill the mother; indeed this is usually necessary before the capture can be carried out," Hagenbeck chillingly wrote. Yet such methods were never fool-proof. "The capture of some of my last walruses nearly cost the hunters their lives; for the young cubs which had been brought on board gave out such appealing cries for help, that a gigantic male was attracted and delivered a furious attack upon the boat, driving three great holes through it with his tusks."

Lilly arrived to Toledo in the early 1900s. Her new home was an outdoor fountain, little more than a swallow saucer of concrete. This was a stark contrast to the Pacific Ocean and its rocky beaches. Where once Lilly could play in the sand, explore kelp beds, and swim among a sea of fish, she now resided in a sterile, lifeless environment. She experienced extreme sensory depravation. Then again, Lilly probably could not see much at all—at least not in summertime. Her fountain had no shade to speak of and the sunlight, and its reflection, would have been blinding. For captive seal lions, the situation has never really improved. In some ways, it has actually deteriorated. Many of today's exhibits, besides being empty of ecological stimuli, are often made with glass and the pool water is saturated with chorine.

At the North Carolina Zoological Park, Sandy suffered for years with swollen and blistered eyes. An official acknowledged that "the condition is not uncommon in captive sea lions due to multiple factors, i.e. lack of salt water, direct sunlight (lack of shade), reflection of light from pool bottom, water quality, etc." For Sandy, the absence of shade proved particularly debilitating. But the zoo chose to continue to keep her in the open and under the blazing southern sun. Visitors prefer it that way. They want a clear, unobstructed view of the animals and they want it sunny. In 1996, during an operation to repair the lesions on Sandy's eyes, she went into cardiac arrest and died. She was only twelve years old. In the ocean, Sandy could have lived well into her twenties.

At the Louisville Zoological Garden in Kentucky, Bo had ulcers on his eyes. His medical records indicated that he had the affliction more than six years and that one of his corneas was peeling off the eyeball. Bo died in 1997 while under anesthesia for a root canal. He was ten. At the Riverbanks Zoo in Columbia, South Carolina, Sophie endured four years of painful abscesses on her face and body. She died in 2002 while under anesthesia for treatment of a chronic ear infection. She was fifteen and hers was the third death of a marine mammal in only four years at the park.

Lilly, for her part, did not intend to wait for such an ominous fate. In 1910, this sea lion clambered out of her fountain and made a daring bid for freedom. Standing in her way were two wrought iron fences, but

SLIPPERY WHEN WET: SEA MAMMALS DREAM OF FREEDOM

somehow Lilly managed to navigate herself over them. Next she had to choose a direction. To the north, west, and south, lay the city. To the east, there was a park and then a river. Lilly chose the river. She made it to the water and swam away. Hers, however, was not the first sea lion escape.

In 1903, Ben fled the Lincoln Park Zoo in Chicago, Illinois. He flopped over a fence and waddled into Lake Michigan. The zoo tried for weeks to capture him. It even offered a reward to local fishermen and made desperate requests to the lake-faring public. "Please, help us catch our sea lion." Ben, though, remained on the loose. It was a full year before they tracked him down. His body had washed up on a Michigan beach.

Four years after that, another prominent escape involving a sea lion occurred—this time at the National Zoo in Washington, DC. It was in the middle of the night on May 26th when an unidentified male made it out of his enclosure and into Rock Creek. He swam south and camped out next to the P Street Bridge. Sometime in the morning, he was spotted. Keepers soon arrived and prepared for what they hoped would be a short chase. Their equipment included fishnets, poles, brickbats, gastronomic delicacies, and a large cage. Local residents and passersby crowded in to watch. It was not long before traffic was backed up in all directions. The keepers, now ready, assembled along the creek and began their attempts. With each one, a chorus of "ahs" and "ohs" could be heard arising from the crowd. This would be followed with loud sea lion honking. As one witness described, "Each time he foiled an attempt to catch him he would honk-honk like a touring car." The morning turned into afternoon and tempers rose. "He's the most derisive seal I ever fished for," a keeper fumed after falling face first into the creek. One observer openly wondered if these men were not going to "beat'em over the head with a club at the finish." Fortunately, it did not come to that. The sea lion was finally netted around 5 o'clock and returned to the zoo unharmed.

Back in Toledo, officials tried all of the same ploys to capture their escaped sea lion. They used poles. They tossed nets. They offered stinky treats. But none of these methods worked. Lilly was too crafty and she remained free. As the days merged into weeks, more sightings were reported to the zoo. The head keeper, Louis Scherer, would venture out each time and make additional attempts to recapture the elusive creature.

Each time Scherer returned empty handed. Months went by, and everyone had given up hope. It was then that Lilly appeared near the town of Port Clinton. Scherer headed out into Lake Erie to give it one more try. He got lucky and caught the sea lion. Lilly was returned in her cement fountain.

It would take nearly five decades before another sea lion made a big splash in the news. His name was Cyril. On June 20, 1958, Cyril arrived from California at his new home in London, Ontario. The place was Storybook Gardens, a newly constructed theme park catering to young children. The park was set to have its grand opening on the following day, and Cyril was meant to play a large part of the festivities. That night, however, the sea lion escaped and made his way into the nearby Thames River.

Cyril swam to the southwest and wound his way through the Oneida Indian Nation and the Munsee-Delaware Nation. Along the route, employees from Storybook Gardens made multiple attempts to catch Cyril but were always thwarted. They even tried playing previously recorded sea lion barks in the slim hopes of luring him to their nets. It didn't work. The *London Free Press*, fearing the worst, offered a $200 reward for his capture, but no one succeeded in claiming the bounty. Not only are sea lions elusive and cunning creatures, they are well-known biters. Woe to the novice trapper who got within arm reach of Cyril. As one modern keeper divulged, sea lions can have "a nasty, treacherous disposition that is totally at odds with their appearance." The first time he ventured into such an arena, for instance, an adult sea lion named Nero took "full advantage" of his inexperience. "Nero snatched me off the floor by my butt. I felt the clamp of jaws, and I was raised and shaken as if I weighed nothing."

Cyril would continue his journey down the Thames for another eighty miles or so until it emptied into Lake St. Clair. From there, he turned south and squeezed between Detroit and Windsor. The city lights must have made an amazing view for a sea lion who had been born just two years earlier on a remote beach. The pollution and dead fish, in contrast, could not have been that endearing. Cyril next entered Lake Erie and decided to follow the contours of the coastline to the south. The path, he had traced up to this point, was once a well-trodden one. It was a key route in the Underground Railroad. Toledo was the next major stop on Cyril's freedom ride.

The sea lion's appearance in the city brought about something of a carnival atmosphere. Newspaper reporters grabbed their cameras. Local citizens rushed to the riverside. Sportsmen jumped in their boats. Everyone wanted a piece of Cyril. The sea lion even earned a nickname: Slippery Sam. But it was the Toledo Zoo who was the most determined to catch the prey. Its staff tracked him to the east to the Lake Erie Islands, to Sandusky Bay, and then to Port Clinton. On June 26th, the keepers finally managed to get a clear shot and hit him with a tranquilizer dart. Cyril, after having traveled a distance of over 400 miles, was captured the following day. He was taken to Toledo and placed on exhibit.

Storybook Gardens, for its part, demanded that its sea lion be returned immediately. The Toledo Zoo refused. "He belongs to us," the director proclaimed, "since we caught him in U.S. waters." On June 29th, 23,000 paying visitors, a one-day record, crammed into the park to see Mr. Slippery. Some came from as far away as Indiana. The zoo kept Cyril through the Fourth of July weekend. Two days later, he was turned over to Canadian authorities and given a police escort back to Ontario. A crowd of nearly 50,000 people awaited him. As the brass band played and majorettes twirled their batons, the sea lion was put back into his enclosure. The city of London declared it "Slippery Day."

Cyril spent the next nine years of his life at the theme park. Over the course of the decade, he would witness the publication of two children's books: *The Day Slippery Ran Away* (1959) and *Slippery: the Wandering Sea Lion* (1963). He would not, however, get to see the 1995 television documentary made in his honor. Cyril died on January 11, 1967. He was eleven years old.

Chuckles

Chuckles was born somewhere in the vast Orinoco watershed of South America. He was an Amazon River dolphin, or boto. The boto is one of three types of freshwater dolphins currently found on the planet.

The other two are the susu from the Ganges River and the bhulan from the Indus. There was a fourth type, the baiji from Yangtze River, but they have, in just the past decade, become functionally extinct—ground under in China's great push for industry and capital. Sadly, with India racing toward a similar kind of pell-mell industrial development, neither the susu nor bhulan have much time left. Soon there will be only one freshwater dolphin left—at least, one who might reside outside of an aquarium.

In 1970, Chuckles was captured in Colombia. He was just two years old and still living with his mother. Nevertheless, his captors packed him up without a thought or concern and shipped him to the United States. It was at this point that Chuckles ceased to be a river dolphin. He was now institutionalized and the proud property of the Pittsburg Zoo and Aquarium. For the next thirty-two years, Chuckles lived in a tank of water.

The Pittsburg Zoo originally bought four botos in total. It was hoped that these specimens would represent a permanent collection at the park. It didn't work out that way. Inexplicably, zoo biologists first placed the botos into a deep-water tank, designed for marine dolphins. In these unfamiliar and inhospitable waters, the animals had to expend a much greater degree of energy to survive. They could never get a decent sleep. They were overly stressed. The botos died. It was not until later that the tank was redesigned with shallows and sloping banks to meet the needs of the river dolphins. But by then only Chuckles remained. In fact, among the over 100 dolphins taken from the Amazon and Orinoco River basins during the late 1960s and early 1970s, Chuckles was among the few to survive beyond a decade in captivity and the only one to last more than sixteen years. Zoos and aquariums have had a miserable record when it comes to keeping these sensitive aquatic mammals alive and well.

At the Oklahoma City Zoo in the 1990s, it was a simple matter of contaminated water. The bacteria levels had gotten too high and park officials knew it. Yet they were either incapable or unwilling to fix the lethal problem. Four Atlantic bottlenose dolphins died in succession. In 2000, a outbreak of deaths occurred at Sea World's now defunct Aurora, Ohio park. Over the course of eleven days, three of its dolphins died.

Biologists were puzzled. Some suspected that a type of bacteria might be behind the fatalities, but nobody could say for sure. They just didn't know.

At the Clearwater Marine Aquarium in Florida, the dolphin tanks were plagued by dangerously high chlorine levels. For two straight years, federal inspectors cited the park for the offense. "Dolphins couldn't fully open their eyes and their skin peeled off," one inspector wrote. Yet no one at the aquarium fixed the problem. In 2001, a twenty-two year old bottlenose dolphin called Sunset Sam died. Records regarding his death were left incomplete, and the toxic situation continued. In August of 2003, Nicholas and Panama were "showing symptoms that are indicative of excessive chlorine levels and/or otherwise detrimental water quality, such as skin sloughing and squinting." In October, Spirit died due to pneumonia caused by a bacterial infection. In 2004, inspectors noted that still another dolphin, Presley, could barely open his eyes and his skin was severely irritated. The aquarium director countered that Presley was just fine.

At the West Edmonton Mall in Alberta, the dolphins developed stress-induced ulcers. Shopping malls are enough to drive most individuals insane, given enough time spent in them. For Edmonton's dolphins, though, there was no escape. Every day was the same. Shows were performed twice a day. The water tanks never got any larger. The light always remained artificial. The crowds of shoppers never stopped coming. The enervating elevator music never stopped playing. So it was hardly surprising that all four of the mall's dolphins suffered from stress-related afflictions. Brought to Canada during the mid-1980s, Maria was the first to die in 2000. Gary followed in 2001 and Mavis in 2003. Howard, languishing with ulcers and extreme weight loss, was kept alone for two years before being shipped off to another facility. He perished soon after the move.

The Miami Seaquarium experienced the same problem in 2000, when a bleeding ulcer killed its fan favorite, Pearl. Regarding her death, park officials refused to answer any questions nor would it allow any public examination of Pearl's medical records. Other aquariums tend to be just as secretive. Records are purposely left incomplete or not released. "I wouldn't want to send a necropsy report out into the public to be kind of tossed around," a senior veterinarian for Sea World commented arrogantly. "It has a lot of information in it, most of which the average person doesn't understand."

Still, these high death rates pose a major challenge for the industry. As the director of conservation and science for the AZA stated bluntly, "these animals are valuable and they are difficult to replace." In the late 1960s, a park could purchase an Atlantic bottlenose dolphin for about $300. Today, that same species will cost more than $100,000. Indeed, this spike in price has forced zoos to change their entire philosophy. "The attitude was these marine mammals were an expendable commodity," a former vice president of Sea World confided. "If these animals perished, you'd just go out and replace them. The ease didn't drive a great deal of research of what they needed to keep them healthy." Nowhere was this reckless attitude more obvious than with the Amazon River dolphins. Chuckles survived more out of sheer luck than any sort of care or concern shown by the Pittsburg Zoo. Yet if "expendability" was the industry's previous philosophy, "reproduction" came to be its new one. The key date for this transition was December 30, 1986.

On that day, Sea World bought Marineland, a mid-sized aquarium based in Los Angeles, California, for 23.4 million dollars. Oddly enough, Sea World had no interest in the park itself, and Marineland was closed less than two months after the acquisition. Sea World's real interest lay in two killer whales: Corky and Orky. At nearly 12 million dollars apiece, it was a steep price to pay for a pair of marine mammals, but they were one of the few reproducing pairs of orca in captivity. Live capture had become a political liability, and Sea World was desperate for a new source of labor supply. Yet, there was one hitch when it came to Corky: none of her calves had ever survived.

The first calf in April of 1977 survived for five weeks. The second in October of 1978 lived only eleven days. At Marineland, the longest lifespan of any of Corky's young was forty-six days. The situation did not improve after her transfer to Sea World. She miscarried in August of 1987 and, soon thereafter, stopped ovulating. Veterinarians did not know what to make of her condition. In an ocean environment, female orcas can produce healthy calves well into their forties. Corky was only in her twenties. What was happening? According to the medical examinations, there was nothing wrong with her physiologically, and she was receiving the best in pre- and post-natal care. Perhaps there was a psychological disorder? A long-time handler of Corky disclosed that the whale never seemed committed to keeping her youngsters alive. Out of her seven pregnancies, all of them ended in either miscarriage, stillbirth, or a brief life for the calf. The zoological industry, for its part, dared not to specu-late any further—for to do so would invite uncomfortable questions about captivity and free will. Was Corky refusing to reproduce? Was this infanticide? Sea World did not want the answers. Instead, the company chose to focus on other, more willing female orcas.

In the case of dolphins, the emphasis on reproduction began a few years later. Aquariums have to date been most successful with the Atlantic bottlenose. Other species have been more difficult, even with the advances in the medical technology. This has been especially so with the white-sided dolphin. After years of failure, the Shedd Aquarium brought in a ringer in 2005 to impregnate its white-sided females. His name was Jump, and he was on loan from Sea World. Officials were sure that he would do the job. Jump did not, and the Chicago facility was forced to try artificial insemination. Ah, success at last. Two females, Kri and Tique, became pregnant. Shedd triumphed the news to anyone who would listen. Finally it would have its calves. Wrong. Kri's calf ended up being a stillborn. And Tique neglected to nurse hers. Was this a refusal to reproduce? The aquarium suggested that it was simply a matter of maternal inexperience. Tique's calf soon died of starvation.

Chuckles at the Pittsburgh Zoo never had sex. He spent much of his life isolated and alone. Yet, he had his own way of showing his displea-sure with captivity. Amazon River dolphins have the unique ability, due to an unfused neck vertebrae, to pivot their heads at a 90-degree angle. Chuckles used this to his advantage. "Every single trainer was bit," a former zoo employee remarked. "I was bit. He got me good a couple times on the fingers." He once grabbed a female trainer and yanked her into the water. Another time, Chuckles clamped down on a patron's arm and only let go after being beaten with an umbrella. Such was the fate to an undisclosed number of visitors who got within reach. People at the park learned to be wary of this dolphin.

While river dolphins are enthusiastic biters, the Atlantic bottlenose prefers to resist in other ways. Marine World of California used to house two infamous bottlenoses: Ernestine and Lucky. Ernestine was known for her prolonged struggles against any attempt to examine her. It could take five burly men anywhere between forty-five minutes to two hours to get a firm hold on her. The trainers were often forced to lower the water level and bring in a net. They would get all pumped up with adrenaline. "Make 'em think God's got 'em," a head trainer would yell to the others. "Don't make your move until you're ready, and then boom! Go all the way, don't hold back." Yet, every encounter with Ernestine, turned into a knock down, drag out fight. She would toss the men into the air. She would roll them underwater. She would do flips and crash down onto their heads. And, when it was all over, Ernestine would calmly swim away as if nothing had happened. "She doesn't look too awful terrified to me," one employee grumped after a particularly long encounter. "Naah," the head man responded, "she just likes to get it on, make it tough for us."

As for Lucky, no number of trainers was enough to constrain him— unless he chose to be constrained. Lucky was one big dolphin. He would bash the men with his head and tail. He would kick for the shins and groin. He once shattered a man's arm with a mere twist. "It looks more like the work of a sledgehammer," the doctor exclaimed upon inspecting the appendage. Lucky also, depending on his mood, could shut down an entire performance. With the stands full of paying visitors, he would just stop in the middle of a show and float about lazily. And the other dolphins would follow suit. The trainer would "blow his whistle till his lips chapped or swing his hand in signal till his arm unscrewed." But it did not matter and an angry audience would begin to shuffle out of the stadium. "One young trainer got so crazy with the frustration of a no-dolphin dolphin show," a long-time employee recalled, "that he jumped into the water with his clothes on and swam through the show himself." Lucky had that kind of effect on people. In fact, after his death, Lucky's acts of resistance became something of a legend at the park. Did Lucky once punch out seven handlers in less than an hour? Did he really leap twenty feet in the air to knock a trainer, whom he hated, from a ladder?

The new terrain for dolphins is "swim-with" programs. Springing up around the globe, these centers can be found in Japan, Hawai'i, Mexico, Bahamas, Florida, New Zealand, and Dubai. Visitors pay anywhere from a couple hundred to a couple thousand dollars to spend a half an hour to several hours in a pool with these animals. For another twenty-five dollars, you can even get your picture taken receiving a dolphin kiss. The parks keep these pools open twelve hours a day, 365 days a year. Visitor after visitor, up to a thousand a day at Sea World's Dolphin Cove, wades in, each with his or her wiggly little fingers extended wanting to touch the pool's cetacean occupants. A single dolphin can generate a million dollars a year in revenue.

At the Dolphin Academy in Curacao, swimmers can participate directly in tricks. It's cute and patrons pay more for the pleasure. In 2008, six visitors were in the pool holding a long pole. They were awaiting a dolphin, who would soon leap into the air, clear the pole, and amaze everyone. That dolphin was Annie, an eleven year old from Honduras. She burst out of the water, turned herself sideways, and landed with her full weight down upon three of the swimmers. Annie had gone off the script, and park personnel reacted in a quick and decisive manner. All cameras were seized and the footage deleted. The Dolphin Academy had been through this before. In a press release, the company only stated that a "little accident" had occurred.

In the aftermath of a serious biting incident at Dolphin Cove in August of 2006, Sea World reluctantly admitted that such unfortunate events are rare but inevitable whenever swimmers and dolphins are mixed together in such close proximity. The best that the park can do is to provide the proper training of its dolphin workforce and to adequately staff and supervise the pool area. The young dolphin involved in the biting incident, to illustrate, would be watched carefully from this point forward and might be removed for further "behavior modification." Sea World, however, was not at liberty to release any details regarding the attack. Nor would it provide any specific information about similar attacks at Dolphin Cove. A spokeswoman would only admit that it has happened "a handful of times."

In truth, most dolphin attacks never make the press. The swim-with dolphins programs' zealously cover them up. Most lawsuits are settled out of court with non-disclosure clauses attached to the monetary deal. On occasion, though, information does leak out. There was the dolphin at a Japanese park who jumped on top of a woman and broke her back. Or there was the case of the TV journalist, who suffered a cervical injury and permanent hearing loss when a dolphin landed on her head. In court, the woman's lawyer argued that the Nassau, Bahamas facility "neither advised nor warned the plaintiff of the potential dangers of a dolphin encounter." Interestingly, there was a recent study done at a New Zealand park, which showed that aggressive behavior was initiated by dolphins against swimmers about 8 percent of the time. It took the form of firm nudges, strong pushes, to full-on rams. Swimming with dolphins, the report concluded, was risky.

The Pittsburgh Zoo and Aquarium would most certainly concur with that assessment. Its star, Chuckles, never allowed any patrons into his pool. The swimmers, if they were able to walk away, would have done so with large chucks of their flesh missing. This was one resistant dolphin. On February 23, 2002, an obituary summed his attitude justly: "Chuckles, the much beloved Amazon River dolphin with the perpetual smile and natural penchant for biting trainers and a few unlucky visitors . . . died yesterday afternoon."

Nootka

It was the first time that a trainer had been killed by a group of captive killer whales. There had been previous attempts, a great many, actually. But the trainers involved, whether through rescue by other employees or a stroke of luck on their part, had always managed to survive. This attack, however, proved to be different and fatal. It occurred on February 21, 1991 at Sealand of the Pacific.

That day's final performance had just ended at the Victoria, British Columbia-based aquarium and the audience was pleased. They got to watch three killer whales, Nootka, Haida, and Tilikum, swim around and perform tricks. It looked like wonderful fun—that is, until a female trainer fell into the water. As she attempted to climb out, an orca latched on to her. "The whale got her foot," an audience member recalled to reporters, "and pulled her in." We do not know which orca it was that started it, but all three, Nootka, Haida, and Tilikum, took their turns dunking the screaming woman underwater. "She went up and down three times," another visitor continued. The Sealand employees "almost got her once with the hook pole, but they couldn't because the whales were moving so fast." Another trainer tossed out a floatation ring, but the whales prevented her from grabbing it. In fact, the closer that such devices got to the young woman, the further out the whales pulled her into the pool. It took park officials two hours to recover her drowned body.

Responding to the death, Sealand dismissed any claims that the whales had hurt the woman on purpose. "It was just a tragic accident," the park manager lamented. "I just can't explain it." A few of the trainers speculated that Nootka, Haida, and Tilikum might have been playing "a game" that simply went wrong, and their coworker was mistakenly killed in the process. There was, however, precedent for a much different interpretation.

In 1989, there had been two violent attacks involving Nootka. The first occurred in April. A trainer was in the middle of a routine activity, scratching the orca's tongue, when that orca decided to turn the tables. Nootka "bit her hand and dragged her into the whale pool." The woman had to be rescued by a fellow employee. Sealand, for its part, chose not to notify the authorities or the press. It believed that, although the trainer received lacerations and needed stitches, Nootka did not really intend to bite the person, and the situation remained in control. The trainer thought differently. Citing "unsafe conditions," she quit her job.

Nootka struck again later that year. A tourist was taking pictures, when he accidentally dropped his camera in the water. The orca quickly noticed the object and put it into her mouth. When a trainer tried to retrieve the camera, Nootka used the opportunity to grab the man's leg and jerk him into the pool. The trainer had to be rescued. Sealand administrators chose, once again, to deny that there was intentionality behind Nootka's actions. No one needed to know. Nevertheless, more trainers resigned their positions. Nootka, they believed, was purposeful and acted with dangerous intent.

Elsewhere in Canada, other theme parks were having their own troubles. About a decade earlier, the Vancouver Aquarium had its hands full with Skana and Hyak. Both orcas were described by their trainer as "moody." Working with Skana was particularly precarious, as the female whale often switched from an obedient disposition to a rebellious one "in minutes." "Skana once showed her dislike by dragging a trainer around the pool," a Vancouver employee explained. "Her teeth sank into his wetsuit but missed the leg."

For Marineland, near picturesque Niagara Falls, a similar story played out with a different pair of whales. There was Kandu. She once yanked a trainer around the pool by the leg after the man fell on his back during a stunt. The employee was evacuated to the hospital and a pale audience stumbled out of the stadium in disbelief. Then there was Nootka, a similarly named but all together unrelated orca to the one at Sealand. During a mid-1980s performance, she struck a trainer in the head with her pectoral fin. Aquarium administrators pronounced that it was an accident. Her trainers knew better. As one of them disclosed, Nootka often leapt out of the water in order to punch her trainers directly in the chest. She wanted to hurt people.

To date, there have been at least five orcas named Nootka. Sea World had one. Marineland had another. And Sealand had the other three. Nootka I was captured in 1973 off the coast of Vancouver Island. She died after nine months. Sealand tried again in 1975 with another female brought from the same waters. She did not fair any better and died within the year. Less than a decade later, Sealand decided to make one more attempt and flew in a young Icelandic female. She, miraculously, survived. Tragically, the average life expectancy during this era for captive orcas stood between one to four years. Aquariums often went through a whole series of whales before just one of them made it into adolescence. Today, the life expectancy of captive killer whales has improved: rising to about ten years. Yet this is still a far cry from the thirty to sixty years that orcas can live in the ocean.

Sea World has owned fifty-one orcas called Shamu. The original Shamu was captured in 1965, after animal collector Ted Griffin harpooned the calf's mother in Puget Sound. Betting with the odds, Sea World chose only to lease the animal at first. Who knew how long she would last? But, when the young orca made it through the year, the park bought her outright for $100,000. Sea World made Shamu the central figure in its operations. All marketing from this point forward was geared towards her. There would be Shamu commercials. There would be Shamu shows. There would be Shamu dolls and t-shirts. Shamu became, in the words of one director, the park's "Mickey Mouse." This iconic orca, however, possessed the power to disrupt these well-laid plans.

In 1971, during a publicity stunt, Shamu was being filmed with a bikini-clad woman riding on her back. Suddenly, the whale tossed the woman off and began dunking her underwater. There were two divers in the small pool, but Shamu shrugged them off like little minnows. The terrifying scene unfolded for a few minutes: a hysterical woman, divers tumbling in the wake, and trainers at the poolside desperately holding out poles. The woman was eventually rescued. But the deed was done and the shocking images made the local news. Shamu was not nearly as friendly or cooperative as the amusement park would have liked us to believe. Sea World had experienced its first major orca attack. At the end of the day, though, the whale's rebellious actions were not enough to bring down the park. Operations continued and, fifty-one Shamus later, Sea World has thrived. It has become a flagship vacation destination with three current locations: San Diego, Orlando, and, oddly, San Antonio. The company owns hotels, restaurants, and roller coasters. It relentlessly hawks merchandise. It offers adventure camps for grade school and high school students. It purveys a multitude of animal exhibitions and performances. It funds extensive breeding and research programs. Shamu has made Sea World's owners very rich.

Back at Sealand, the situation was not as rosy. The attack by Nootka, Haida, and Tilikum left the park in a public relations freefall. Administrators promised changes. New safety procedures would be initiated. Physical contact between the trainers and whales would no longer be allowed. Guardrails would be installed along the poolside to prevent slips or bites. But the public pressure did not let up. Between the daily protests at the park's front gates, national demands that the orcas be released back to the ocean, and the city council's entrance into the debate, Sealand's will crumbled. In August of 1991, the park reached a startling decision. "After a lot of thought and discussion," the director clarified, "it was decided killer whales should be phased out." Less than a year later, Sealand shut down its entire operations. The twenty-nine year old institution closed permanently.

The three whales, along with Haida's newborn calf, were sold to Sea World for five million dollars. The sale was made in secret, and the export permits were granted behind closed doors. Tilikum was shipped out under the cover of night to Orlando, where he still resides. Nootka soon followed him to Florida. She died in 1994 at the age of thirteen. Haida and her calf, Ky, were shipped off to the desert in San Antonio, Texas. Three years after the death of his mother in 2001, Ky made news of his own. During a July performance in front a thousand people, the orca jumped on top of his trainer and repeatedly pushed the man underwater. Afterwards, Sea World tried to pass the incident off as a bit of rough play, saying that at no time was the trainer in any real danger. That's not how it appeared to the stunned audience. As one of witness explained, "the whale was staying between the [exit] ramp and the trainer and finally the trainer jumped on top of the whale's back and leaped over him and another trainer caught him…the whale turned around and slammed down on the ramp and he was pretty upset that the trainer got out of the pool."

Orky and Kasatka

Sometimes a single violent encounter can trigger a wave of enormous and lasting proportions. In late 1987, one such wave washed over Sea World, San Diego and sent the entertainment park's owner, Harcourt Brace Jovanovich, tumbling in the wake. The media investigated park operations. Protesters picketed the front gates. Lawsuits drained the corporate coffers. Even the normally tame OSHA got in on the act and issued a report censuring the park. In the end, Sea World had to sacrifice its own staff to survive. The park president, chief trainer, zoological director, and public relations chief were all fired. It was a little less than two years later when the wave finally receded and claimed its last victim. Harcourt Brace Jovanovich quit the aquarium business and sold its parks.

The incident, which initiated this whole affair, happened during a weekend performance on November 21st. A trainer was riding on the back on a killer whale, when another orca leapt into air and landed squarely upon the individual. The man, who had been training orcas for two years, was crushed. His ribs, pelvis, and femur were all broken into pieces. He would survive, but only barely. "It was a timing problem," a spokesperson stated afterwards. "It was absolutely not an aggressive act on the part of the whale." Orky, the whale in question, had simply made a mistake. Yet others were not so sure.

As the pressure mounted on Sea World, new facts started to emerge. It was soon reported that three trainers had been injured in the previous three months. According to the park, these were only minor scrapes. No big deal. Later, though, more numbers leaked out. There had been fourteen separate injuries in past the five months. Some were not overly serious, such as bites to the hands. But others were more troubling. Trainers had been rammed while in the water. In fact, among the fourteen injuries at the San Diego park, at least three had involved neck and back trauma. In June, an orca named Kandu jumped on top of a person during a rehearsal. In March, Orky snatched a trainer during a performance and pulled the person down to bottom of the thirty-two foot deep tank. He then rushed to the surface and spat the trainer out. Moments later another whale slammed into the individual. With the person floundering about, Orky grasped onto the man once again and pulled him back under. The attack lasted two and half minutes, and the trainer was taken to the hospital with broken ribs, a ruptured kidney, and a lacerated liver.

Subsequent lawsuits disclosed the next round of revelations about Sea World. The documents showed that the company's trainers considered the orcas to have "dangerous propensities." As one trainer spoke candidly about the attacks: "it's not [a question of] if but a when." Orky was revealed to be partially blind and had other severe health problems. Yet Sea World forced the whale to perform anyway. So damning was the evidence presented in the trial for the November 21st incident that Harcourt and Brace lawyers cleared the courtroom beforehand and had the majority of the records sealed from public view at the conclusion. But the trouble did not stop there. Now it was OSHA's turn. The agency's report, which was later made public, concluded that Sea World's orcas were under a tremendous amount of stress and that this factor could have been a central cause in the attacks. This was not an unsubstantiated hypothesis.

Sea World orcas work as many as eight shows a day, 365 days a year. In the ocean, these whales can swim up to ninety miles a day. In captivity, the tanks are measured in feet. In the ocean, orcas have highly evolved and cohesive matriarchal cultures. Generations of family members, combining both females and males, spend their entire lives together—with each family, or pod, communicating its own unique dialect. In captivity, little to none of this exists. Orca culture is effectively destroyed. Lawyers for Harcourt and Brace wasted little time in dealing with OSHA. The federal office was threatened, told to withdraw its findings, and required to make a public mea culpa. OSHA backed down. But the damage had already been done.

Sea World was forced to admit that it had a problem. "A series of accidents [had occurred] that are more serious than we've had in a short period before," a high-ranking corporate official stated for the record. The theme park would, he went on to promise, thoroughly review each of the incidents, so that "new safety measures" could be devised and implemented. In the meanwhile, the orca shows would continue, but no trainers would be allowed in the water. "I don't know," the individual continued, "how long it will be" before they are permitted back in. Behind the scenes, Sea World was grappling with a different issue. Namely, what it was going to do with Orky—for all of this trouble began in the spring when he first arrived in San Diego.

Orky and Corky had been the star attractions at Marineland since the early 1970s. Located in the Palos Verdes section of Los Angeles, the ocean-aquarium was California's first aquatic theme park. Orky and Corky themselves came to Marineland in 1968 after being captured off the coast of British Columbia. They were just a year or two old. From the sea zoo's perspective, this is the most convenient age to nab orcas. When whales reach adolescence, controlling them becomes far more difficult. Orcas begin to resist. In the case of Orky, he became, in the words of one trainer, "gruff," "stubborn," and plain "exasperating." The most notable incident involving the whale took place on May 2, 1978.

Orky was in the middle of rehearsing a new routine, when he suddenly stopped and flipped the trainer off his back. He then pushed the woman to the bottom of the twenty-three foot deep tank and pinned her there for almost four minutes. It was the head curator and an assistant who finally pulled the unconscious body out of the water. They were able to revive the woman with CPR. While in the hospital, the trainer was asked why the whale did what he did. "I guess," she joked, "he just overestimated how long I could hold my breath." More seriously, she added, it was the first time "in months and months" that anyone had ridden the whale. Maybe he didn't like it. As for her return, she was going to "play it by ear."

Ironically in northern part of California, two similar scenes transpired around the same time, both involving a whale named Kianu. On one occasion, Kianu purposely lowered her immense body down upon a Marine World diver. "All but his little arm disappeared," one co-worker remembered. The whale eventually released the diver with no apparent physical damage done. Even so, the man immediately "gathered his gear and left the park." He was never seen again. In a second incidence, a trainer was trying to ride on Kianu. "She threw him off," a senior official described, "and chased him out." No one was certain what would have happened if she had caught the trainer. Indeed, Marine World employees confessed that they worked in a certain amount of fear. Some of them had been sharply bitten. Some had been bumped or rammed. Others had been "yanked from stages and detained underwater." Trainers had the scars on their legs and arms to prove it. Working with orcas was always dangerous, and parks have had to figure out ways to minimize the perils.

The most common method of orca control is through the reward or withholding of fish. At Sealand of the Pacific the trainers often withheld 25 to 35 percent of their orcas' daily food allowance to compel discipline. Marineland tried to do this with Orky, but it was not successful. After one particularly poor performance, the whale's trainer decided to "dock his pay" and refused to give him any fish. Orky would have none of this. He "shrieked angrily and jerked his head at lightning-quick speed." The whale then gave the man the "red eye." Translated, it means anger; and when it happens, trainers run for their lives. In this specific case, the man tossed a large quality of fish towards Orky and then promptly left the scene. This orca had a way of manipulating those around him. "Several times," a senior employee explained, "I've seen Orky take advantage of a single trainer on a specific point over a period of several days." He would take a brief swim between routines. This delay would, as the days progressed, grow longer and longer. Eventually, there was barely any show to speak of. To gentice Orky to return to performing at full effort, Marineland had to greatly increase his payment of fish.

All of Sea World's parks, in fact, have alternative plans built-in to their performances to deal with whale work stoppages. "You have to make allowances for the animal," one administrator acknowledged, "because they can recognize the show ending…They will just stop and refuse to perform." To prevent such strikes from ruining the show, he continued, "a lot of variability and flexibility is built into our shows." If trainers are losing control of a situation, they will often switch whales. If this doesn't help, they will distract the audience by giving a lecture about orcas and the oceans, or they will start a video on the Jumbotron. New mothers are especially notorious in their refusal to work. To combat this, the calves themselves are brought into the show. Yet, for parks like Marineland or Sea World, attacks on trainers represent a higher level of struggle and risk.

For its part, Marineland decided that Orky's punishment for his May of 1978 assault would be isolation. "No one is going near Orky for three days," a spokesperson bristled. "Yes, you could say that Orky is in solitary confinement." As for Sea World, after the series of 1987 attacks, it decided to scrap its entire training program. Called "the Sea World Method," the program emphasized less predictably. The payment of fish was regularly replaced with toys, games and tactile stimulation. The point was to keep the orcas guessing and thereby turn them into better, more reliable performers. But in the battle over the control of production, the orcas ultimately won out. The Sea World Method was replaced with a version that relied much more upon the direct reward of fish. The switch seemed to have immediate results, and the park's trainers were allowed back in the water in May of 1988, just in time for Sea World's 25th anniversary. Matters improved for Sea World when the primary troublemaker, Orky, died four months later. An autopsy revealed that the 30-year-old had the organs of an orca twice his age. Orky had been literally worked to death. Nevertheless, Harcourt and Brace was done with the whale business. The company finalized its sale in September of the following year. Anheuser-Busch was now the owner of Sea World.

Over the next several years, relations between the Sea World performers and their trainers remained relatively calm. This would, however, begin to change when another orca, Kasatka, matured into adulthood. Kasatka was born in 1976 off the coast of Iceland. Her subsequent capture and sale represented something of a change for Sea World. In prior decades, the park seized the majority of its whales from the Puget Sound area. Yet in 1976, it was banned from further capture operations. The key event for that prohibition happened in March of that year.

Ralph Munro was sailing one day when he witnessed a flotilla of boats, a seaplane, and a fishing trawler driving a pod of orcas into a cove. As he motored over to get a closer look, the hunters "yelled at us to get back and we asked them what authority they had to chase these whales. They screamed back at us that they had permits and to get the hell out of the way." Munro, a future Secretary of State in Washington, refused and witnessed what happened next:

> The whales were frantic with no place to go. As the whales realized that they were at the end of the inlet and into shallow water, they swung around and headed back out to deeper water. But the troller had already set a net across much of the harbor and the whales ran square into the net. As the captors started to close the nets around some of the pod, a torch was lit on the stern of the fastest chase boat.

> Then the captors started to light the underwater explosives (seal bombs). As fast as they could light them, these were dropped in the water to drive the whales into the circling nets. It was a tragic scene. Some whales were inside the net and some were outside. The whales were crying out to each other. Explosives were going off, motors were being revved up full, captors were using pike poles to push and drive the whales into the nets. I was so disgusted that I wanted to throw up. We were furious.

Sea World's long-time collector, Ted Griffin, admits "whales die in the hunt." "If I have dead whales," he went on, "I'm going to conceal it from the public, which is what I did." His favored technique is to slit open their bellies, fill the whales' with rocks, and sink them to the bottom. As for Munro, he not only would file a lawsuit against Sea World for its actions, but would win the case and prohibit the capture of orcas in the Puget Sound. "The people are sick and tired of these Southern California amusement parks taking our wildlife down there to die," he stated to the press. "They keep naming the whales the same name, but they're not fooling anybody. Their bottom-line there is commercial profit. Their scientific studies are baloney."

Less than a decade later, Sea World tried to get Alaska to sign an agreement for the capture of 100 orcas—ten of which they would put into captivity. The park needed more whales, and it was not afraid to push hard to get its wish. Sea World's owner lobbied state officials and took out full-page advertisements. It promoted the necessity of scientific testing. It highlighted how its biologists would perform blood work, extract teeth, and take liver biopsies and stomach samples. Some orcas would be fitted with radio transmitters, while the rest would be branded for future identification. Alaska's citizens bought into none of this and rejected the petition. Iceland, for the time being, would remain Sea World's only option for its labor supply.

Between 1976 and 1987, a grand total of eight orcas were captured in those icy Atlantic waters. Among them, Kasatka would become the most infamous. Troubles with her began to appear in 1993, when she tried to bite a trainer during a show. It was an aggressive act and one which, if done successfully, might have injured or even killed the individual. Sea World cautiously wrote it off as an anomaly. Six years later, Kasatka made a similar public attempt. With the employee escaping with only an inch to spare, it was too close for comfort. "She definitely tried to bite the trainer," a spokesperson confessed. Kasatka was sent back for some additional training and behavior modification. Until then, she would continued to perform "but not in parts of the show while a trainer is in the water." The next incident took place on November 29, 2006. It was during the final performance of the evening, when Kasatka decided to alter the script. Instead of rising up out of water, so that her trainer could dive off her nose, the whale grabbed a hold of the man, pulled him under, and pinned him to the bottom of the pool. The sixteen-year veteran managed to wiggle free, only to be dragged under once again. While he had been able to evade Kasatka's jaws a few years earlier, he had no such luck this time.

In the aftermath of the attack, Sea World went into full crisis mode. The news had already made the national and international wires. And it was just a matter of time before new information began to leak out. At first, the park tried to convince the public that this was just an isolated incident. But then Kasatka's earlier episodes were brought to light. Next, Sea World confessed that Kasatka did have a history, especially with the one trainer, but that its orca program was firmly under control. This too turned out to be false.

It was only fourteen days earlier when Orkid, a seventeen-year-old captive-born whale, had crunched a senior trainer's ankle during a show and yanked the person to the bottom of a tank. In 2002, Orkid broke another trainer's arm in a similar attack. Then there were the recent incidents at other Sea World locations. In April of 2005, Taku—also captive-born—hospitalized his Orlando trainer with a vicious blow to the body. That previous summer, another orca jumped on top of his San Antonio trainer. Sea World, however, choose not to divulge any of this information.

As for Kasatka, she was sent back to work almost immediately. "She's been one of our strongest, most consistent performers," the park emphasized. There will be restrictions with her, as she will be limited to performing those stunts that do not directly involve trainers. The show, nonetheless, will triumphantly go on. Behind the scenes, though, Sea

World officials once again crossed their fingers and hoped that business would return to normal. It did, for five months. In April of 2007, Orkid made the news once again. During a routine medical examination, she had pushed her trainer off a high retaining wall. Sea World claimed that it was just an accident.

WHEN ORCAS RESIST

WHEN ORCAS RESIST THEIR EXPLOITATION, THEY DO SO WITH MEASURED levels of intensity and warning. What starts with a look of anger will precede a bruising bump. The grabbing of limb can be followed by repeated dunking underwater. In the final act, orcas will hold or pin their trainer at the bottom of pool until that person drowns. These are highly intelligent creatures. They have come to understand the fragility and weaknesses of their human counterparts. They know that they can hold their breath far longer than we human, a useful bit of intelligence that one orca, in particular, has put to use more than once.

Sea World was warned about Tilikum, when the park purchased him in 1991. He had already been involved in the drowning death of a trainer and was known to be difficult to work with. Officials took precautions from the start. Only the most experienced trainers were allowed to handle him. No one was allowed to swim with him. All interactions took place on shallow ledges, three to five inches deep with water. Orcas routinely propel themselves up onto these aquatic platforms to amaze and entertain the audience. For the trainers, this "dry" form of contact has an added advantage, as they can "easily retreat if they see any signs that the animal is about to stop following directions." These ledges, by design, both enhance the performances and lessen the chance of attacks.

On February 24, 2010, Tilikum figured out a way around this. With his trainer leaning over the shallow ledge, he surfaced and grabbed her. This was supposed to be a "relationship" session: with the handler and orca interacting good-naturedly and appearing somewhat close to one another. The orca would then be signaled to swim down to an underwater window and pause for photographs. Tilikum, however, had his own plan. He chose to use his understanding and experience to reverse the situation. He chose to take advantage of his trainer's vulnerabilities, both in terms of her position and inability to hold her breath. He chose to drown the woman. These actions were done with intent and purpose.

Tilikum's clear intention was to kill his trainer. After obtaining a firm grip, the orca shook the woman so violently that he fractured her back, ribs, legs, and arms. He then held her underwater for five minutes. Employees attempted the entire time to get Tilikum "under control," as they would explain in the initial sheriff's report. But the enraged orca "was not giving up." The "confrontation" lasted for over a half an hour. Even after the staff had trapped and netted him, Tilikum refused to let go of the body. They had to pry the corpse out of his mouth with a pole. Then they had to pry out the trainer's arm, which had been ripped off in the melee. There is no question that Tilikum wanted this person dead.

As to his ultimate purpose, this was a clear, pronounced demonstration of his dislike of captivity and all that it entails: from the absence of autonomy to the exploitative relations to the ever-increasing workload. Visitors reported that during the earlier show the orcas were not responding to directions and appeared agitated. Tilikum refused to obey the command to splash the audience. Another refused to do a trick. The trainers told the crowd that the orcas "were having an off day, that they were being ornery." This should have been taken as an ominous warning.

Sea World officials knew, for instance, that it was only two months previous when a trainer had been killed at Loro Parque in the Canary Islands. Keto, a captive-born orca who was on lease from Sea World, was rehearsing a routine when he decided to violently ram into his handler's ribs and drown the person. The almost exact same thing happened in 2007 at the island park, when another captive-born whale, Tekoa, slammed into his trainer's chest and repeatedly dunked the women underwater before finally letting her go. Another message left unheeded.

After Tilikum's lethal attack, everyone had a theory. Many trotted out the usual excuses. The orca was a testosterone-driven male, wild and unpredictable. Others referred to his species common-name, "killer whale," and believed that he was just following his natural instinct. Some pointed to his history of prior attacks and branded him a dangerous "serial killer." A few got more complex and suggested that Tilikum suffered from Post Traumatic Stress Disorder.

Long used as a diagnosis for humans, PTSD was first applied to elephants in order to provide an explanation for their aggressive behavior. The theory goes that, if an elephant attacks a human, it was because he or she had "cracked up" due to some past trauma. He or she might have witnessed the killing of family members or been extensively abused. For Tilikum, since he had been snatched from his Atlantic pod and thrown into captivity, people theorized that he too was suffering from PTSD. There is, however, a significant problem with this direction in thinking.

Resistance is not a psychological disorder. Indeed it is often a moment of distinct clarity. This is not to say that Tilikum and others are not suffering from clinical depression or stress-related ailments. Rather the point is that captive animals have used their intelligence, ingenuity, and tenacity to overcome the situations and obstacles put before them. Their actions have had intent and purpose. If anything, these animals are psychologically strong, not weak. They are choosing to fight back.

As for Sea World, it trotted out its own explanation for that day. "What you need to remember is," the corporate curator began, "we've done thousands of interactions with this animal with no incidents whatsoever." Furthermore, the park's head trainer added, "there wasn't anything to indicate to us that there was a problem." The orcas during the previous performance were in fact being "very cooperative." What happened was an accident. The trainer's long braid of hair had swung down into the water and flowed into Tilikum's mouth. He grasped onto it, like a child takes a hold of a new toy. He was just being curious and playful.

As in the Kurosawa film "Rashomon," most of the approximately fifty guests who were present at that show reported different versions of the attack. Tilikum, one person described, "took off really fast in the tank and he came back, shot up in the air, grabbed the trainer by the waist." Several others, including a park security guard, said that the woman was initially seized by the arm. Another visitor thought it was by the shoulder. All of the witnesses detailed the shocking violence with which the orca then shook the trainer. Tilikum, in their view, was definitely not playing around and this was no accident.

Despite these discrepancies, Sea World stuck with its story and followed the standard public relations script. Shows resumed three days later. This was a risky but not surprising move. As a theme park consultant assessed, "Sea World operations are built around Shamu and the orca. So quantitatively they mean literally hundreds of millions of dollars to that company." Remember, the six million annual visitors who come to the Orlando location do not pay $78.95 a piece to watch fish swim in an aquarium. They come to be entertained. Blackstone, the private equity firm that bought the park in October of 2009, understood this and put the orcas back to work.

As for Tilikum, he remained behind the scenes and isolated. Sea World was treading carefully. Park officials stated repeatedly how essential and valuable Tilikum had been to their operations. This is true. Zoos and circuses are a business, and Blackstone paid 2.3 billion dollars for its purchase. The most productive employees in that business, in terms of labor and revenue, are the orcas themselves. Tilikum has performed for almost nineteen years in Orlando, sired thirteen calves, and produced in the range of a billion dollars in revenue. Nevertheless, Sea World did not believe that Tilikum had earned the right to retire. None of that billion dollars would be used to build an ocean sanctuary for older captive orcas. They do not deserve it. Tilikum was going nowhere.

The zoo industry is full of such contradictions. It helps people learn about the importance of animals, but not what is vitally important to the animals themselves. Sea mammals, elephants, and primates are capable of so many amazing feats, but they are incapable of demonstrating their intentions and making their own choices. The industry encourages you to think that these animals are intelligent, but not intelligent enough to have the ability to resist. The industry encourages you to care about them, so that you and your children will return for a visit. But it does not want you to care so much that you might develop empathy and begin to question whether these animals actually want to be there.

Tilikum has made two pronounced statements about his captivity. The first was in 1991 and the second in 2010. Other animals have made their own: from Tyke, to Ken Allen, to Kasatka. There is a long history to this struggle, which stretches back centuries. Zoos and circuses live in fear of it and the historical changes that it can bring. We, however, do not have to be afraid. Instead, we can recognize this struggle, learn from it, and choose a side. Where does Tilikum want to be? Certainly not confined in the lonely and sterile tanks of Sea World.

ACKNOWLEDGEMENTS

I WISH TO THANK PETER LINEBAUGH, MY TEACHER. DIANE BRITTON, for firmly reminding the Toledo Zoo that, because it was a public institution, I must be allowed into its archives. Manuel Yang for help in the preliminary stages of this project. *CounterPunch* and its editors, Jeffrey St. Clair and Alexander Cockburn, for the room to express my ideas. Teresa Marshall and Jennifer O'Connor for the mountain of photocopied primary sources that saved me a year's worth of work. Gail Laule for corrections on protected contact. Jeff Howison for his keen knowledge of chess. Ralph Munro for sharing his experience. *Now Magazine* (Toronto). The Local History Department at the Toledo/Lucas County Library and Greg Miller. I wish to give a special note of gratitude to Tracey Briggs, for wading through every draft of this book. And to my parents, for their continued faith.

INDEX

AK Press

ORDERING INFORMATION

AK Press
674-A 23rd Street
Oakland, CA 94612-1163
USA
(510) 208-1700
www.akpress.org
akpress@akpress.org

AK Press
PO Box 12766
Edinburgh, EH8 9YE
Scotland
(0131) 555-5165
www.akuk.com
ak@akedin.demon.co.uk

The addresses above would be delighted to provide you with the latest complete AK catalog, featuring several thousand books, pamphlets, zines, audio products, video products, and stylish apparel published & distributed by AK Press. Alternatively, check out our websites for the complete catalog, latest news and updates, events, and secure ordering.

Also Available from AK Press

The first audio collection from Alexander Cockburn on compact disc.

Beating the Devil
Alexander Cockburn, ISBN 13: 9781902593494   •   CD   • $14.98

In this collection of recent talks, maverick commentator Alexander Cockburn defiles subjects ranging from Colombia to the American presidency to the Missile Defense System. Whether he's skewering the fallacies of the war on drugs or illuminating the dark crevices of secret government, his erudite and extemporaneous style warms the hearts of even the stodgiest cynics of the left.

Available from CounterPunch/AK Press

Call 1-800-840-3683 or order online from
www.counterpunch.org or www.akpress.org

The Case Against Israel

by Michael Neumann

Wielding a buzzsaw of logic, Professor Neumann dismantles plank-by-plank the Zionist rationale for Israel as religious state entitled to trample upon the basic human rights of non-Jews. Along the way, Neumann also offers a passionate amicus brief for the plight of the Palestinian people.

Other Lands Have Dreams: From Baghdad to Pekin Prison

by Kathy Kelly

At a moment when so many despairing peace activists have thrown in the towel, Kathy Kelly, a witness to some of history's worst crimes, never relinquishes hope. Other Lands Have Dreams is literary testimony of the highest order, vividly recording the secret casualties of our era, from the hundreds of thousands of Iraqi children inhumanely denied basic medical care, clean water and food by the US overlords to young mothers sealed inside the sterile dungeons of American prisons in the name of the merciless war on drugs.

Dime's Worth of Difference: Beyond the Lesser of Two Evils

Edited by Alexander Cockburn and Jeffrey St. Clair

Everything you wanted to know about one-party rule in America.

Whiteout: the CIA, Drugs and the Press

by Alexander Cockburn and Jeffrey St. Clair, Verso.

The involvement of the CIA with drug traffickers is a story that has slouched into the limelight every decade or so since the creation of the Agency. In Whiteout, here at last is the full saga.

Been Brown So Long It Looked Like Green to Me: the Politics of Nature

by Jeffrey St. Clair, Common Courage Press.

Covering everything from toxics to electric power plays, St. Clair draws a savage profile of how money and power determine the state of our environment, gives a vivid account of where the environment stands today and what to do about it.

Imperial Crusades: Iraq, Afghanistan and Yugoslavia

by Alexander Cockburn and Jeffrey St. Clair, Verso.

A chronicle of the lies that are now returning each and every day to haunt the deceivers in Washington and London, the secret agendas and the underreported carnage of these wars. We were right and they were wrong, and this book proves the case. Never leave home without it.

Born Under a Bad Sky

By Jeffrey St. Clair

"Movement reporting on a par with Mailer's Armies of the Night"—Peter Linebaugh, author of *Magna Carta Manifesto* and *The Many-Headed Hydra*.

These urgent dispatches are from the frontlines of the war on the Earth. Gird yourself for a visit to a glowing nuclear plant in the backwoods of North Carolina, to the heart of Cancer Alley where chemical companies hide their toxic enterprise behind the dark veil of Homeland Security, and to the world's most contaminated place, the old H-bomb factory at Hanford, which is leaking radioactive poison into the mighty Columbia River.

With unflinching prose, St. Clair confronts the White Death in Iraq, the environmental legacy of a war that will keep on killing decades after the bombing raids have ended. He conjures up the environmental villains of our time, from familiar demons like James Watt and Dick Cheney to more surprising figures, including Supreme Court Justice Stephen Breyer (father of the cancer bond) and the Nobel laureate Al Gore, whose pieties on global warming are sponsored by the nuclear power industry. The mainstream environmental movement doesn't escape indictment. Bloated by grants from big foundations, perched in high-rent office towers, leashed to the neoliberal politics of the Democratic Party, the big green groups have largely acquiesced to the crimes against nature that St. Clair so vividly exposes.

All is not lost. From the wreckage of New Orleans to the imperiled canyons of the Colorado, a new green resistance is taking root. The fate of the grizzly and the ancient forests of Oregon hinge on the courage of these green defenders. This book is also a salute to them.

Available from CounterPunch.org and AK Press
Call 1-800-840-3683
$19.95

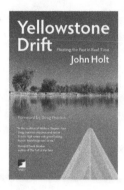

Printed in the USA
CPSIA information can be obtained
at www.ICGtesting.com
LVHW010425050124
768078LV00003B/152

9 781849 350266

Second Edition

GREAT AMERICAN STORIES 1

An ESL/EFL Reader

beginning-intermediate to intermediate levels

C.G. Draper

PRENTICE HALL REGENTS
Englewood Cliffs, New Jersey 07632

Acquisitions editor: Nancy Leonhardt
Production supervision, interior design
  and desktop composition: Noël Vreeland Carter
Desktop production supervision: Molly Pike Riccardi
  and Shari Toron
Cover design: Jayne Conte
Cover and interior art: Len Shalansky
Pre-press buyer: Ray Keating
Manufacturing buyer: Lori Bulwin
Scheduler: Leslie Coward

© 1993 by Prentice Hall Regents
Prentice-Hall, Inc.
A Paramount Communications Company
Englewood Cliffs, New Jersey 07632

Printed in the United States of America

10 9 8

0-13-364381-6

Prentice-Hall International (UK) Limited, *London*
Prentice-Hall of Australia Pty. Limited, *Sydney*
Prentice-Hall of Canada Inc. *Toronto*
Prentice-Hall Hispanoamericana, S.A., *Mexico*
Prentice-Hall of India Private Limited, *New Delhi*
Prentice-Hall of Japan, Inc. *Tokyo*
Simon & Schuster Asia Pte. Ltd., *Singapore*
Editora Prentice-Hall do Brasil, Ltda., *Rio de Janeiro*

CONTENTS

TO THE READER

This book starts at the beginning-intermediate level. It ends at the intermediate level. The first story in the book will be easy for you. The vocabulary list for the first four stories has 600 words. The list for the last four stories has 1,000 words. The longest sentences in the first story have 10 words. In the last stories, they have 18 words. There is new grammar in each story.

By working on this book, you will improve your
    reading
    speaking and discussion
    vocabulary
    knowledge of word forms
    writing

These stories were written many years ago by eight of America's most famous writers. You will read about the writers' lives before you read their stories. Special exercises will introduce you to the world of each story before you read it. And after each story you will find
    2 reading exercises
    2 vocabulary and word form exercises
    2 discussion and language activity exercises
    1 writing exercise

Good luck and good reading!

TO THE TEACHER

GREAT AMERICAN STORIES I consists of eight careful adaptations of famous stories by classic American writers and exercises on each story in reading skills, vocabulary, discussion, word forms, language activity, and writing. Prereading exercises introduce the student to the world of the story; and one of the prereading exercises in each lesson is based on a biographical paragraph about the story's author that appears on the story's title page.

The book is both graded and progressive—that is, the vocabulary, grammar, and internal structure of the stories increase in difficulty from the first story (which is at the beginning-intermediate level of proficiency) to the last (which is at the intermediate level). Structural, lexical, and sentence-length controls have been used throughout the book. The head-word list for the first four stories contains 600 words, while that used for the final four contains 1,000. Maximum sentence length increases from 10 words in the first story to 18 in the final four. New grammatical structures are added gradually, story by story. And words from outside the head-word lists are introduced in a context that makes their meaning clear; used again within the next 100 words of text; and then repeated at least three more times before the end of the story.

The exercises are so designed that the student must often return to the text to check comprehension or vocabulary. In addition, skimming and scanning exercises in the prereading sections often involve rereading of the writers' biographies. In short, an objective of the book is to involve the reader deeply in the text of each story and the world of its author, and, toward that end, to present exercises that are difficult if not impossible to complete without a thorough understanding of the text.

Finally, the book is designed for use either in or out of class—as a core reading text, ancillary text, or simply for pleasure reading. Its in-class use can take a number of different forms: teacher-student, student-student (pairs or small groups), student alone, or student-tutor.

C.G.D.

THE GIFT OF THE MAGI

Before You Read the Story . . .

1. *A Life*

Read the paragraph about O. Henry on page 3. To you, what is the most interesting thing about his life?

2. *The Pictures*

This story is "The Gift of the Magi." (MAY-jai) The word "Magi" means "wise men." The three kings on page 7 are the Magi. Each king is carrying a gift. What do you think these gifts are?

Look at the pictures on page 5 and page 8. The same woman is in both pictures. Look at her face, her hair, and her clothes. What is the same? What is different?

On page 8, the man is holding something in his hands. What is it?

3. *Thinking About It . . .*

"The Gift of the Magi" happens at Christmas (December 25). In many countries, people give gifts at this time of year. At what other times of the year do people give gifts? When do you give gifts? Why do you give gifts?

4. *Scanning*

Read the questions below. The answer to each question can be found in the paragraph about O. Henry on page 3. Read the paragraph quickly, looking for the information that will answer each question. You do not need to understand everything in the paragraph. But you must read carefully enough to find the answer to each question. This kind of reading to find information is called *scanning*. Try to answer each question in 30 seconds or less.

a. In what town was O. Henry born?
b. How old was he when he left school?
c. Why did he go to prison?
d. What is O. Henry famous for?
e. What is *The Four Million*?
f. How old was O. Henry when he died?

2

THE GIFT OF THE MAGI

adapted from the story by
O. HENRY

O. Henry's real name was William Sydney Porter. He was born in Greensboro, North Carolina, in 1862. He left school at the age of fifteen and worked in many different places. He also spent three years in prison because he took money from a bank. He started to write stories while he was in prison. O. Henry is famous for his stories with surprise endings. "The Gift of the Magi" is his most famous story. It is from the book *The Four Million*, stories about the everyday people of New York City. O. Henry died in 1910.

Della counted her money three times. She had only one dollar and eighty-seven cents. That was all. And tomorrow would be Christmas. What Christmas gift could she buy with only one dollar and eighty-seven cents? Della lay down on the old bed and cried and cried.

2 Let's leave Della alone for a while and look at her home. The chairs and tables were old and poor. Outside there was a mailbox without mail, and a door without a doorbell. The name on the door said MR. JAMES DILLINGHAM YOUNG—Della's dear husband Jim.

3 Della knew that Jim would be home soon. She dried her eyes and stood up. She looked in the mirror. She began to comb her hair for Jim. She felt very sad. She wanted to buy Jim a Christmas gift—something good. But what could she do with one dollar and eighty-seven cents? She combed her hair in the mirror and thought. Suddenly she had an idea.

4 Now, Jim and Della had only two treasures. One was Jim's gold watch. The other was Della's hair. It was long and brown, and fell down her back. Della looked in the mirror a little longer. Her eyes were sad, but then she smiled. She put on her old brown coat and her hat. She ran out of the house and down the street. She stopped in front of a door which said, MME. SOPHRONIE. HAIR OF ALL KINDS. Madame Sophronie was fat and seemed too white. The store was dark.

5 "Will you buy my hair?" Della asked.

6 "I buy hair," said Madame. "Take off your hat. Let's see your hair."

7 Della took off her hat. Her hair fell down like water. Mme. Sophronie lifted Della's hair with a heavy hand. "Twenty dollars," she said.

8 "Give me the money now!" said Della.

9 Ah! the next two hours flew past like summer wind. Della shopped in many stores for the right gift for Jim. Then she found it—a chain for his gold watch. It was a good chain, strong and expensive. Della knew the chain would make Jim happy. Jim had a cheap chain for his watch, but this chain was much better. It would look good with the gold watch. The chain cost twenty-one dollars. Della paid for the chain, and ran home with eighty-seven cents.

10 At seven o'clock Della made coffee and started to cook dinner. It was almost dinner time. Jim would be home soon. He was never late. Della heard Jim outside. She looked in the mirror again. "Oh! I hope Jim doesn't kill me!" Della smiled, but her eyes were wet. "But what could I do with only one dollar and eighty-seven cents?"

11 The door opened, and Jim came in and shut it. His face was thin and quiet. His coat was old, and he had no hat. He was only twenty-two. Jim stood still and looked at Della. He didn't speak. His eyes were strange. Della suddenly felt afraid. She did not understand him. She began to talk very fast. "Oh, Jim, dear, why do you look so strange? Don't look at me like that. I cut my hair and sold it. I wanted to buy you a Christmas gift. It will grow again—don't be angry. My hair grows very fast. Say 'Merry Christmas,' dear, and let's be happy. You don't know what I've got for you—it's beautiful."

12 "You cut your hair?" Jim spoke slowly.

13 "I cut it and sold it," Della answered. "Don't you like me now? I'm still me, aren't I?"

14 "You say that your hair is gone?" Jim asked again.

15 "Don't look for it, it's gone," Della said. "Be good to me, because it's Christmas. Shall we have dinner now, Jim?"

16 Jim seemed to wake up. He smiled. He took Della in his arms.

17 Let us leave them together for a while. They are happy, rich or poor. Do you know about the Magi? The Magi were wise men who brought Christmas gifts to the baby Jesus. But they could not give gifts like Jim's and

Della's. Perhaps you don't understand me now. But you will understand soon.

18 Jim took a small box out of his pocket. "I love your short hair, Della," he said. "I'm sorry I seemed strange. But if you open the box you will understand." Della opened the box. First she smiled, then suddenly she began to cry. In the box were two beautiful combs. Combs like those were made to hold up long hair. Della could see that the combs came from an expensive store. She never thought she

would have anything as beautiful! "Oh, Jim, they are beautiful! And my hair grows fast, you know. But wait! You must see your gift." Della gave Jim the chain. The chain was bright, like her eyes. "Isn't it a good one, Jim? I looked for it everywhere. You'll have to look at the time one hundred times daily, now. Give me your watch. I want to see them together."

19 Jim lay back on the bed. He put his hands under his head, and smiled. "Della," he said, "let's put the gifts

away. They are too good for us right now. I sold the watch to buy your combs. Come on, let's have dinner."

20 The Magi, as we said, were wise men—very wise men. They brought gifts to the baby Jesus. The Magi were wise, so their gifts were wise gifts. Perhaps Jim and Della do not seem wise. They lost the two great treasures of their house. But I want to tell you that they *were* wise. People like Jim and Della are always wiser than others. Everywhere they are wiser. They are the magi.

THE GIFT OF THE MAGI
EXERCISES

A. Understanding the Main Ideas

Answer the following questions with complete sentences.

1. Why did Della want to buy a gift for Jim?

2. Were Della and Jim rich? How do you know?

3. What were Jim's and Della's greatest treasures?

4. How did Della get enough money for Jim's gift?

5. How did Jim get enough money for Della's gift?

6. Who were the Magi, and what did they do?

7. Why does the writer think Della and Jim were wise?

B. Close Reading

If the sentence is true, write "T" next to it. If it is not true, write "F" for false. If the sentence is false, change one word and make it true.

1. ____ Della and Jim had a door without a doorbell.

2. ____ Della was very happy before Christmas.

3. ____ Madame Sophronie gave Della two dollars for her hair.

4. ____ Jim had an expensive chain for his watch.

5. ____ Jim was young, but his coat was old.

6. ____ Della laughed when Jim gave her the combs.

7. ____ Jim didn't show Della his watch.

C. Discussion

1. The writer, O. Henry, tells us that the Magi were wise. He also says that Jim and Della were wise. Why does he say this? Were they all wise in the same way? Do you agree with O. Henry?

2. A gift is one way of showing love. Do you think it is a very important way? Why or why not?

3. Do you give gifts to everyone you love? Do you ever give gifts to people you don't love? If so, why? If not, why not?

D. Vocabulary Practice

For each space in the sentences below, choose the best word from the following list:

merry	watch	wise	
mirror	gift	count	treasures

1. Della needed to _____ her money many times.

2. People say "_____ Christmas!" on December 25.

3. When Della looked in the _____, she saw her long hair.

4. Della's _____ to Jim was a chain for his watch.

5. Della's hair and Jim's watch were their two great _____.

6. At the beginning of the story, Jim has a cheap chain for his _____. At the end, he has no chain.

7. Jim's and Della's door had no _____.

8. Were Jim and Della _____ to give the gift of love?

E. Word Forms: Nouns and Adjectives

Put the correct form of the word on the left in the blank spaces on the right.

1. (sad / sadness) Della's _____ came from not having enough money to buy Jim a present. But she was not _____ to lose the great treasure of her hair. Why?

2. (wise / wisdom) People say that great _____ comes with great age. But I know children who are very _____, and old people who are not.

3. (happy / happiness) When she was _____, all the people around her were merry. Her _____ was like sun after a long rain.

4. (heavy / heaviness) The _____ of Della's hair surprised Madame Sophronie. "With hair this _____," she thought, "I will make a lot of money."

5. (expensive / expense) Cars are an _____ that John doesn't like to have. So he always buys old, cheap cars. But it is _____ to keep an old car on the road. So in the end he spends a lot of money on cars that he doesn't like.

F. Language Activity: Interview

What is your greatest treasure?
When did you get it?
How did you get it?

Why is it such a treasure to you?
Would you ever sell it?
Would you ever give it away?

Write down your answers to these questions. Then, ask two other people the same questions. Tell them about your own treasure, to help them understand what you want to learn. Write down their answers. Then tell your classmates what you learned from the people you talked with.

G. Writing: Madame Sophronie Speaks

In this exercise, you are Madame Sophronie. Answer each question below. Use complete sentences. When there are two questions together, join your answers using the words in parentheses.

Example:

What is your name? Do you have a store in the city, or in the country? (and)

My name is Madame Sophronie, and I have a store in the city.

1. Do you buy hair, or do you buy gold chains? Do you sell hair, too, or don't you? (and)
2. One day, did a young woman come into your store, or was it her husband?
3. Did she want to sell her hair, or buy it? Did you tell her to take her hat off, or to put it on? (and)
4. Was her hair beautiful, or ugly? Did you tell her that, or not? (but)
5. How much did you tell her you would pay?
6. Did she need the money, or didn't she? Did she take it, or not? (so)
7 Did you take her money, or did you take her hair? Did you want to buy it later, or sell it later? (because)

After you have answered the questions above, put your seven answers together into one paragraph. Then add another paragraph, about this:

Then a rich woman came into your store. She wanted to buy some hair. What did she say to you? What did you say to her? Did you show her the young woman's beautiful hair? Did she like it? How much did she pay for it?

LOVE OF LIFE

Before You Read the Story...

1. *A Life*

Read the paragraph about Jack London, the writer, on page 15. Why do you think he wrote adventure stories?

2. *The Pictures*

Look closely at the pictures on pages 17, 19, 21, and 22. Without reading the story, try to answer the questions below. If possible, do this exercise with a classmate, and report your answers to the class.

In the first picture, is one man walking away from the other, or toward him? Why is one man on the ground? Describe the man's clothes. What is he carrying? Where are the two men? Describe the land.

In the picture on page 19, the bones of an animal are on the ground. Why do you think the man is reaching for the bones?

In the picture on page 22, do you think the animal is friendly? Is the man in the picture sleeping, or dead?

In the picture on page 21, what does the man see in the distance? What does his face tell you?

3. *Thinking About It...*

Tell your own story about the man in the four pictures. Use all four pictures in your story.

4. *Skimming*

Sometimes we want to have a general idea about a piece of writing before we read it carefully. This exercise will show you one way of doing that.

Read the first two sentences of each paragraph in "Love of Life." Take one minute (60 seconds) to do this. This kind of fast reading for the general idea is called *skimming*. Next, try to answer the following questions. Do not look back at the story to answer them.

a. How many men are in the story at the beginning?

b. Does the man hurt his foot or his hand?

c. Is the man hungry, or thirsty? Warm, or cold? Sick, or well?

d. Who finally finds the man? Is he alive, or is he dead?

14

LOVE
OF
LIFE

adapted from the story by
JACK LONDON

Jack London was born of a poor family in San Francisco, in 1876. He left school at fourteen, and became a sailor, a hunter, and an explorer. His first long trip was to Japan. When he was eighteen he returned to high school for one year. Then he went to the University of California at Berkeley. But again he left after one year and began to write seriously. In 1897 he went to the Klondike in Canada. Many men went there to find gold. London found adventures that he put into his most famous stories and novels. London continued to travel until a few years before his death in 1916.

Two men walked slowly through the low water of a river. They were alone in the cold, empty land. All they could see were stones and earth. It was fall, and the river ran cold over their feet. They carried blankets on their backs. They had guns, but no bullets; matches, but no food.

2 "I wish we had just two of those bullets we hid in the camp," said the first of the men. His voice was tired. The other man did not answer.

3 Suddenly the first man fell over a stone. He hurt his foot badly, and he cried out. He lay still for a moment, and then called: "Hey, Bill, I've hurt my foot." Bill didn't stop or look back. He walked out of the river and over the hill. The other man watched him. His eyes seemed like the eyes of a sick animal. He stood up. "Bill!" he cried again. But there was no answer. Bill kept walking.

4 "Bill!"

5 The man was alone in the empty land. His hands were cold, and he dropped his gun. He fought with his fear, and took his gun out of the water. He followed slowly after Bill. He tried to walk lightly on his bad foot.

6 He was alone, but he was not lost. He knew the way to their camp. There he would find food, bullets, and blankets. He must find them soon. Bill would wait for him there. Together they would go south to the Hudson Bay Company. They would find food there, and a warm fire. Home. The man had to believe that Bill would wait for him at the camp. If not, he would die. He thought about the food in the camp. And the food at the Hudson Bay Company. And the food he ate two days ago. He thought about food and he walked. After a while the man found some small berries to eat. The berries had no taste, and did not fill him. But he knew he must eat them.

7 In the evening he hit his foot on a stone and fell down. He could not get up again. He lay still for a long

time. Later, he felt a little better and got up. He made a fire. He could cook only hot water, but he felt warmer. He dried his shoes by the fire. They had many holes. His feet had blood on them. His foot hurt badly. He put his foot in a piece of his blanket. Then he slept like a dead man.

8 He woke up because he heard an animal near him. He thought of meat and took his gun. But he had no bullets. The animal ran away. The man stood up and cried out. His foot was much worse this morning. He took out a small bag that was in his blanket. It was heavy—fifteen pounds. He didn't know if he could carry it. But he couldn't leave it behind. He had to take it with him. He had to be strong enough. He put it into his blanket again.

9 That day his hunger grew worse, worse than the hurt in his foot. Many times he wanted to lie down, but hunger made him go on. He saw a few birds. Once he tried to catch one, but it flew away. He felt tired and sick. He forgot to follow the way to the camp. In the afternoon he found some green plants. He ate them fast, like a horse. He saw a small fish in a river. He tried to catch it with his cup. But the fish swam away into a hole. The man cried like a baby, first quietly, then loudly. He cried alone in that empty world.

10 That night he made a fire again, and drank hot water. His blanket was wet, and his foot hurt. He could think only of his hunger. He woke up cold and sick. The earth and sky were gray. He got up and walked, he didn't know where. But the small bag was with him. The sun came out again, and he saw that he was lost. Was he too far north? He turned toward the east. His hunger was not so great, but he knew he was sick. He stopped often. He heard wolves, and knew that deer were near him. He believed he had one more bullet in his gun. It was still empty. The small bag became too heavy. The man opened the bag. It was full of small pieces of gold. He put half the gold in a piece of his blanket and left it on a rock. But he kept his gun. There were bullets in that camp.

11 Days passed, days of rain and cold. One day he came to the bones of a deer. There was no meat on the

bones. The man knew wolves must be near. He broke the bones and ate like an animal. Would he, too, be only bones tomorrow? And why not? This was life, he thought. Only life hurt. There was no hurt in death. To die was to sleep. Then why was he not ready to die? He could not see or feel. The hunger, too, was gone. But he walked and walked.

12 One morning he woke up beside a river. Sunlight was warm on his face. A sunny day, he thought. Perhaps he could find his way to the camp. His eyes followed the river. He could see far. The river emptied into the sea. He saw a ship on that silver sea. He shut his eyes. He knew there could be no ship, no seas, in this land. He heard a noise behind him, and turned back. A wolf, old and sick, was following him. I know *this* is real, he thought. He turned again, but the sea and the ship were still there. He didn't understand it. He tried to remember. What did the men at the Hudson Bay Company say about this land? Was he walking north, away from the camp, toward the sea? The man moved slowly toward the ship. He knew the sick wolf was following him. In the afternoon, he found more bones left by wolves. The bones of a man! Beside the bones was a small bag of gold, like his own. Ha! Bill carried his gold to the end, he thought. He would take Bill's gold to the ship. He would have the last laugh on Bill. His laughing sounded like the low cry of an animal. The wolf cried back to the man, and the man stopped laughing. How could he laugh about Bill's bones? He could not take Bill's gold. He left the gold near the bones.

13 The man was very sick, now. He walked more and more slowly. His blanket was gone. He lost his gold, then his gun, then his knife. Only the wolf stayed with him hour after hour. At last the man could go no further. He fell down. The wolf came close to him. It weakly bit his hand. The man hit the wolf and it went away. But it did not go far. It waited. The man waited. After many hours the wolf came back again. It was going to kill the man. But the man was ready. He held the wolf's mouth closed, and he got on top of the sick wolf. He held the animal still. Then he bit it with his last strength. He tasted the wolf's blood in his mouth.

Only love of life gave him enough strength. He held the wolf with his teeth and killed it. Later he fell on his back and slept.

14 The men on the ship saw a strange thing on the land. It did not walk. It was lying on the ground, and it moved slowly toward them—perhaps twenty feet an hour. The men went close to look at it. They could not believe it was a man.

15 Three weeks later the man felt better. He could tell them his story. But there was one strange thing. He could not believe there was enough food on the ship. The men told him there was a lot of food. But he only looked at them with fear. And slowly he began to grow fat. The men thought this was strange. They gave him less food, but still he grew larger and larger—each day he was fatter. Then one day they saw him put a lot of bread under his shirt. They looked in his bed, too, and saw bread under his blanket. The men understood, and left him alone.

LOVE OF LIFE
EXERCISES

A. Understanding the Main Ideas

Read the sentence (or sentences) from the story. Then answer the question about the sentence.

1. "Bill didn't stop or look back." (paragraph 3)
   Who was Bill? Why do you think he didn't stop or look back?
2. "He took out a small bag that was in his blanket." (paragraph 8)
   What was in this bag? Did the man keep it, or leave it? Why?
3. ". . . the fish swam away into a hole. The man cried like a baby, first quietly, then loudly." (paragraph 9)
   Why did the man cry about losing the fish?
4. "He saw a ship on that silver sea." (paragraph 12)
   Did he think the ship was real? Why, or why not? Was the ship real?
5. "But he only looked at them with fear." (paragraph 15)
   Was the man safe on the ship? Did he have enough food to eat? Why was he still afraid?
6. "Love of Life."
   This is the title of the story. What does it mean? How does the man show that he loves life?

B. Close Reading

Choose the right word to complete each sentence.

1. The man could not walk quickly because he hurt his
   a. back
   b. foot
   c. hand
2. The man wanted to find the camp because of the
   _____ there.

   a. gold

   b. water

   c. bullets and food

3. One day the man found and ate the bones of a

   a. deer

   b. fish

   c. wolf

4. The wolf could not kill the man because the wolf, too, was

   a. hungry

   b. thirsty

   c. weak

5. The man found Bill's

   a. hat and gloves

   b. bones and gold

   c. blanket and bullets

6. The men on the ship did not take the man's hidden

   a. meat

   b. blanket

   c. bread

7. The men on the ship understood why the man was always

   a. hungry

   b. angry

   c. laughing

C. Discussion

1. When the man finds Bill's gold, why does he laugh? Why does he stop laughing? Why does he leave the gold where he found it?

2. Do you know land that is "empty" — that has almost no people in it? Where is it? Describe it. Have you ever walked there? Did you like it? Would you like to live there?

D Vocabulary Practice (Antonyms)

Find a word in column A that means the OPPOSITE of a word in column B. (good-bad, big-little, etc.) Write the number of the word from column A next to the right word in column B.

A	**B**
1. weak	_____ life
2. lost	_____ open
3. laugh	_____ full
4. death	_____ thin
5. follow	_____ cry
6. empty	_____ loudly
7. quietly	_____ strong
8. closed	_____ found
9. fat	_____ lead

E. Word Forms: Adjectives and Adverbs

Put the correct form of the words on the left in the blank spaces in the sentences on the right.

1. (slow/slowly) The man walked very _____. But the sick wolf was _____, too.

2. (sudden/suddenly) Bill had a _____ thought: "If I die _____, what will happen to my gold?"

3. (tired/tiredly) The man was hungry and _____. When he walked _____ onto the ship, the men there watched him without speaking.

4. (weak/weakly) The wolf was _____, like the man, and could only bite him _____.

5. (hungry/hungrily) The man ate the bones _____ like an animal. He was so _____ he could think only of food.

F. Language Activity: Riddles

For each sentence below, choose a word from the list which fits the sentence.

Example:

<u>bag</u>   He carried his gold in it.

bag	blanket	hunger	camp
strength	bullet	wolf	bones

1. _____ Without this little thing, he could not use the big thing he carried with him.

2. _____ He made pieces of it—one for his hurt foot, one for his gold.

3. _____ He killed it the way it wanted to kill him.

4. _____ He ate them, and he thought he might die and become them.

5. _____ He didn't want it, but every day he had more of it.

6. _____ He needed it, but every day he had less of it.

7. _____ It had everything he wanted, but he couldn't find it.

G. Writing A Letter Home

You are one of the men on the ship in "Love of Life." Write a letter to your family at home. Tell them the strange story of the man you found.

Where did you find him?
What did he look like on that first day?

Did you think he would live, or not?
On the ship, little by little, what happened to him?
And what was strange about him?
Why did he look at the other men with fear?
One day, what did you see him do?
What did you find in his bed?
Why, then, did you leave him alone?
What do you think will happen to him?

THE STORY OF AN HOUR

Before You Read the Story . . .

1. *A Life*

Read the paragraph about Kate Chopin on page 29. Look up the word "shocking" in the dictionary. Why were Chopin's stories almost forgotten until recently?

2. *The Pictures*

The same woman is in the pictures on page 31 and page 34. What is she feeling in the first picture? How has she changed in the second?

What do you think is happening in the picture on page 32?

3. *Thinking About It . . .*

"The Story of an Hour" is about a marriage more than a hundred years ago. Have marriages changed in the past 100 years? In what ways? In what ways have they not changed?

4. *Scanning Two Different Sources of Information*

For this exercise, use the paragraphs about Jack London, on page 15, and Kate Chopin, on page 29.

After you read each question below, quickly scan the paragraphs about the two writers. Find the answer to the question. You do not need to find any other information as you read. Try to do the exercise in less than three minutes.

a. Which writer was born earlier?
b. Which writer was born to a rich family?
c. Which writer started writing when young?
d. Which writer traveled a lot?
e. Which writer died later?
f. Which writer died older?

THE STORY OF AN HOUR

adapted from the story by
KATE CHOPIN

Kate Chopin was born in 1851 in St. Louis, Missouri. Her family was rich. She married, and had six children. She lived a family life like other rich ladies in those days. But she was well educated and liked to read and write. After her husband died, in 1883, she began to write stories. She wrote a book called *The Awakening*. This book, and many of her stories, shocked her readers at that time. She wrote about the freedom of women at a time when most women lived only for the family. Because the stories were so shocking, people did not read them for many years after her death in 1904. Now Kate Chopin's writing has been discovered again. People are interested in her life and work.

They knew that Louise Mallard had a weak heart. So they broke the bad news softly. Her husband, Brently, was dead.

2 "There was a train accident, Louise," said her sister Josephine, quietly.

3 Her husband's friend, Richards, stood with Josephine. Richards brought the news, but Josephine told the story. She spoke in broken sentences.

4 "Richards . . . was at the newspaper office. News of the accident came. Louise . . . Louise, Brently's name was on the list. Brently . . . was killed, Louise."

5 Louise did not hear the story coldly, like some women would. She could not close her mind or her heart to the news. Like a sudden storm, her tears broke out. She cried loudly in her sister's arms. Then, just as suddenly, the tears stopped. She went to her room alone. She wanted no one with her.

6 In front of the window stood an empty chair. She sat down and looked out the window. She was very tired after her tears. Her body felt cold, her mind and heart were empty.

7 Outside her window she could see the trees. The air smelled like spring rain. She could hear someone singing far away. Birds sang near the house. Blue sky showed between the clouds. She rested.

8 She sat quietly, but a few weak tears still fell. She had a young, strong face. But now her eyes showed nothing. She looked out the window at the blue sky. She was not thinking, or seeing. She was waiting.

9 There was something coming to her. She was waiting for it with fear. What was it? She did not know; she could not give it a name. But she felt it coming out from the sky. It reached her through the sound, the smell, the color of

the air.

10 Slowly she became excited. Her breath came fast, her heart beat faster. She began to see this thing. It wanted to find her and take her. She tried to fight against it. But she could not. Her mind was as weak as her two small white hands. Then she stopped fighting against it. A little word broke from her lips.

11 "Free," she said. "Free, free, free!" The emptiness and fear left her. Her eyes showed her excitement. Her heart beat fast, and the blood warmed her body. A sudden feeling of joy excited her.

12 She did not stop to ask if her joy was wrong. She saw her freedom clearly. She could not stop to think of smaller things.

13 She knew the tears would come again when she saw her husband's body. The kind hands, now dead and still. The loving face, now still and gray. But she looked into the future. She saw many long years to come that would belong to her alone. And now she opened her arms wide to those years in welcome.

14 There would be no one else to live for during those years. She would live for herself alone. There would be no strong mind above hers. Men and women always believe they can tell others what to do and how to think. Suddenly Louise understood that this was wrong. She could break away and be free of it.

15 And yet, she loved him—sometimes. Often she did not. What did love mean now? Now she understood that freedom is stronger than love.

16 "Free! Body and mind free!" she said again.

17 Her sister Josephine was waiting outside the door.

18. "Please open the door," Josephine cried. "You will make yourself sick. What are you doing in there, Louise? Please, please, let me in!"

19 "Go away. I am not sick." No, she was drinking in life through that open window.

20 She thought joyfully of all those days before her. Spring days, summer days. All kinds of days that would be her own. She began to hope life would be long. And just

yesterday, life seemed so long!

21 After a while she got up and opened the door. Her eyes were bright, her cheeks were red. She didn't know how strong and well she looked—so full of joy. They went downstairs, where Richards was waiting.

22 A man was opening the door. It was Brently Mallard. He was dirty, and tired. He carried a suitcase and an umbrella. He was not killed in the train accident. He didn't even know there was an accident. He was surprised at Josephine's sudden cry. He didn't understand why Richards moved suddenly between them, to hide Louise from her husband.

23 But Richards was too late.

24 When the doctors came, they said it was her weak heart. They said she died of joy—of joy that kills.

THE STORY OF AN HOUR
EXERCISES

A. Understanding the Main Ideas

Answer the following questions with complete sentences.

1. What news did Richards tell Louise?

2. How did Louise act when she first heard the news?

3. What was Louise waiting for?

4. Why did she feel joy?

5. When Brently came home, why was everyone surprised?

6. "They said she died of joy." Did she? If not, why not?

B. Close Reading

Choose one of the two words in parentheses to make a correct sentence.

1. Louise Mallard had a (sad / weak) heart.

2. They said (Brently /Richards) was killed in a train accident.

3. Sitting near the window, Louise was waiting to understand (her feelings / her husband).

4. At first, Louise (welcomed / fought against) the strange feeling that came to her.

5. She understood that freedom is (stronger / weaker) than love.

6. She knew she could live her life (with Josephine / alone).

7. After her husband died, she hoped that her life would be (short / long).

8. Richards tried to hide Louise from (Brently / Josephine).

C. Discussion

1. What does Louise discover about herself in this story?

2. Louise thinks, "Men and women always believe they can tell others what to do and how to think." Why do you think she believes this? Do you agree with her? How do people try to tell other people what to do and how to think?

3. What does Louise mean when she says, "Free, free!"? Free from what? Today, are women more free than men, or less free? Why?

D. Vocabulary Practice

Find words or phrases in the story that mean almost the same as the underlined words or phrases.

1. Chopin's stories made her readers feel *surprised and angry*. (See paragraph about Kate Chopin on page 29.)

2. She spoke in *short phrases*. (See paragraph 3.)

3. She couldn't *hide her thoughts and feelings*. (See paragraph 5.)

4. She saw many long years ahead that would *be her own.* (See paragraph 13.)

5. She was *enjoying* life. (See paragraph 19.)

6. She thought *happily* of all those days *in front of* her. (See paragraph 20.)

E. Word Forms

Put the correct form of the word on the left in the blank spaces in the sentences on the right.

1. (broke / broken / brokenly) Josephine spoke _____ to Louise about Brently's death. She cried, too, when Louise's tears _____ out. Josephine thought Louise's heart was _____.

2. (understand / understanding / understandingly) "Please open the door. You will make yourself sick!" Josephine said to her sister _____. But when Louise came out, Josephine couldn't _____ why she looked so strong and well. Are you more _____ of Louise?

3. (joy / joyful / joyfully) The _____ Louise felt surprised her. She spoke _____to her sister, and lifted _____ eyes to Richards.

F. Language Activity: Class Project on the Role of Women

In pairs or groups, find examples of the role of women today, as shown in magazines, newspapers, and television. What do the "want-ads" (job advertisements) tell you? What do advertisements for clothes tell you? What do television programs about families tell you? Report to the class on what you find

G. Writing: Josephine's Diary

You are Louise's sister, Josephine. Every day, you write in a diary. You write what happened every day, and how you feel about it. Now, you will write about what happened on the day Louise died.

Dear Diary,

Our friend Richards brought the saddest news today:_____

_____

_____

_____.

After Louise heard about it, she_____

_____.

Then she_____

_____

I was so worried about her! I called and called outside her door, and_____

_____.

I couldn't understand why she looked

_____

_____

_____

_____.

We went downstairs to see Richards. Suddenly, the door opened and Brently_____

_____.

We couldn't understand what had happened. I_____, Richards_____, and Louise_____

_____. Later,

the doctors_____

_____.

I don't know what Brently thought. But I think

_____

_____

_____

_____

_____.

THE TELL-TALE HEART

Before You Read the Story . . .

1. *A Life*

   Read the paragraph about Edgar Allan Poe on page 41. Was Poe's life an unhappy one?

   What does the word "detective" mean? the word "horror?"

   A "tale" is a story. What does the title mean: "The Tell-Tale Heart?"

2. *The Pictures*

   Look at the picture on page 43. What word can you use to describe the man's face? There is a light shining on the man's face. Where is the light coming from? What is the other man holding?

   There are three policemen in the picture on page 47. What words can you use to describe their faces? Who are they looking at?

3. *Thinking About It . . .*

   What do you think small children are most afraid of? The dark? Large, strange animals? Sudden, loud noises? Things they do not understand? Are older people afraid of the same things? Do most people talk easily about their fears?

4. *Skimming*

   Take 60 seconds to skim "The Tell-Tale Heart." (Quickly read the first two or three sentences of each paragraph.)

   Do not look back at the story. Look at the three groups of words below. Which group fits the general idea you got from skimming the story—group **A**, **B**, or **C** ?

A	B	C
machine	flower	house
tomorrow	today	yesterday
study	enjoy	kill
new	young	old
thinking	happy	mad
noon	morning	midnight

THE TELL-TALE HEART

adapted from the story by
EDGAR ALLAN POE

Edgar Allan Poe was born in 1809 in Boston, Massachusetts. He is one of America's most important and famous writers. Poe's parents died when he was a child. He was raised by people named Allan. They were rich, but Poe was poor all his life. He lost several jobs because he drank too much. People remember Poe for his poetry, for his detective stories, and for his horror stories like "The Tell-Tale Heart." Poe died unhappily at the age of forty, in 1849.

True! Nervous. I was nervous then and I am nervous now. But why do you say that I am mad? Nothing was wrong with me. I could see very well. I could smell. I could touch. Yes, my friend, and I could hear. I could hear all things in the skies and in the earth. So why do you think that I am mad? Listen. I will tell you the story. I will speak quietly. You will understand everything. Listen!

2 Why did I want to kill the old man? Ah, this is very difficult. I liked the old man. No, I loved him! He never hurt me. He was always kind to me. I didn't need his gold; no, I didn't want that. I think it was his eye—yes, it was this! He had the eye of a bird. It was a cold, light-blue eye—a horrible eye. I feared it. Sometimes I tried to look at it. But then my blood ran cold. So, after many weeks, I knew I must kill the old man. His horrible eye must not live. Do you understand?

3 Now here is the point. You think that I am mad. Madmen know nothing. But I? I was careful. Oh, I was very careful. *Careful,* you see? For one long week, I was very kind to the old man. But every night, at midnight, I opened his door slowly, carefully. I had a lantern with me. Inside the lantern there was a light. But the sides of the lantern hid the light. So, first I put the dark lantern through the open door. Then I put my head in the room. I put it in slowly, very slowly. I didn't want to wake the old man. Ha! Would a madman be careful, like that? There was no noise, not a sound. I opened the lantern carefully—very carefully—and slowly. A thin light fell upon the old man's eye. I held it there. I held it there for a long time. And I did this every night for seven nights. But always the eye was closed. And so I could not do my work. I was not angry at the old man, you see. I was angry only at his horrible eye. And every morning I went into his room happily. I was friendly with him. I asked about his night. Did he sleep well? Was he all

right? And so, you see, he knew nothing.

4 On the eighth night, I was more careful than before. I know you don't believe me, but it is true. The clock's hand moved more quickly than my hand. I opened the door slowly. I put the lantern in the room. The old man moved suddenly in his bed. But I did not go back. The room was very dark. I knew he could not see me. I put my head in the room. I began to open the lantern, but my hand hit the side. It made a loud noise.

5 The old man sat up quickly in bed. "Who's there?" he cried.

6 I stood still and said nothing. For one long hour I did not move a finger. And he did not lie down. He sat in his bed. He listened. I knew his fear!

7 And soon I heard another sound. It came from the old man. It was a horrible sound, the sound of fear! I knew that sound well. Often, at night, I too have made that sound. What was in the room? The old man didn't know. He didn't want to know. But he knew that he was in danger. Ah, yes, he knew!

8 And now I began to open the lantern. I opened it just a little. A small thin light fell upon the horrible blue eye.

9 It was open—wide, wide open. I could not see the old man's face or body. But I saw the eye very well. The horrible bird's eye. My blood ran cold. At the same time, anger began to grow inside me.

10 And now, haven't I told you that I could hear everything? Now a low, quick sound came to my ears. It was like the sound of a small wooden clock. I knew *that* sound well, too. It was the beating of the old man's heart!

11 My fear and anger grew. But I did not move. I stood still. I held the light on the old man's eye. And the beating of the heart grew. It became quicker and quicker, and louder and louder every second! I knew that his fear was very great. *Louder*, do you hear? I have told you that I am nervous. And this is true. My fear was like the old man's. But I did not move. I held the light on his eye. But the beating grew louder, LOUDER! And now a new fear came to

me. Someone in the next house would hear! The old man must die! This was his hour! With a loud cry, I opened the lantern wide. I ran into the room! The old man cried loudly once—once only. His fear, his fear killed him! In a second I pulled him from the bed. He lay still. I smiled a little. Everything was all right. For some minutes, I heard his heart beat softly. Then it stopped. I put my hand on his body. He was cold. He was like a stone. The old man was dead. His eye would never look upon me again!

12 And now I was very, very careful. I worked quickly but quietly. I used a good, new knife. I cut off the old man's arms and legs and head. Then I took three boards from the floor of the room. I put everything below the floor. Then I put the boards in their place again. I cleaned the floor. There was no blood. Nothing was wrong. I was *careful,* you see? Ha! Can you still think that I am mad?

13 I finished. It was four o'clock—still dark as midnight. Suddenly there was a beating on the door. Someone was there. But I went down with a happy heart. I had nothing to fear. Nothing.

14 Three policemen came into the house. They said that someone in the next house heard a cry. Was something wrong? Was everyone all right?

15 "Of course," I said. "Please come in." I was not nervous. I smiled at the men. I told them that the old man was in another town. I said he was with his sister. I showed them his money, his gold. Everything was there, in its place.

16 I brought chairs. I asked the men to sit. I sat, too. I sat on the boards over the dead man's body! I talked easily. The policemen smiled.

17 But after some minutes I became tired. Perhaps I was a little nervous. There was a low sound in my head, in my ears. I didn't like it. I talked more loudly, more angrily. Then suddenly I understood. The sound was not in my head or in my ears. It was there in the room!

18 Now I know that I became *very* nervous. *It was a low quick sound. It sounded like a small wooden clock!* My eyes opened wide. Could the policemen hear it? I talked in a louder voice. But the noise did not stop. It grew! I stood up

and talked angrily, dangerously. I walked across the floor and back again. Why wouldn't the men leave? There was a storm inside my head! And still the noise became louder— LOUDER—LOUDER! I beat my hands on the table. I said dangerous things in a loud voice. But still the men talked happily and smiled. Couldn't they hear? Was it possible? Oh, God! No, no! They heard! They knew! They laughed at my hopes, and smiled at my fears. I knew it then and I know it now. I couldn't keep still! Anything was better than their smiles and laughing! And now—again!—listen! louder! LOUDER! LOUDER!

19 "Stop!" I cried. "Enough! Enough! Pull up the boards! Below the floor! Here, here!—It is the beating of his horrible heart!"

THE TELL-TALE HEART
EXERCISES

A. Understanding the Main Ideas: Cause and Effect

Complete each sentence below by choosing **a**, **b**, or **c**. The first half of each sentence tells about something that happened in the story (*the effect*). The second half should tell why it happened (*the cause*).

1. The young man wanted to kill the old man because
    a. he loved the old man.
    b. he didn't like the old man's eye.
    c. he wanted the old man's gold.

2. He opened the old man's door carefully because
    a. the old man was mad.
    b. he thought the old man was horrible.
    c. he didn't want to wake the old man.

3. Every morning the young man was friendly because
    a. he held a thin light over the old man's eye.

b. he didn't want the old man to think anything was wrong

c. he was angry at the old man.

4. The police came to the house because

   a. someone in the next house heard a cry.

   b. they knew the young man was mad.

   c. they wanted to sit, talk, and laugh.

5. The young man talked louder and louder to the police because

   a. they couldn't hear him.

   b. he thought they would hear the beating of the old man's heart.

   c. he was very angry at them.

6. The young man killed the old man and then told the police because

   a. they all laughed and smiled at him.

   b. the old man's heart beat louder and louder.

   c. the young man was mad.

B. Close Reading

Read the first half of a sentence in column A. Then draw a line from it to the second half in column B that best completes the meaning. The first one is done for you.

A	B
1. The madman thought	when he heard a low, quick sound
2. He wanted to kill the old man	after the young man ran into the room
3. The old man woke up	that he could hear all things in the earth and in the sky

4. The old man died	when the young man's hand hit the lantern
5. The young man told the police	because he was afraid of the beating of the heart below the floor
6. The young man became nervous	that the old man was in another town
7. He told the police about the killing	because he hated his cold blue eye

C. Discussion

1. The old man was dead. His body, in pieces, was below the floor. But the young man believed that he could hear the old man's heart beating. Why?
2. What do you think will happen to the man after the police take him away? Should he go to prison? To a doctor? Should he be killed?
3. Do you enjoy horror stories? Do you enjoy horror movies? Why, or why not?

D. Vocabulary Practice: Words for Unpleasant People and Things

Choose the word below that best completes the description of the person or thing in the sentences that follow:

mad   horrible   angry   fear   danger   nervous

1. The young man couldn't sit still. He talked quickly, loudly. His eyes moved all over the room. His hands

shook. He was very _____.

2. The eye was cold, light blue, the eye of a bird. His blood ran cold when he looked at it. He thought the eye was _____.

3. He killed the old man, cut him in pieces, and put the pieces below the floor. But he believed that the old man's heart was still beating. Surely he was

_____.

4. When the policemen came, he took them into the old man's room. He sat on the boards over the dead man's body. He tried to talk easily. But truly he was in

_____.

5. He said he loved the old man. The old man was kind to him. The old man never hurt him. It was only the old man's eye that made him so _____.

6. What really killed the old man? It wasn't a knife. It wasn't even the open lantern, or the young man's loud cry. It was his own _____.

E. Word Forms: Adjective or Adverb?

Put the correct form of the word on the left in the blank space in the sentence.

1. (horrible / horribly) The old man's eye seemed _____ to the young man.

2. (careful / carefully) He didn't want to make any noise, so he opened the lantern _____.

3. (dangerous / dangerously) The police thought the young man might be _____, so they were careful in the way they spoke to him.

4. (quick / quickly) The heart beat _____.

F. Language Activity: The Police

Choose one of the following activities. Prepare to speak about your topic to a classmate, a small group, or the entire class.

1. Find and read a newspaper or magazine article about police activity.
2. Talk about the role of the police in a t.v. program or movie you have seen recently.
3. Talk to a policeman or policewoman about his or her job.
4. In an encyclopedia, read about the history of the police.

G. Writing: A Police Report

You are one of the policemen in "The Tell-Tale Heart." You must write a report about the killing. In your report, you should answer some or all of the following questions:

What time was it when you went to the young man's house?
Why did you go there?
Did he meet you at the door?
How did he seem — friendly? Nervous? Angry?
Did he ask you to come in?
Did you ask about the old man?
What did he say about the old man?
Where did he take you?
Did he ask you to sit, or to stand?

Did he sit or stand?
How did he talk?
After some minutes of this, how did he seem?
How did he talk then?
Finally, what did he say?
What did you find below the boards?
What happened then?

A CUB-PILOT'S EDUCATION

Before You Read the Story . . .

1. *A Life*

Read the paragraph about Mark Twain on page 55. What are his most famous books about?

2. *The Pictures*

Look at the picture on page 57. It is a picture of a steamboat. In the 19th century, these boats traveled on the Mississippi River, the longest river in the United States. The steamboats were large. Can you tell why these boats were important?

In the picture on page 58, what is the boy doing? Where would he be doing this in the picture on page 62?

3. *Thinking About It . . .*

A pilot is someone who drives (or steers) a boat or plane. A cub-pilot is a young person who is learning to be a pilot. He watches the pilot at his job. Then he tries to do the job. Do you think this is a good way for a young person to learn?

4. *Scanning for Specific Information*

Sometimes we scan a piece of writing to find one or two pieces of information. We don't read everything. We don't even need to get a general idea about the piece of writing. We need only the information.

We do this by reading very quickly. Our eyes move across and down the page, looking for a single word or number. When we find it, we stop and read more carefully.

In this exercise, you will try to answer the questions below by scanning a page of the story "A Cub-Pilot's Education." The answer to each question can be found on the page given. In front of each question is an underlined word or phrase. Let your eyes move quickly across and down the page. When they find the underlined name or number, stop. Read more carefully, and find the answer to the question. Try to answer each question in 30 seconds or less.

a. page 56 <u>Keokuk</u> Did the steamboat come up-river or down river from Keokuk?

b. page 56 <u>New Orleans</u> How old was the boy when he ran away to New Orleans?

c. page 59 <u>Twelve-Mile</u> <u>Point</u> Was the boy interested in Twelve-Mile Point?

d. page 61 <u>Apple</u> <u>Bend</u> Did the boy know the shape of Apple Bend?

e. page 62 <u>Island</u> <u>66</u> Was the bend there easy, or difficult?

A CUB-PILOT'S EDUCATION

adapted from the story by
MARK TWAIN

Mark Twain's real name was Samuel Langhorne Clemens. He was born in 1835 in Missouri. As a boy, he lived in a small town on the Mississippi River. His most famous books, *The Adventures of Tom Sawyer* and *The Adventures of Huckleberry Finn*, are about boyhood and the Mississippi. Because of these books, Mark Twain became America's most famous and best-loved writer. He died in 1910 at the age of seventy-five. The following story is from his book *Life on the Mississippi*.

I

All the boys in my village wanted to be the same thing: a steamboat pilot. Our village lay on the great Mississippi River. Once a day, at noon, a steamboat came up from St. Louis. Later, at one o'clock, another came down from Keokuk. Before these hours, the day was full and bright with waiting. After them, the day was a dead and empty thing.

2 I can see that old time now. The white town sleeps in the morning sun. The streets are empty. Some animals walk near the buildings. The waters of the Mississippi are quiet and still. A man who has drunk too much lies peacefully near the river. Other men sit outside their stores in chairs. They look at the town and don't talk much.

3 Then a worker cries, "S-t-e-a-m-boat coming!" And everything changes! The man who has drunk too much gets up and runs. Suddenly the streets are full. Men, women, and children run to the steamboat landing. The animals make a hundred different noises. The town wakes up!

4 The steamboat that comes toward the town is long and pretty. Her big wheel turns and turns. Everybody looks at her and at the men who live on her. The pilot stands tallest, the center of everything, the king. Slowly the steamboat comes to the landing. Men take things off the boat and bring other things on. In ten minutes she is gone again. The town goes back to sleep. But the boys of the town remember the boat. They remember the pilot. And they don't forget.

5 I was fifteen then, and I ran away from home. I went to New Orleans. There I met a pilot named Mr. Bixby. I said I wanted to be his cub-pilot, or learner. He said no—but only once. I said yes a hundred times. So in the end I won. He said he would teach me the river. He didn't smile or

laugh, but I was the happiest boy in that city.

6 We left New Orleans at four o'clock one afternoon. Mr. Bixby was at the wheel. Here at the beginning of the river, there were a lot of steamboats. Most of them were at landings on the sides of the river. We went past them quickly, very close to them. Suddenly Mr. Bixby said, "Here. You steer her." And he gave me the wheel. My heart was in my mouth. I thought it was very dangerous, close to those other boats. I began to steer into the middle of the river. In the middle, there was enough water for everybody.

7 "What are you doing?" Mr. Bixby cried angrily. He pushed me away and took the wheel again. And again he steered us near the other boats. After a while, he became a little cooler. He told me that water runs fast in the middle of a river. At the sides, it runs slow. "So if you're going up-river, you have to steer near the sides. You can go in the middle only if you're going down-river." Well, that was good enough for me. I decided to be a down-river pilot only.

8 Sometimes Mr. Bixby showed me points of land. "This is Six-Mile Point," he said. The land pointed like a finger into the water. Another time, he said, "This is Nine-Mile Point." It looked like Six-Mile Point to me. Later, he said, "This is Twelve-Mile Point." Well, this wasn't very interesting news. All the points seemed the same.

9 After six hours of this, we had supper and went to bed. Even bed was more interesting than the "points." At midnight, someone put a light in my eyes. "Hey, let's go!"

10 Then he left. I couldn't understand this. I decided to go back to sleep. Soon the man came again with his light; now he was angry. "Wake up!" he called. I was angry, too, and said, "Don't put that light in my eyes! How can I sleep if you wake me up every minute?"

11 All the men in the room laughed at this. The man left again, but came back soon with Mr. Bixby. One minute later I was climbing the steps to the pilot-house. Some of my clothes were on me. The rest were in my hands. Mr. Bixby walked behind me, angry. Now, here was something interesting: Pilots worked in the middle of the night!

12 And that night was a bad one. There was a lot of

mist on the river. You could not see through it. Where were we going? I was frightened. But Mr. Bixby turned the wheel easily and happily. He told me we had to find a farm. Jones Farm. To myself I said, "Okay, Mr. Bixby. You can try all night. But you'll never find anything in this mist."

13 Suddenly Mr. Bixby turned to me and said, "What's the name of the first point above New Orleans?"

14 I answered very quickly. I said I didn't know.

15 "Don't *know?*"

16 The loudness of his voice surprised me. But I couldn't answer him.

17 "Well, then," he said, "What's the name of the next point?"

18 Again I didn't know.

19 "Now, look! After Twelve-Mile Point, where do you cross the river?"

20 "I-I-I don't know."

21 "You-you-you don't know? Well, what *do* you know?"

22 "I—nothing, it seems."

23 "Nothing? *Less* than nothing! You say you want to pilot a steamboat on the river? My boy, you couldn't pilot a cow down a street! Why do you think I told you the names of those points?"

24 "Well, to-to—be interesting, I thought."

25 "What?! To be *interesting?*" Now he was *very* angry. He walked across the pilot-house and back again. This cooled him down. "My boy," he said more softly, "You must get a little notebook. I will tell you many names of places on this river. You must write them all down. Then you must remember them. All of them. That is the only way to become a pilot."

26 My heart fell. I never remembered things easily in school. But also I didn't fully believe Mr. Bixby. No one, I thought, could know all of the Mississippi. No one could put that great river inside his head.

27 Then Mr. Bixby pulled a bell. A worker's voice came up from below.

28 "What's this, sir?"

29 "Jones Farm," Mr. Bixby said.

30 I could see nothing through the mist. And Mr. Bixby could see nothing. I knew that. So I didn't believe him. How could I? We were in the middle of nowhere! But soon the boat's nose softly hit the landing. Workers' voices came up to us. I still couldn't believe it, but this was Jones Farm!

II

31 And so, slowly, I began to put the Mississippi River inside my head. I filled a notebook—I filled two notebooks—with names from the river. Islands, towns, points, bends in the river. The names of all these things went into my notebooks. And slowly some of them began to go into my head. Then more of them. I began to feel better about myself. I was beginning to learn the river.

32 Then one day Mr. Bixby said to me, "What is the shape of Apple Bend?"

33 "The shape of Apple Bend?"

34 "Yes, of course."

35 "I know the *name* of Apple Bend. I know where it is. Don't tell me I have to know the shape of it, too!"

36 Mr. Bixby's mouth went off like a gun, bang! He shot all his bad words at me. Then, as always, he cooled. "My boy," he said, "You must learn the shape of this river and everything on it. If you don't know the shape, you can't steer at night. And of course the river has two shapes. One during the day, and one at night."

37 "Oh, no!"

38 "Oh, yes. Look: How can you walk through a room at home in the dark? Because you know the shape of it. You can't *see* it."

39 "You mean I must know this river like the rooms at home?"

40 "No. I mean you must know it *better* than the rooms at home."

41 "I want to die."

42 "My boy, I don't want you to be sad or angry. But there is more."

43 "All right. Tell me everything. Give it to me!"

44 "I'm sorry, but you must learn these things. There is

no other way. Now, a night with stars throws shadows. Dark shadows change the shape of the river. You think you are coming to a bend, but there *is* no bend. And this is different from a night with no stars. On a night with no stars, the river has a different shape. You think there are no bends, but there *are* bends. And of course, on a night with mist, the river has no shape. You think you are going to steer the boat onto the land. But then suddenly you see that it's water, not land. Well. Then you have your moonlight nights. Different kinds of moonlight change the shape of the river again. And there are different kinds of shadows, too. Different shadows bring different shapes to the river. You see—"

45 "Oh, stop!" I cried. "You mean I have to learn the thousand million different shapes of this river?"

46 "No, no! You only learn *the* shape of the river. The *one* shape. And you steer by that. Don't you understand? You steer by the river that's in your head. Forget the one that's before your eyes."

47 "I see. And you think that's easy."

48 "I never said it was easy. And of course the river is always, always changing shape. The river of this week is different from the river of last week. And next week it will be different again."

49 "All right. Goodbye. I'm going home.'

50 But of course I didn't go home. I stayed. I wanted to learn. I *needed* to learn. And day by day, month by month, I did learn. The river was my school. Slowly I began to think I was a good student. I could steer the boat alone, without Mr. Bixby's help. I knew the river like the rooms of my house—no, better. I could steer at night, by the shape of the river in my head. No cub-pilot was better, I thought. Oh, my nose was very high in the air!

51 Of course, Mr. Bixby saw this. And he decided to teach me another lesson.

52 One beautiful summer's day we were near the bend above Island 66. I had the wheel. We were in the middle of the river. It was easy water, deep and wide.

53 Mr. Bixby said, "I am going below for a while. Do

you know how to run the next bend?"

54 A strange question! It was perhaps the easiest bend in the river. I knew it well. It began at a little island. The river was wide there, and more than a hundred feet deep. There was no possible danger.

55 "Know how to *run* it? Why, I can run it with my eyes closed!"

56 "How much water is there in it?"

57 "What kind of question is that? There's more water there than in the Atlantic Ocean."

58 "You think so, do you?"

59 He left, and soon I began to worry. There was something in his voice. . . .

60 I didn't know it, but Mr. Bixby had stayed close to the pilot-house. I couldn't see him, but he was talking to some of the men. Soon a worker came and stood in front of the pilot-house. He looked a little worried. We were near the island at the beginning of the bend. Another man came and stood with the first. He looked worried, too. Then another. They looked at me, then at the water, then at me again. Soon there were fifteen or twenty people out there in front of me. No one said anything. The noise of the engines suddenly seemed loud to me.

61 Then one of them said in a strange voice, "Where is Mr. Bixby?"

62 "Below," I said. The man turned away and said nothing more.

63 Now I became *very* worried. I steered a little to the right. I thought I saw danger! I steered to the left. More danger! I wanted to go slower. I wanted to stop the engines. I didn't know *what* I wanted.

64 In the end I called down to the engine room. "How deep is it here? Can you tell me soon? Please be quick!"

65 "Forty feet," came the voice. He had the answer already! Forty feet! It couldn't be! Why, the water there was as deep as. . . .

66 "Thirty-five," he said in a worried voice. "Thirty-two! Twenty-eight!"

67 I couldn't believe it! I ran to the wheel, pulled a

bell, stopped the engines.

68 "Eighteen!" came the voice. "Fifteen! Thirteen! Ten!"

69 Ten feet! I was filled with fear now. I did not know what to do. I called loudly down to the man in the engine room. "Back!" I called. "Please, Ben, back her! Back her! Oh, Ben, if you love me, back her now!"

70 I heard the door close softly. I looked around, and there stood Mr. Bixby. He smiled a sweet smile at me. Then all the people in front of the pilot-house began to laugh. I understood it all now, and I felt two feet tall. I started the engines again. I steered to the middle of the river without another word. After a while, I said, "That was kind and loving of you, *wasn't* it? I think I'll hear that story the rest of my life."

71 "Well, perhaps you will. And that won't be a bad thing. I want you to learn something from this. Didn't you know there was a hundred feet of water at that bend?"

72 "Yes, I did."

73 "All right, then. If you know a thing, you must believe it—and deeply. The river is in your head, remember? And another thing. If you get into a dangerous place, don't turn and run. That doesn't help. You must fight fear, always. And on the river there is always fear."

74 It was a good lesson, perhaps his best lesson. And I never forgot it. But I can tell you, it cost a lot to learn it. Every day for weeks and weeks I had to hear those difficult words: "Oh, Ben, if you love me, back her!"

A CUB-PILOT'S EDUCATION
EXERCISES

A. Understanding the Main Ideas

Answer the following questions with complete sentences.

1. Why did all the boys in Twain's village want to be steamboat pilots?
2. What did the village look like before the steamboat came every day?
3. Why did Mr. Bixby give the boy the wheel on their first trip up the river? Why did he take it back again?
4. Why was the boy surprised when the boat reached Jones Farm?
5. Did the boy learn slowly or quickly? Why?
6. What was the "best lesson" the boy learned from Mr. Bixby? How did Mr. Bixby teach this lesson?

B. Close Reading

Read the sentence from the story. Then answer the question about the sentence.

Note: Questions 1-6 are about Part I (pages 56-61). Questions 7-12 are about Part II (pages 61-65).

1. "Then a worker cries 'S-t-e-a-m-boat coming!' And everything changes!" (paragraph 3)
   What were some of these changes?

2. "So in the end I won." (paragraph 5)
   What did the boy win? How did he win it?

3. "I began to steer into the middle of the river." (paragraph 6)
   Why did the boy do this?

4. "Well, that was good enough for me. I decided to be a down-river pilot only." (paragraph 7)
   Why did the boy decide this? Why was it easier to steer

down-river than up-river?

5. "All the men in the room laughed at this."
   (paragraph 11)
   What did the men laugh at?

6. "My heart fell." (paragraph 26)
   What does this mean? Why did it happen?

7. "And so, slowly, I began to put the Mississippi River
   inside my head." (paragraph 31)
   What made the boy decide to do this? How did he do
   it?

8. "You steer by the river that's in your head. Forget the
   one that's before your eyes." (paragraph 46)
   Did Mr. Bixby say this about daytime steering or
   nighttime steering? Why?

9. "Oh, my nose was very high in the air!"
   (paragraph 50)
   Why did the boy feel so good about himself?

10. "Eighteen!" came the voice. "Fifteen! Thirteen! Ten!"
    (paragraph 68)
    Why did these numbers frighten the boy? Why did
    they surprise him?

11. "I understood it all now, and I felt two feet tall."
    (paragraph 70)
    What did the boy understand? Why did he feel so
    small?

C. Discussion

1. A Chinese thinker named Confucius said, "I hear, I
   forget. I see, I remember. I do, I understand." Does
   Ben learn most by hearing, seeing, or doing? Do you

learn best by hearing, seeing, or doing? How do most schools try to teach students?

2. Do you think Mr. Bixby was a good teacher or a bad teacher? Why? Describe the best teacher you had when you were young. What made her or him a good teacher?

D. Vocabulary Practice

Match each word in Column A with the phrase in Column B that has a similar meaning. Write the number of the word next to the correct phrase.

A	B
1. pilot	_____machine
2. steer	_____troubled in the mind
3. shape	_____not safe
4. worried	_____outline; form; appearance
5. engine	_____give direction to
6. dangerous	_____"driver" of a boat or plane

E. Word Forms

From the chart below, choose the form of the word that best fits the sentence that follows it.

Example:

(kind) They showed me a lot of <u>kindness</u> at their home.

Noun	Adjective	Adverb	Verb
kindness	kind	kindly	
peace	peaceful	peacefully	
point	pointed	pointedly	point
worry	worried	worriedly	worry

coolness	cool	coolly	cool
danger	dangerous	dangerously	
loudness	loud	loudly	
easiness	easy	easily	ease
interest	interesting	interestingly	interest

1. (peace) The man who has drunk too much lies _____ near the river.

2. (point) In some places, the land _____ like a finger into the river.

3. (worry) The men in front of the pilot-house haD _____ faces.

4. (cool) He was very angry at first, but after a while, he _____.

5. (danger) The river can be very _____ when it is covered with mist.

6. (loud) The _____ of his voice surprised the boy.

7. (easy) It was the _____ bend in the river.

8. (interest) I didn't tell you those things just to be _____.

F. Language Activity: Crossword Puzzle

On the following page, find the word that explains or completes the sentence, or answers the question. Write the word in the right boxes, one letter for each box. Some words go across, some down. The first letter of each word is given.

Number 1 Across has been done for you.

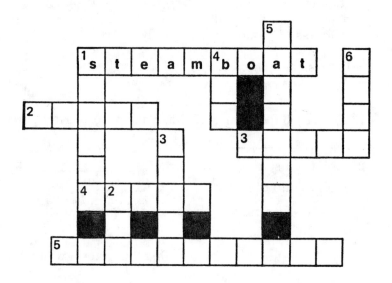

Across

1. One way to travel down the Mississippi River (S)

2. If you don't know the _____ of the river, you can't find your way at night. (S)

3. Mr. Bixby (P)

4. The boy turned it to the left and to the right. (W)

5. "Why do you think I told you the names of all those points? To be _____?" (I)

Down

1. It can change the shape of the river. (S)

2. Mr. Bixby would usually get _____ before he got cool. (H)

3. What did the boy begin to do with the boat on his first day as cub-pilot? (S)

4. What was the boy in, when Mr. Bixby got him at midnight? (B)

5. The nose of the boat softly touched the _____ at Jones Farm. (L)

6. No one could see through the _____ on the river. (M)

G. Writing: Mr. Bixby and Ben Make Plans

In the story, Ben is the man in the engine room. When the boy calls down to him to ask how deep the water is, he answers "forty feet" — but really the water is much deeper than that. Mr. Bixby has made a plan with Ben to fool the boy.

Write a dialogue between Ben and Mr. Bixby. In your dialogue, show how they made their plan. What do they say, exactly, when they decide that

- they will teach the young cub a lesson
- they will make him think that the deep water is not deep
- they will leave him alone in the pilot house
- they will tell the other workers to come and stand in front of the pilot-house and look worried
- the boy will get worried
- one of the workers will ask for Mr. Bixby. The boy will get even more worried
- he will try to steer away from danger
- he will call down to the engine room to find how deep the water is
- Ben will say "forty feet" at first — then less and less
- the boy will try to stop the boat
- then he . . .
- then . . .

THE LADY, OR THE TIGER?

Before You Read the Story . . .

1. *A Life*

   Read the paragraph about Frank Stockton on page 73. In what magazine was this story first published? Who read this magazine? Why do you think the story caused so much excitement?

2. *The Pictures*

   Look at the picture on page 75. From their clothes, who are they? When did they live?

   The title of the story asks a question. Think about what question it is asking. Now look at the picture on page 79. What does the picture show? Where is the man going? Why is he looking back?

3. *Thinking About It*

   A phrase you will read early in the story is: "the first law of Chance." This phrase suggests that chance – or luck – follows certain laws, or rules. Do you agree? Which is more important to you in your life: laws and rules, or chance and luck? Why do you think so?

4. *Skimming*

   Look over the following questions. Then skim the story. Read only the first sentence or two of each paragraph. Next, return to the questions below and write an answer to each one. Do not reread. Write only from memory. Skim the story and write answers to the questions in no more than 10 minutes. Compare your answers to those of another student.

   Does the story take place in our times, or long ago?

   Are the people in the story rich, or poor?

   Does the story ask a question, or give an answer?

   Is the story like a newspaper article, or a folk tale?

   Is the story about peace, or the opposite of peace?

   Do you think you will enjoy reading the story? Why or why not?

   What are a few interesting words or phrases that you remember reading?

THE LADY, OR THE TIGER?

adapted from the story by
FRANK STOCKTON

Frank R. Stockton was born in 1834. His most famous stories are in the form of fairy tales, ghost stories, or romances. But in all of them his humor has an edge like a knife. When "The Lady, or the Tiger?" was published in *Century Magazine* in 1882, it caused excitement all over the country. Hundreds of people wrote letters to the magazine or to their newspapers about it. Many letters demanded an answer to the question that the story asks. Others asked if the story was really about government, or psychology, or the battle of the sexes, or something else. Wisely, Stockton never answered any of the letters. The story remains as fresh today as it was then. Frank Stockton died in 1902.

Along, long time ago, there was a semi-barbaric king. I call him semi-barbaric because the modern world, with its modern ideas, had softened his barbarism a little. But still, his ideas were large, wild, and free. He had a wonderful imagination. Since he was also a king of the greatest powers, he easily turned the dreams of his imagination into facts. He greatly enjoyed talking to himself about ideas. And, when he and himself agreed upon a thing, the thing was done. He was a very pleasant man when everything in his world moved smoothly. And when something went wrong, he became even more pleasant. Nothing, you see, pleased him more than making wrong things right.

2 One of this semi-barbaric king's modern ideas was the idea of a large arena. In this arena, his people could watch both men and animals in acts of bravery.

3 But even this modern idea was touched by the king's wild imagination. In his arena, the people saw more than soldiers fighting soldiers, or men fighting animals. They enjoyed more than the sight of blood. In the king's arena, the people saw the laws of the country at work. They saw good men lifted up and bad men pushed down. Most important, they were able to watch the workings of the first law of Chance.

4 Here is what happened when a man was accused of a crime. If the king was interested in the crime, then the people were told to come to the arena. They came together and sat there, thousands of them. The king sat high up in his king's chair. When he gave a sign, a door below him opened. The accused man stepped out into the arena. Across from him, on the other side of the arena, were two other doors. They were close together and they looked the same. The accused man would walk straight to these doors and open one of them. He could choose either one of the

doors. He was forced by nothing and led by no one. Only Chance helped him—or didn't help him.

5 Behind one of the doors was a tiger. It was the wildest, biggest, hungriest tiger that could be found. Of course, it quickly jumped on the man. The man quickly—or not so quickly—died. After he died, sad bells rang, women cried, and the thousands of people walked home slowly.

6 But, if the accused man opened the other door, a lady would step out. She was the finest and most beautiful lady that could be found. At that moment, there in the arena, she would be married to the man. It didn't matter if the man was already married. It didn't matter if he was in love with another woman. The king did not let little things like that get in the way of his imagination. No, the two were married there in front of the king. There was music and dancing. Then happy bells rang, women cried, and the thousands of people walked home singing.

7 This was the way the law worked in the king's semi-barbaric country. Its fairness is clear. The criminal could not know which door the lady was behind. He opened either door as he wanted. At the moment he opened the door, he did not know if he was going to be eaten or married.

8 The people of the country thought the law was a good one. They went to the arena with great interest. They never knew if they would see a bloody killing or a lovely marriage. This uncertainty gave the day its fine and unusual taste. And they liked the fairness of the law. Wasn't it true that the accused man held his life in his own hands?

9 This semi-barbaric king had a daughter. The princess was as beautiful as any flower in the king's imagination. She had a mind as wild and free as the king's. She had a heart like a volcano. The king loved her deeply, watched her closely, and was very jealous of her. But he could not always watch her. And in his castle lived a young man. This young man was a worker. He was a good worker, but he was of low birth. He was brave and handsome, and the princess loved him, and was jealous of him. Because of

the girl's semi-barbarism, her love was hot and strong.

Of course, the young man quickly returned it. The lovers were happy together for many months. But one day the king discovered their love. Of course he did not lose a minute. He threw the young man into prison and named a day for his appearance in the arena.

10 There had never been a day as important as that one. The country was searched for the strongest, biggest, most dangerous tiger. With equal care, the country was searched for the finest and most beautiful young woman. There was no question, of course, that the young man had loved the princess. He knew it, she knew it, the king knew it, and everybody else knew it, too. But the king didn't let this stand in the way of his excellent law. Also, the king knew that the young man would now disappear from his daughter's life. He would disappear with the other beautiful lady. Or he would disappear into the hungry tiger. The only question was, "Which?"

11 And so the day arrived. Thousands and thousands of people came to the arena. The king was in his place, across from those two doors that seemed alike but were truly very different.

12 All was ready. The sign was given. The door below the king opened, and the lover of the princess walked into the arena. Tall, handsome, fair, he seemed like a prince. The people had not known that such a fine young man had lived among them. Was it any wonder that the princess had loved him?

13 The young man came forward into the arena, and then turned toward the king's chair. But his eyes were not on the king. They were on the princess, who sat to her father's right. Perhaps it was wrong for the young lady to be there. But remember that she was still semi-barbaric. Her wild heart would not let her be away from her lover on this day. More important, she now knew the secret of the doors. Over the past few days, she had used all of her power in the castle, and much of her gold. She had discovered which door hid the tiger, and which door hid the lady.

14 She knew more than this. She knew the lady. It was

one of the fairest and loveliest ladies in the castle. In fact, this lady was more than fair and lovely. She was thoughtful, kind, loving, full of laughter, and quick of mind. The princess hated her. She had seen, or imagined she had seen, the lady looking at the young man. She thought these looks had been noticed and even returned. Once or twice she had seen them talking together. Perhaps they had talked for only a moment. Perhaps they had talked of nothing important. But how could the princess be sure of that? The other girl was lovely and kind, yes. But she had lifted her eyes to the lover of the princess. And so, in her semi-barbaric heart, the princess was jealous, and hated her.

15 Now, in the arena, her lover turned and looked at her. His eyes met hers, and he saw at once that she knew the secret of the doors. He had been sure that she would know it. He understood her heart. He had known that she would try to learn this thing which no one else knew—not even the king. He had known she would try. And now, as he looked at her, he saw that she had succeeded.

16 At that moment, his quick and worried look asked the question: "Which?" This question in his eyes was as clear to the princess as spoken words. There was no time to lose. The question had been asked in a second. It must be answered in a second.

17 Her right arm rested on the arm of her chair. She lifted her hand and made a quick movement towards the right. No one saw except her lover. Every eye except his was on the man in the arena.

18 He turned and walked quickly across the empty space. Every heart stopped beating. Every breath was held. Every eye was fixed upon that man. Without stopping for even a second, he went to the door on the right and opened it.

19 Now, the question is this: Did the tiger come out of that door, or did the lady?

20 As we think deeply about this question, it becomes harder and harder to answer. We must know the heart of the animal called man. And the heart is difficult to know.

Think of it, dear reader, and remember that the decision is not yours. The decision belongs to that hot-blooded, semi-barbaric princess. Her heart was at a white heat beneath the fires of jealousy and painful sadness. She had lost him, but who should have him?

21 Very often, in her thoughts and in her dreams, she had cried out in fear. She had imagined her lover as he opened the door to the hungry tiger.

22 And even more often she had seen him at the other door! She had bitten her tongue and pulled her hair. She had hated his happiness when he opened the door to the lady. Her heart burned with pain and hatred when she imagined the scene: He goes quickly to meet the woman. He leads her into the arena. His eyes shine with new life. The happy bells ring wildly. The two of them are married before her eyes. Children run around them and throw flowers. There is music, and the thousands of people dance in the streets. And the princess's cry of sadness is lost in the

sounds of happiness!

23 Wouldn't it be better for him to die at once? Couldn't he wait for her in the beautiful land of the semi-barbaric future?

24 But the tiger, those cries of pain, that blood!

25 Her decision had been shown in a second. But it had been made after days and nights of deep and painful thought. She had known she would be asked. She had decided what to answer. She had moved her hand to the right.

26 The question of her decision is not an easy one to think about. Certainly I am not the one person who should have to answer it. So I leave it with all of you: Which came out of the opened door—the lady, or the tiger?

THE LADY, OR THE TIGER?
EXERCISES

A. Understanding the Main Ideas

If the sentence below is true, write "T" next to it. If it is not true, write "F" for false, then rewrite the sentence so that it is true.

____ **1.** The king and the princess were civilized people.

____ **2.** The king believed that questions of right and wrong should be decided by chance.

____ **3.** There were three doors in the arena. Behind one stood the king, behind the second stood the princess, and behind the third stood the tiger.

____ **4.** The people of the land thought the king was fair.

____ **5.** The king was pleased that the princess and the young man were in love. He wanted them to be married in the arena.

____ **6.** The princess was very upset because she couldn't help her lover choose the right door.

____ **7.** The young man didn't know which door to choose.

B. Close Reading: Understanding Pronouns

In the following sentences, the words <u>this</u>, <u>that</u>, and <u>it</u> have been underlined. Find the sentence in the story (paragraph numbers are given). Then tell what words or ideas are meant by <u>this</u>, <u>that</u>, or <u>it</u>.

Examples:

"The young man quickly returned <u>it</u>." (paragraph 9)

"<u>It</u> means: the princess's love.

"She knew more than <u>this</u>." (paragraph 14)

"<u>This</u>" means: which door hid the tiger, and which door hid the lady.

1. The king did not let little things like <u>that</u> get in the way of his imagination. (paragraph 6)

2. <u>This</u> was the way the law worked in the king's semi-barbaric country. (paragraph 7)

3. <u>This</u> uncertainty gave the day its fine and unusual taste. (What uncertainty?) (paragraph 8)

4. But the king didn't let <u>this</u> stand in the way of his excellent law. (paragraph 10)

5. But how could the princess be sure of <u>that</u>? (paragraph 14)

6. He had been sure that she would know <u>it</u>. (paragraph 15)

7. Certainly I am not the one person who should have to answer <u>it</u>. (paragraph 26)

C. Discussion

1. "Which came out of the opened door — the lady, or the tiger?" What do you think? Did the princess send her lover to the lady or to the tiger? Why?

2. The end of "The Lady, or the Tiger?" is about the princess's decision: that is, whether to send her lover to the lady or to the tiger. But doesn't the lover, too, have a decision to make? Look at the picture on page 75. The lover is about to open one of the doors. In this picture, he turns and takes a final look at the princess. With a movement of her hand, she has told him to open the door on the right. This leads us to a final question. Remember, the lover knows that the princess knows which door hides the lady, and which door hides the tiger. How well does the lover know the princess? Will he open the door she has chosen? Or, believing it hides the tiger, will he open the other one? Why, finally, did he open the door on the right?

3. Do you think people are less barbaric now than they were hundreds of years ago? In what ways? Are they more barbaric? In what ways? Or are they exactly the same? Give specific examples to help others understand your thoughts.

D. Vocabulary Practice

Choose the best word from the list below, and fill in the blanks in the sentences.

volcano	imagination
accused	jealous
arena	chance
fair	semi-barbaric

1. The _____ laws of that land were made by the king.

2. People gathered in the _____ to see what

would happen to the young man.

3. Only _____ helped a man decide which door to choose.

4. If someone broke a law, he was _____ of the crime. Then he had to come before the king in the arena.

5. The king had some modern ideas. But his ideas were touched by his wild _____.

6. The love in the princess' heart was a strong as a hot _____.

7. The princess felt _____ of the beautiful, gentle lady in the castle.

8. Everyone thought the working of chance was _____ because a man's life was in his own hands.

E. Word Forms: Verb, Noun, Adjective

Put the correct form of the word on the left into the blank spaces in the sentences.

1. (marry / marriage / married) Although the princess loved the young man, the king was against their _____. If an accused man chose the door with the lady behind it, he had to _____. It didn't matter if he was already _____.

2. (accuse / accusation / accused) It was a matter of chance whether the _____ chose the lady or the tiger. The king _____ the young man of loving his daughter. Neither the princess nor the young man denied the _____.

3. (imagine / imagination / imaginative) The king was an _____ man. His laws reflected his wild _____. Can you _____ how people would feel about such a law today?

4. (search / search / searching) The young man gave the princess a _____ look. He was sure she must know which door hid the tiger. The princess _____ her heart to decide which door to show him. No matter which door he chose, she would have to continue her own _____ for a husband.

5. (disappear / disappearance) The accused would _____ into the tiger's mouth, or into the lady's arms. Which _____ do you think was worse for the princess?

6. (Succeed / success / successful) The princess _____ in giving her lover a sign. But the reader doesn't know whether the young man makes a _____ choice. And we don't know which choice would seem like a _____ to the princess.

F. Language Practice: Pair Work on Composition

With a partner, read over the instructions for the Writing exercise (Exercise G) below. Share the ideas you both have about each of the three paragraphs. Take notes as you talk. Plan each paragraph separately. Next, working alone, write the three paragraphs. Then, exchange your paragraphs with the paragraphs of your partner. Correct your partner's paragraphs. Make suggestions for the improvement of the paragraphs your partner wrote. Discuss the suggestions your partner makes on your paragraphs. Then rewrite them.

G. Writing: Three-paragraph Composition

"Which came out of the opened door, the lady or the tiger?"

Write down the above question. Then write a paragraph that begins with the sentence, "Perhaps it was the lady who came out." Give at least three reasons why the princess chose the lady for her lover.

Then write a second paragraph that begin, "On the other hand, perhaps it was the tiger." Give at least three reasons why the princess chose the tiger.

Then write a third paragraph that begins with the words, "Personally, I think . . ." Give your own choice. Which of the reasons that you have written is the most important to you? Why?

AN OCCURRENCE AT OWL CREEK BRIDGE

Before You Read the Story . . .

1. *A Life*

   Read the paragraph about Ambrose Bierce on page 87. How many years did Bierce go to school? Which other writers in this book had little or no school education?

2. *The Pictures*

   Look at the pictures on pages 89 and 92. On page 89, we see a man with a rope around his neck. How would you describe his clothes? What sort of a man does he seem to be, judging by these clothes? On page 92, we see where the man is standing. How would you describe the clothes of the other man in the picture? What does his profession seem to be, judging by these clothes?

   What is the name of the bridge in the picture on page 92? (Hint: the title tells you.) What is a synonym for the word "occurrence" in the title?

3. *Thinking About It . . .*

   The paragraph about Ambrose Bierce on page 87 mentions "the Civil War between the North and the South." This war took place in the United States between 1861-1865. In a civil war, people of the same community fight against each other. What do you think are the worst effects of a civil war?

4. *Scanning*

   You are asked to find Ambrose Bierce's age, in years, at some of the major events in his interesting life. To the left of each statement below, write Bierce's age at the time the event took place. To do this, you will have to scan the paragraph about Bierce on page 87 and make calculations based on the information you find. Try to complete the entire exercise in three minutes or less.

   _____ Bierce joins the army.

   _____ His first short story is published.

   _____ He goes with his wife to London.

   _____ He returns to the United States.

   _____ He disappears in the Mexican War.

   _____ "An Occurrence at Owl Creek Bridge" is

   published in a collection of stories.

AN OCCURRENCE AT OWL CREEK BRIDGE

adapted from the story by
AMBROSE BIERCE

Ambrose Bierce was born in Ohio in 1842. He went to school, a military academy, for just one year. In 1864, during the Civil War between the North and the South, Bierce joined the Army. After the war he went to California. He wrote political pieces for newspapers. His first short story was published in 1871. That same year he married and went to live in London. After five years in London he returned to the United States. He worked for the Hearst Newspaper Company on the West Coast. He went to write about the Mexican War in 1914, where he disappeared in the fighting. "An Occurrence at Owl Creek Bridge" appeared in a collection of short stories, *Tales of Soldiers and Civilians*, in 1891. A second collection, *Can Such Things Be?*, was published in 1893.

I

A man stood upon a railroad bridge in northern Alabama. He looked down into the river below. The man's hands were tied behind his back. A rope circled his neck. The end of the long rope was tied to part of the wooden bridge above his head.

2 Next to the man stood two soldiers of the Northern army. A short distance away stood their captain. Two soldiers guarded each end of the bridge. On one bank of the river, other soldiers stood silently, facing the bridge. The two guards at each end of the bridge faced the banks of the river. None of the soldiers moved. The captain, too, stood silent. He watched the work of the two soldiers near him, but he made no sign. All of them were waiting silently for Death. Death is a visitor who must be met with respect. Even soldiers, who see so much death, must show respect to Death. And in the army, silence and stillness are signs of respect.

3 The man with the rope around his neck was going to be hanged. He was about thirty-five years old. He was not dressed like a soldier. He wore a well-fitting coat. His face was a fine one. He had a straight nose, strong mouth, and dark hair. His large eyes were gray, and looked kind. He did not seem like the sort of man to be hanged. Clearly he was not the usual sort of criminal. But the Army has laws for hanging many kinds of people. And gentlemen are not excused from hanging.

4 When the two soldiers were ready, they stepped away. The captain faced the condemned man. They stood face to face on a piece of wood. The middle of the board rested against the edge of the bridge. When the captain stepped off the board, the piece of wood would fall down into the river. The condemned man would fall down after the board. Only the rope around his neck would stop him. He

would be hanged by the neck until dead. The man's face had not been covered. His eyes were open. He looked down at the river below. He saw a small piece of wood floating along with the river. How slowly it moved! What a gentle river!

5 He closed his eyes and thought of his wife and children. Until now, other things had filled his mind: the water, painted gold by the sun . . . the soldiers . . . the floating wood. After a little while he heard a new sound. A strange metallic sound kept beating through the thoughts of his family. He wondered what it was. It sounded far away, and yet very close. It was as slow as a death-bell ringing. The sound came louder and louder. It seemed to cut into his brain like a knife. He was afraid he would cry out. But it was only his own watch making its little sound.

6 He opened his eyes. He saw again the water below him. "If I could free my hands," he thought, "I might throw off the rope. I could jump into the river. If I swam quickly underwater, I could escape the bullets. I would reach the river bank, run into the woods and go home. My home, thank God, is still safe from the Northern Army." These thoughts must be written in words here. But they passed as quickly as light through the condemned man's mind.

7 And then the captain stepped off the board.

II

8 The condemned man's name was Peyton Farquhar. He was a rich farmer, the last son in an old Alabama family. He owned slaves who worked on his farm. Like other Southern farmers, he believed that slaves were necessary to Southern farming. The Northern government had said that it was against the law to have slaves. Now, the North and the South were at war.

9 Certain work had kept Peyton Farquhar from joining the Southern Army at the beginning of the war. But he was at heart a soldier. He did everything he could to help the South. No job was too low, no adventure too dangerous. One evening, Farquhar and his wife were sitting in the garden. A soldier rode up to the house. He was dressed like

other soldiers in the Southern Army. While Mrs. Farquhar went to get him a drink of water, the soldier spoke with Farquhar.

10 "The Northerners are rebuilding the railroads," the soldier said. "They are getting ready for another advance. They've reached Owl Creek Bridge. They've fixed the bridge and moved in a lot of soldiers. Anyone who attacks the railroad or tries to destroy the bridge will be hanged."

11 "How far is it to Owl Creek Bridge?" Farquhar asked.

12 "About thirty miles."

13 "Are there soldiers on this side of the bridge?"

14 "Only a few guards."

15 "Suppose that a man went around the guards?" Farquhar smiled. "What could he do to stop the advance?"

16 The soldier thought a moment. Then he said, "I was at the bridge a month ago. I saw a lot of wood that the river had washed against one end of the bridge. It's very dry now, and the wood would burn quickly and well."

17 The lady had now brought the water. The soldier drank. He thanked her, bowed to Farquhar, and rode away. An hour later, after nightfall, he passed Farquhar's farm again. He went North in the direction he had come from. He was a Northern soldier.

III

18 Peyton Farquhar fell down from the bridge. He lost consciousness. He was like one already dead. He was awakened—hours later, it seemed to him—by the great pain in his neck. Pain passed through his body like rivers of fire. He was conscious of a fullness in his head. He could not think. He could only feel. He was conscious of motion. He seemed to be falling through a red cloud. Then suddenly the light flew upward with the noise of a loud splash. A fearful noise was in his ears. All was cold and dark. The power of thought came back to him. He knew the rope had broken, and he had fallen into the river. The rope around his neck was cutting off the air. To die of hanging at the bottom of a river! No! Impossible! He opened his eyes

in the darkness. He saw light far, far above him. He was still going down, for the light grew smaller and smaller. But then it grew brighter, and he knew he was coming back up to the top of the river. Now he felt sorry to be coming out of the water. He had been so comfortable. "To be hanged and drowned," he thought. "That is not so bad. But I do not want to be shot. No, I will not be shot. That's not fair!"

19 He was not conscious of his actions until he felt pain in his hands. Then he realized that he was trying to free his hands. At last the rope fell off. His arms floated upward; he could see his hands. He watched with interest. His hands were trying to untie the rope around his neck. They pulled off the rope and it floated away. "Put it back, put it back," he felt himself crying. His neck hurt badly. His mind was on fire, his heart beat wildly enough to leave his body. His whole body was in great pain. But his hands pushed him up out of the water. And he took a great breath of air.

20 Now he was fully conscious. His five senses seemed unusually clear. The pain his body had felt made him see and feel the beauty around him. He felt the water against his skin. He heard the soft sound as it hit his neck and shoulders. He looked into the forest on the bank and could see each tree, each leaf. He could even see small forest animals between the trees. A fish swam before his eyes. He noticed how the sunlight shone on the fish's silver skin.

21 He was facing away from the bridge when his head came out of the water. Now he turned around. He saw small men on the bridge, dark against the blue sky. They cried out and pointed at him. The captain took out his gun but did not shoot.

22 Then, suddenly, he heard a loud bang. Something hit the water near his head. Water splashed in his face. He heard a second shot and a light blue cloud rose from the gun. Then Farquhar heard the captain call to the men: "Ready, men . . . Shoot!"

23 Farquhar swam deep under the water. The water sounded loud in his ears. But even above the sound of the water he heard the shots. He swam down the river.

24 Later he swam to the top again. He saw he was quite far from the bridge. The soldiers were still pointing their guns at him.

25 "The captain will not order them to shoot together again," he thought. "It's as easy to escape many bullets as one. He'll order them to shoot as they wish. God help me, I cannot escape them all."

26 Suddenly he was caught by a strong current in the river. The current pulled him under the water. It carried him down the river and turned him over and over. At last the force of the current pushed him up onto the bank.

27 He lay on the bank, crying with happiness and tiredness. He dug his fingers into the river bank. The small stones felt like jewels. The trees looked to him like a forest of gold. The air smelled clean and sweet, and a pink light shone through the trees.

28 The sound of bullets in the trees awoke him. He rose to his feet, frightened again, and disappeared into the forest.

29 All that day he traveled. The forest seemed endless. He could find no road. He hadn't realized before now that he lived near such a wild place.

30 When night began to fall, he was very tired and hungry. The thought of his wife and children helped him to continue. At last he found a road that seemed to lead in the right direction. It was as wide and straight as a city street. But it seemed untraveled. There were no fields, no houses nearby. The big black trees formed a straight wall on both sides. Overhead, great golden stars shone in the sky. The stars looked unfamiliar. He was sure that they were grouped in some strange order which meant bad luck. From inside the forest came strange noises. Among them he heard people talking in an unknown language.

31 His neck was in pain. He knew that the rope had left a black circle on his skin. He could not close his eyes. His tongue was dry; he felt very thirsty. Grass seemed to cover the road now; it was soft under his feet.

32 Did he fall asleep while he was walking? Now he sees something else. Perhaps he was wakened from a

dream. Now he stands not far from the door of his own house. Everything looks just as he left it, bright and beautiful in the morning sunshine. He must have traveled through the whole night. As he walks toward the door, his wife appears to meet him. She stands waiting, cool and sweet, silent and still. She holds out her arms to him with a smile of happiness. Ah! how beautiful she is! He moves toward her with open arms. He moves slowly, closer, closer. At the moment he touches her, he feels a great pain at the back of his neck. A while light flames all about him. . . .

33 There was a loud bang, then silence. All was darkness . . .

34 Peyton Farquhar was dead. His body, with a broken neck, hung from a rope beneath Owl Creek Bridge.

AN OCCURRENCE AT OWL CREEK BRIDGE EXERCISES

A. Understanding the Main Ideas

Answer the following questions with complete sentences.

1. At the beginning of the story, where is the man named Farquhar standing?
2. Why were all the soldiers so silent?
3. What would happen when the captain stepped off one end of the board?
4. What sounded so loud to Farquhar? Why?
5. Who was Peyton Farquhar? What role did he play in the war?
6. When Farquhar fell from the bridge, did the rope around his neck break, or did his neck break? What really happened? How do you know?
7. In your opinion, what is the "loud bang" that Farquhar hears (at the very end of the story)?
8. How long do you think it took for Farquhar's escape and adventure to pass through his mind?

B. Close Reading: Adverbial Clauses

To do the exercise below, you will need to read Part II of the story (pages 90-91) carefully. The first half of each sentence below is joined to the second half by an adverb. The adverb tells the relationship of the first half of the sentence to the second half. Make sure that the whole sentence, and not just the separate halves of it, are true.

Finish each sentence below with clause **a**, **b**, **c**, or **d**.

1. Peyton Farquhar owned slaves

    a. until he understood that it was against the law.

    b. before he was a rich farmer.

    c. because he thought the South needed slaves.

    d. while the slaves wanted to work for him.

2. A man dressed like a Southern soldier came to Farquhar's house

    a. because he knew that Farquhar had helped the South in the war.

    b. before Farquhar had helped the South in the war.

    c. since he wanted to burn Owl Creek Bridge.

    d. when he learned that the North and South were at war.

3. Farquhar decided to burn the bridge

    a. while the Northerners were rebuilding the railroads.

    b. before the Northerners fixed the bridge and moved in some soldiers.

    c. because Owl Creek Bridge was thirty miles from his home.

    d. after the soldier told him about the dry wood.

4. The soldier rode north

    a. until night came

    b. before Mrs. Farquhar could bring him a drink of water

    c. because he wanted to tell the Northern army about Farquhar.

d. since he wanted to attack the Northern army.

C. Discussion

1. Did the end of the story surprise you? Why, or why not?

2. Find five things that Farquhar thought about before the captain stepped off the board. (see especially paragraphs 4, 5, and 6.) Why do you think that Bierce tells us that these thoughts "passed as quickly as light through the condemned man's mind?" What are the other signs that Farquhar's five senses are working unusually quickly or sharply?

3. In Part III (pages 91-95), what seems very realistic? (Give at least three examples of realistic writing.) What seems unrealistic, dreamlike, or strange? (Give at least three examples of this dreamlike writing.)

D. Vocabulary Practice

The following phrases are definitions of words in the reading. Find the appropriate word, then write it in the blank.

1. To look up to, or admire, something or someone greater than yourself (paragraph 2)

_____

2. A person who breaks the law (paragraph 3)

_____

3. To be allowed *not* to do something (paragraph 3)

_____

4. A person who the law has decided to punish (paragraph 4)

_____

5. To get away from something dangerous (paragraph 6)

_____

6. A move forward (paragraph 10)

_____

7. Of a clear head, clear mind (paragraph 18)

_____

8. Tell someone to do something (paragraph 25)

_____

9. The strong motion of a river or sea (paragraph 26)

_____

10. Vanished, went out of sight (paragraph 28)

_____

11. Empty of traffic or people (paragraph 30)

_____

E. Word Forms: Nouns and Adjectives

Choose the noun or adjective from the left that best fits the sentence to the right.

1. (metal / metallic) Farquhar's watch ticked with a
_____ sound.

2. (circle / circular) The rope made a _____ path
around Farquhar's neck.

3. (respect / respectful) The soldiers waited in
_____ silence for Farquhar's death.

4. (condemnation / condemned) After his _____
Farquhar was sentenced to death by hanging.

5. (danger / dangerous) Farquhar wanted to help the
Southern army. He was not afraid of _____.

6. (consciousness / conscious) When he fell from the
bridge, Farquhar lost _____ as the rope
tightened around his neck.

7. (traveler / traveled) The road to Farquhar's house was
not much _____.

8. (order / orderly) The soldiers stood in an
_____ line, pointing their guns at
Farquhar.

F. Language Activity: Images for a Silent Movie

Work in pairs or small groups. You will present to the
class 6-10 pictures that tell a part of the story of "An
Occurrence at Owl Creek Bridge." Choose a section of
the story from either Part I (pages 88-90) or Part III
(pages 91-95).

Try to imagine what the camera would see in a silent
movie (a movie without words) of this part of the story.
You do not have to be an artist to draw the pictures. Use
simple lines and "stick figures" to give the idea (see
example, below). If you can, draw the pictures on large
pieces of paper so that they are easy to see.

When you present your pictures to the class, describe what is happening in each one. What does the audience see? What do you want the audience to feel?

G. Writing: A Summary

A summary tells in a few words what someone else said or wrote in many words.

Write a summary of Part I, Part II, or Part III of "An Occurrence at Owl Creek Bridge." Begin your summary with the first sentence of the section you have chosen:

A man stood upon a railroad bridge in Alabama.

or

The condemned man's name was Peyton Farquhar.

or

Peyton Farquhar fell down from the bridge.

In no more than 6 or 8 sentences, tell what happens in the rest of the section you have chosen. Try to include the facts you think are the most important for a general understanding of that section.

A WHITE HERON

Before You Read the Story...

1. *A Life*

Read the paragraph about Sarah Orne Jewett on page 103. What subjects does she write about? Where do her stories take place? What other writers in this book write mostly about one particular place?

2. *The Pictures*

Look at the picture on page 105. What can you tell about the place they live in? What is the young man holding?

In the picture on page 108 the girl is at the top of a tall pine tree. What will she be able to do from so high? What kind of bird is flying past her? (Hint: The title tells you.) What do you know about this bird? What can you find out about it?

3. *Thinking About It...*

"A White Heron" takes place more than a hundred years ago. The story's main characters live deep in the country, far from cities or towns or even villages. How do you feel about the wild country? Have you spent time there? Would you like to live there? Why, or why not?

4. *Rapid Scanning*

Sometimes we have to quickly scan an entire book, or sections of a book, for specific information. In this exercise, you are asked to scan the biographies of all the writers in GREAT AMERICAN STORIES I. First, read the questions below. Then scan the biographies of the writers to find the answers. Try to do the entire exercise in no more than five minutes.

a. Did these writers write in the 19th century, or in the 20th century?

b. List which ones were men. List which ones were women.

c. How many of them died in the 20th century?

d. How many traveled outside the United States for long periods of time?

e. How many of them were known for their stories about specific places within the United States?

102

A
WHITE HERON

adapted from the story by
SARAH ORNE JEWETT

Sarah Orne Jewett was born in 1849 in South Berwick, Maine. She lived there quietly near the sea most of her life. She wrote stories about the simple lives of the country people around her. Her stories show her love of nature, as well as human nature. The woods, fields, and animals of Maine are almost like characters in her stories. Her best-known book is called *Country of the Pointed Firs*. Maine is well known for its pine and fir trees. In 1909, Sarah Orne Jewett died in the same house in which she had been born and raised.

I

The woods were already filled with shadows one June evening just before eight o'clock. Sylvia was driving her cow home. They turned deep into the dark woods. Their feet knew the way. The birds in the trees above her head seemed to sing "good night" to each other quietly. The air was soft and sweet. Sylvia felt a part of the gray shadows and the moving leaves. To Sylvia, it seemed as if she hadn't really been alive before she came to live with her grandmother in this beautiful place.

2 Suddenly she heard a call. Not a bird's call, which would have had a friendly sound. It was a young man's call, sudden and loud. Sylvia left the cow alone and hid behind some leaves. But the young man saw her.

3 "Halloa, little girl. How far is it to the road?"

4 Sylvia was afraid. She answered in a soft voice, "A good ways . . ."

5 "I'm hunting for some birds," the young man said kindly. He carried a gun over his shoulder. "I am lost and need a friend very much. Don't be afraid. Speak up, and tell me what your name is. Do you think I can spend the night at your house and go out hunting in the morning?"

6 Sylvia was more afraid than ever. But she said her name, and dropped her head like a broken flower.

7 Her grandmother was waiting at the door. The cow gave a "moo" as the three arrived.

8 "Yes, you should speak for yourself, you old cow," said her grandmother. "Where was she hiding so long, Sylvy?"

9 Sylvia didn't speak. She thought her grandmother should be afraid of the stranger.

10 But the young man stood his gun beside the door. He dropped a heavy gun-bag beside it. He said good evening and told the old woman his story.

11 "Dear me, yes," she answered. "You might do better if you went out to the road a mile away. But you're welcome to what we've got. I'll milk the cow right away. Now, you make yourself at home. Sylvy, step round, and set a plate for the gentleman!"

12 Sylvia stepped. She was glad to have something to do, and she was hungry.

13 The young man was surprised to find such a comfortable, clean house in the deep woods of Maine. He thought this was the best supper he had eaten in a month. After supper the new-made friends sat in the shadowed doorway to watch the moon come up. The young man listened happily to the grandmother's stories. The old woman talked most about her children. About her daughter, Sylvia's mother, who had a hard life with so many children. About her son, Dan, who left home for California many years ago.

14 "Sylvy is like Dan," she said happily. "She knows every foot of the woods. She plays with the woods animals and feeds the birds. Yes, she'd give her own meals to them, if I didn't watch her!"

15 "So Sylvy knows all about birds, does she?" asked the young man. "I am trying to catch one of every kind."

16 "Do you keep them alive?" asked the old woman.

17 "No. I stuff them in order to save them," he answered. "I have almost a hundred of them. And I caught every one myself."

18 Sylvia was watching a toad jump in the moonlight.

19 "I followed a bird here that I want to catch. A white heron. You would know a heron if you saw it, Sylvy," he said, hopefully. "A strange, tall white bird with long, thin legs."

20 Sylvia's heart stopped. She knew that strange white bird.

21 "I want that bird more than anything," the young man went on. "I would give ten dollars to know where its nest is."

22 Sylvia couldn't believe there was so much money in the world. But she watched the toad and said nothing.

23 The next day Sylvia went with the young man into the woods. He was kind and friendly, and told her many things about the birds. She wasn't afraid of him anymore. Perhaps in her heart a dream of love was born. But she couldn't understand why he killed and stuffed the birds he liked so much.

II

24 At the edge of the woods a great pine tree stood. Sylvia knew it well. That night she thought of the tree. If she climbed it early in the morning, she could see the whole world. Couldn't she watch the heron fly, and find its hidden nest? What an adventure it would be! And how happy her friend would be! The young man and the old woman slept well that night, but Sylvia thought of her adventure. She forgot to think of sleep. At last, when the night birds stopped singing, she quietly left the house.

25 There was the tall pine tree, still asleep in the moonlight. First she climbed a smaller tree next to it. Then she made the dangerous step across to the old pine. The birds in the woods below her were waking up. She must climb faster if she wanted to see the heron as it left its nest. The tree seemed to grow taller as she went up. The pine tree must have been surprised to feel this small person climbing up. It must have loved this new animal in its arms. Perhaps it moved its branches a little, to help her climb. Sylvia's face shone like a star when she reached the top. She was tired, but very happy. She could see ships out to sea. Woods and farms lay for miles and miles around her. The birds sang louder and louder. At last the sun came up. Where was the heron's nest? Look, look, Sylvia! A white spot rises up from the green trees below. The spot grows larger. The heron flies close. A wild, light bird, wide wings, and a long thin neck. He stops in the tree beyond Sylvia. Wait, wait, Sylvia! Do not move a foot or a finger, to frighten it away!

26 A moment later, Sylvia sighs. A large company of noisy birds comes to the tree, and the heron goes away. It flies down to its home in the green world below. Sylvia

knows its secret now. She climbs back down. Now she is almost crying. Her fingers hurt, and her feet slip. She wonders what the young man will say to her. What will he think when she tells him how to find the heron's nest?

27 "Sylvy, Sylvy," her grandmother called, but nobody answered.

28 The young man woke up and dressed. He wanted to begin hunting again. He was sure Sylvia knew something about the white heron. Here she comes now. Her small face is white, her old dress is torn and dirty. The grandmother and the young man wait at the door to question her. The time has come to tell about the heron's nest.

29 But Sylvia does not speak. The young man looks into her eyes. He will make them rich. She wants to make him happy. He waits to hear the story she can tell.

30 No, she must keep silent! What is it that keeps her quiet? This is the first time the world has put out a hand to her. Does she have to push it away because of a bird? She hears again the wind blowing in the pine tree. She remembers how the white heron flew through the golden air. She remembers how they watched the sea and the morning together. Sylvia cannot speak. She cannot tell the heron's secret and give its life away.

31 Poor Sylvia! She was sad when the young man went away. She could have helped him. She would have followed him like a dog. She would have loved him as a dog loves! Many nights afterwards Sylvia remembered his "Halloa" as she came home with the cow. She forgot the sharp sound of his gun. She forgot the birds, wet with blood. Were the birds better friends than the hunter? Who can tell?

32 Oh, Woods! Oh, Summertime! Remember what riches were lost to her. Bring her your riches instead, your beauties and your gifts. Tell all your secrets to this lonely country child!

A WHITE HERON
EXERCISES

A. Understanding the Main Ideas

Answer the following questions with complete sentences.

1. At the beginning of the story, why was Sylvia afraid of the young man?
2. How does the grandmother act with the young man?
3. Why is the young man killing birds?
4. Why does he say he will pay ten dollars?
5. Why does he think Sylvia can help him?
6. Why does she watch the toad so carefully?
7. Why does she leave the house before the sun comes up?
8. Why does she climb the tall pine tree?
9. What is the heron's secret?
10. Why can't she give the heron's secret away?

B. Close Reading: A Question of Time

Complete the sentences below by choosing **a**, **b**, or **c**. The first part of the sentence tells you something that happened in the story. The second part tells you when it happened.

1. Sylvia went to bring home the cow
   a. when the cow was ready to eat.
   b. just as it began to get dark.
   c. just after her grandmother was ready to eat.
2. Sylvia began to feel frightened
   a. at the same time that she heard the young man call out.
   b. after it began to get dark.
   c. when she lost the cow.
3. The young man wanted to stay with Sylvia and her grandmother

a. before they ate dinner.

b. while it began to get dark, but not after.

c. during the time that he hunted for birds.

4. They sat in the doorway

a. as the moon came up.

b. before it began to get dark.

c. while the birds sang softly.

5. Sylvia decided to find the heron's nest

a. as she was watching the toad.

b. before it was dark.

c. sometime during the night.

6. She had to climb the pine tree

a. after the young man woke up.

b. while it began to get dark.

c. shortly before the sun came up.

7. She decided not to tell the young man where the heron lived

a. after he said he would pay ten dollars.

b. just before it began to get dark.

c. because she saw how beautiful the heron was.

C. Discussion

1. What do you think about what the young man is doing? Is it work or play? This story was written about 100 years ago. Would you feel differently about him if he were hunting today? Why, or why not?

2. As you were reading the story, what did you think Sylvia would do? Do you think she should have helped the young man? Why, or why not?

3. The story says that Sylvia "couldn't understand why he killed the birds he liked so much." Explain her feelings for the birds, compared to the feelings of the young man. The young man tells her grandmother, "I stuff them to save them." In what way does he "save" the birds?

D. Vocabulary Practice

The underlined phrases in column B mean the same as a word or phrase in column A. Match the phrase in column A to the sentence with the same meaning in column B. Then write the new sentence.

Example:

A	B
getting darker	The woods were already <u>filled</u> <u>with</u> <u>shadows</u>.

<u>The woods were already getting darker</u>.

A	B
quite far away	1. She knows <u>every foot of</u> the woods.
faithfully	2. Sylvy, <u>step round</u> and set a plate for the gentleman.
lowered	3. You might <u>do better</u> if you went out to the road.
happily	4. This is the first time the world has <u>put out its hand</u> to her.
hurry up	5. The road is <u>a good ways</u> from here.
a lot about	6. Sylvia's face shone <u>like a star.</u>
have more success	7. She <u>dropped</u> her head like a broken flower.
tried to help	8. From the top of the tree Sylvia could see <u>the whole world.</u>
for miles	9. She would have loved him <u>as a dog loves.</u>

Write the new sentences here

1. _____

_____

2. _____

_____

3. _____

_____

4. _____

_____

5. _____

_____

6. _____

_____

7. _____

_____

8. _____

_____

9. _____

_____

E Word Forms

From the chart below, choose the form of the word that best fits the sentences below.

noun	adjective	adverb	verb
surprise	surprising	surprisingly	surprise
secret	secretive	secretly	secrete
hunter	hunted		hunt
shadow	shadowy		shadow
comfort	comfortable	comfortably	
stuffing	stuffed		stuff

1. (surprise) By the second day of his visit, Sylvia was
_____ friendly with the young man.

2. (secret) Sylvia was a _____ child,
perhaps because she was alone so much of the time.

3. (hunt) The young man was an unusual kind of
_____.

4. (shadow) Neither Sylvia nor the cow were afraid of the
_____ darkness. They were used to
the woods.

5. (comfort) The three new-made friends were
_____ with each other.

6. (stuff) What kind of _____ did the
young man use inside his birds?

F. Language Activity: A Class Project on Wildlife Protection

In pairs or teams, investigate local environmental groups
that work with wildlife protection, endangered species,
and other environmental questions related to animals:
animal rights, animal research, etc. Take notes, and
make an oral report to the class.

G. Writing

Write a narrative (story) of your own. Choose one of the
suggestions below:

1. You are Sylvia. You have told the young man where to
find the heron. You go with him to hunt the bird.
What happened then? How did you feel about it?
What did you do?

2. You are the young man. When you see that Sylvia
won't tell you where to find the bird, you try to
persuade her to tell you. What happened then? Did

she tell you, finally? What did you do? How did you feel?

3. You are the grandmother. The day after the hunter left you found "Sylvy" in tears. Years later, you tell the story of what happened to Sylvia. Did she remain sad, or become happy again. Why? What became of her when she got older?